SharePoint Online Power User Playbook

*Next-Generation Approach for Collaboration,
Content Management, and Security*

Deviprasad Panda

Distributors:

BPB PUBLICATIONS
20, Ansari Road, Darya Ganj
New Delhi-110002
Ph: 23254990/23254991

DECCAN AGENCIES
4-3-329, Bank Street,
Hyderabad-500195
Ph: 24756967/24756400

MICRO MEDIA
Shop No. 5, Mahendra Chambers,
150 DN Rd. Next to Capital Cinema,
V.T. (C.S.T.) Station, MUMBAI-400 001
Ph: 22078296/22078297

BPB BOOK CENTRE
376 Old Lajpat Rai Market,
Delhi-110006
Ph: 23861747

Published by Manish Jain for BPB Publications, 20 Ansari Road, Darya Ganj, New Delhi-110002 and Printed by him at Repro India Ltd, Mumbai

Dedicated to

Parents, Elder Brother, Younger Brother, Wife, and Lord Jagannath – Most important in my life. Thanks for everything you do

About the Author

Mr. Deviprasad Panda is currently working as a Lead SharePoint administrator having almost 9-year relevant experience in SharePoint. He is having strong experience in SharePoint 2010, SharePoint 2013, SharePoint 2016, SharePoint 2019 on-premises production farm, SharePoint online, hosting SharePoint in azure. He completed certifications in *"70-573: Microsoft SharePoint Application Development"*, *"70-667: Microsoft SharePoint Configuration"*, *"70-668: Microsoft SharePoint 2010Administrator"*, *"70-331: Core Solutions of Microsoft SharePoint Server 2013"*, *"70-332: Advanced Solutions of Microsoft SharePoint Server 2013"*, *"70-339: Managing Microsoft SharePoint Server 2016"*, *"70-533: Implementing Microsoft Azure Infrastructure Solutions"*. He has huge production experience in multiple reputed companies in India. He is the founder of **SharePointTechnicalSupport** a website to support SharePoint related queries to people. He is a trainer, YouTuber having channel **Deviprasad Panda** as well. He is very passionate about the work that he steps into, and his dedication to providing quality work as committed is highly appreciated.

Acknowledgments

I would like to acknowledge my parents and my elder brother *"Prabhu Prasad Panda"* for their every small sacrifice so as to give higher education to me and put me in a place where I am capable enough to take the right decision and drive my life for better future – I can never forget and fulfill your sacrifices in my life. Thank you!

I would like to acknowledge my younger brother, *"Hara Prasada Panda,"* who is my best friend, a guide at every step in my career. Thank You!

I would like to acknowledge my lovely wife, who is with me at every ups and downs in life; all her encouragement and supports brought me success. Thank You!

Most importantly, blessings from Lord Jagannath to share true values to society and grow together. I strongly believe without the blessings of God, nothing is possible.

Finally, I would like to thank the BPB Team for giving me this wonderful opportunity to write my first book for them. Thank You!

Preface

We are moving very fast in the digital world. Its digital revolution and content play an important role. It is very important to manage content effectively, make content secure, targeted, collaborate more to work together to save cost, time, improve quality with more produce works. SharePoint is the giant of providing a collation tool when managing everything related to content comes into the picture. SharePoint Online by Microsoft is one of the finest software as a service (SaaS) that provides smart features and keeps on upgrading tools, rolling out new features to manage content smartly, with more security.

The primary goal of this book is to providea clear concept of sharepoint online. The book covers each and every newly introduced smart setting in the SharePoint Online site, like a user manual or field guide which you can follow to do the task, with very simple words but advanced-level production task experience as the outcome. Every setting in SharePoint is covered as a screenshot, so there will not be any problem if you are not accessing any SharePoint site. You will not face any problem since all images are taken considering user understanding step by step. This book is divided into 13 chapters, and it provides a detailed description of SharePoint Online basics to new advanced level settings. Over the 13 chapters in this book, you will learn the following:

Section I: Introduction and New Features in SharePoint Online

Chapter 1: Introduction and Site Information, covers, rewind SharePoint content concept, what is the scope of power user role, Revised SharePoint templates, Creating sites and subsites using site template, Getting started with site settings, basic modification in the site and how to select the right template for right business work

Chapter 2: Library and List Smart Management, cover about the default site contents and site features available, Upgraded new features in list and library for smart management, Information about Apps management, discussion about each list and library settings.

Section II: Application of SharePoint Features

Chapter 3: Content Approval Concept, covers specific about what content approval is, settings responsible for content approval, how content approval works, how can we automate content approval using traditional workflow or modern power automate, and its benefits over the manual approval process.

Chapter 4: Configure Information Management Policy focusing specifically on information management policy settings. Introduction to information management policies, how to activate the dependent feature, apply site policies, how to create content type policy templates. Describes how to enable retention, auditing, barcodes, labels policies, applying policy in content types, library, folder, list. Discussion about dependent timer job.

Chapter 5: Configure Document ID Service covers document id overview, dependent feature for document id service, how to add a column to the library, modify document id settings, document id service test case.

Chapter 6: Document Sets Feature describes document set overview, dependent feature for the document set. Creating site content type, content type columns, edit document set settings. Creating library, views, and adding content type to the library. creating a modern document set and how it is different from the classic document Set.

Chapter 7: Content Organizer Feature covers about content organizer overview, dependent feature for the content organizer, how to configure content organizer settings, create content organizer rules and how documents are routing based on rules and conditions.

Chapter 8: Manage Permission, focuses specific to permission overview, default groups in SharePoint, groups dependent on features, different permission levels, different settings available for permission management, modern experiences in permission management

Chapter 9: Managed Metadata Concept, focuses specific to managed metadata overview. How to create a new group, term set, term. Application of reuse terms, copy term set, merge terms, move term set. How to create metadata column, application of metadata in navigation settings and filtering, create and apply metadata navigation.

Chapter 10: SharePoint Server Publishing Infrastructure Feature, focuses specifically on how to activate the features and what are the changes happening in the site after activating the publishing infrastructure feature.

Section III: Site Designing and External Content Type Integration

Chapter 11: Application of Business Connectivity Services, focus specifically on how to create an external content type and how to integrate external content type with sharepoint.

Chapter 12: Site Designing and Enhancement describes how to create and edit site pages. what are section layouts and terminologies, add and configure new modern webparts in details. How structural navigation cache works, how to register hub site, associate other sites with a hub site, and application of webparts in the hub site.

Section IV: Usage and Analytics

Chapter 13: Manage Site Usage, explains how to monitor activities under site usage, analyze file activity reports, analyze site usage reports, analyze using site activity webpart, understand traditional audit log reports, analyze storage metrics.

Table of Contents

1, Introduction and Site Information 1

Structure 1

Objective 2

Rewind SharePoint Content Concept 2

Scope of power user role 2

Templates revised 3

Site templates out of box 4

Content templates 6

Creating sites and subsites using a site template 7

Modern communication site 8

Modern team site 10

Team site as subsite 13

Start page 15

Hub Site 16

Getting started with Site settings 17

Basic modification in Site 18

Change the look 18

Modify Site Information 20

Selecting the Right Template 21

Modern Team Site 21

Communication site 21

Blog Site (Collaboration) 21

Developer Site (Collaboration) 22

Project Site (Collaboration) 22

Community Site (Collaboration) 23

Document Center Site (Enterprise) 24

eDiscovery center site (Enterprise) 24

Records Center Site (Enterprise) 25

Business Intelligence Center Site (Enterprise) 25

Compliance Policy Center Site (Enterprise) 26

Community Portal Site (Enterprise) 27

Visio Process Repository Site (Enterprise) 27

Publishing Site (Publishing) 28

Enterprise Wiki Site (Publishing) 28

Default SharePoint Online Templates 29

Conclusion 30

Points to remember 30

2. Library and List Smart Management 31

Structure 31

Objective 32

Default Site Contents and Site Features..32

    Modern Team Site Contents..32

    Modern Communication Site Contents 34

    Blog Site Contents..35

    Developer Site Contents 35

    Project Site Contents 36

    Community Site Contents 37

    Document Center Site Contents..38

    eDiscovery Center Contents 38

    Record Center Site Contents..39

    SharePoint Online Configuration Site Contents......................................40

    Business Intelligence Center Site Contents 40

    Compliance Policy Center Site Contents 41

    Community Portal Site Contents 42

    Visio Process Repository Contents 42

    Publishing Portal Site Contents..43

    Enterprise Wiki Site Contents 44

Creating a New Document Library 45

Creating New List...46

    Upgraded new features for smart management 52

    Modern Document Library Smart Features 52

Command Bar 52

    New 53

    Upload 55

    Quick edit 56

    Sync 56

    Export to Excel 58

    PowerApps 58

    Automate 59

    Switch view options...61

    Filters pane..63

    Details pane 63

    Expand content..64

    Add column simplified..65

Move to/Copy to option 66

    Pin to top option 66

    Saved for later 67

Check out/Check in multiple files..67
Submit for approval...68
Publish 68
Change the document file group..69
Hover card...70
Modern list smart features 71
Create new item..71
Request sign-off..73
Apps Management 75
Understand List and Library Settings is Must............................75
General Settings..77
List name, description and navigation..78
Versioning settings..78
Advanced Settings 82
Validation Settings 85
Rating Settings 86
Audience Targeting 87
Form Settings 87
Permissions and Management...87
Delete this document library 88
Permissions for this document library.......................................89
Manage files which have no checked in version........................89
Workflow Settings..90
Enterprise Metadata and Keywords Settings..............................90
Communications..91
Columns 91
Create column...92
Add from existing site columns..94
Column ordering..94
Indexed columns 95
Views 95
Content Types...98
Enhanced Features in Quick Edit Mode 100
Conclusion 101
Points to Remember... 101
3. Content ApprovalConcept 103
Structure 103
Objective 104
Content approval overview 104
Enable content approval process first 104

How Content Approval works... 106

Approval Workflow in the content approval process 109

Activate a feature first 109

Create Approval Workflow... 111

    How the approval workflow works 115

    Benefits of Approval Workflow 118

Approval flow using Power Automate 119

Conclusion 126

Points to Remember.. 126

4. Configure Information Management Policy **127**

Structure 127

Objective 128

Activate Feature First 128

Apply Site Policies 129

Content Type Policy Templates Creation.. 133

    Enable Retention 134

    Enable Auditing.. 137

    Enable Barcodes 137

    Enable Labels 138

Applying Information Management Policy 139

    Applying Policy in Content Types 139

    Applying Policy in Library.. 144

    Applying Policy in Folder... 145

    Applying Policy in List 146

Timer Job Action... 146

Conclusion 146

Points to remember... 146

5. Configure Document ID Service **147**

Introduction 147

Structure 147

Objective 148

Activate feature first 148

Edit View to Add Column.. 149

Document ID settings configuration... 150

Different testing scenarios... 152

    Move file to folder in the same library.. 152

    Move the file to a different library in the same site collection 153

    Move the file to a different site collection 154

    Copy to folder or library... 155

    Copy to a different site collection 156

Find by Document ID Webpart 156
Document ID Value Document property 157
Conclusion 157
Points to remember 158

6. Document Sets Feature **159**
Structure 159
Objective 160
Activate feature first 160
Creating a new content type of type document set 161
   Creating site columns 162
   Document set settings 164
   Create a document library 165
   Allow management of content types 166
Adding content type to the library 167
   Change the default content type 168
   Delete content type from the library 169
   Creating a document set view 170
   Create a modern document set 171
Conclusion 176
Points to remember 177

7. Content Organizer Feature **179**
Structure 179
Objective 180
Activate feature first 180
   Content organizer settings 181
   Create a new site content type 184
   Create a document library 186
   Allow management of content types 187
   Adding content type to the library 188
Content organizer rules 190
How do the content organizer rules work? 192
Conclusion 196
Points to remember 196

8. Manage Permission **197**
Introduction 197
Structure 197
Objective 198
SharePoint groups by default 198
   Permission levels 200
   Read permission level 201
   View only permission level 203

Edit permission level 204

Contribute permission level... 205

Full control permission level.. 206

Design permission level... 207

Approve permission level 209

Manage hierarchy permission level.. 210

Restricted read permission level... 211

Restricted interfaces for translation permission level............................. 212

Records center web service submitters permission level......................... 213

Custom permission level 213

Access request settings.. 214

Site collection administrators 216

Check user permission 217

Remove user permission 217

Edit user permissions 218

Grant permissions 218

Create a group 219

Permission inheritance.. 221

Permission management modern experience 223

Invite people... 223

Add members to the group 223

Share site only... 224

Sharing options... 225

Conclusion 227

Points to remember... 228

9. Managed Metadata Concept.. **229**

Structure 229

Objective 230

Term store administration 230

Creating a term set... 232

Creating a term 235

Reuse terms... 237

Copy term set... 238

Merge terms 239

Move term set 240

Creating a metadata column... 240

Metadata column with submission policy closed 240

Metadata column with submission policy open 244

Creating local term set 245

Creating a global term set from the site collection 247

Metadata navigation settings 248
   Activate feature first 248
   Create metadata site columns 249
   Create a site content type 249
   Add columns to content type 250
   Allow management of content types in the library 251
   Add site content types to the library 251
Configure metadata navigation settings 252
   Testing metadata navigation settings 253
Metadata navigation 255
   Enable term set for site navigation 256
   Set term driven pages 256
Configure site navigation settings 259
Conclusion 261
Points to remember 261

10. SharePoint Server Publishing Infrastructure Feature 263
Structure 263
Objective 264
Activate Feature First 264
Changes in Site Contents 265
Changes in Content Type 265
Changes in Site Column 267
Changes in Look and Feel 267
Changes in Page Layouts 269
Change in permission levels 273
Changes in Webparts 274
Change in Site Settings options 274
Conclusion 276
Points to remember 276

11. Application of Business Connectivity Services 277
Structure 277
Objective 277
Create an external content type 278
Application of external content type 282
Conclusion 283
Points to remember 283

12. Site Designing and Enhancement 285
Structure 285
Objective 286
Site page 286

Section layout.. 292
    Add a new section 293
    Edit section.. 294
    Move section 294
    Duplicate section 294
    Delete section 295
    Add a new webpart in column 295
Modern site webparts 295
Featured webparts 297
    Text 297
    Image 298
    File viewer 299
    Link 300
    Embed 301
    Highlighted content 301
    Text, media, and content webparts.. 304
Bing Maps 304
    Call to Action.. 305
    Divider 305
Image Gallery.. 306
    Office 365 Video 307
    Spacer 307
    Stream 308
    Weather 309
    YouTube 309
    Kindle Instant Preview... 309
    Discovery 310
    Document Library.. 310
Hero 311
List 313
    List Properties... 314
    Page Properties... 315
Quick Links 316
    Recent Documents... 319
    Sites 320
    Communication and collaboration.. 320
    Conversations 320
    Events 323
    Group Calendar.. 325
    Highlights 326
    Microsoft Forms 326

News 327

People 329

Twitter 330

Planning and process 331

Planner 331

Business and Intelligence 332

Site Activity 332

Quick Chart 333

Power BI 333

Connectors 334

Google Analytics 334

Others 335

Button 336

Code Snippet 336

Countdown Timer 336

Markdown 337

World Clock 338

Saved For Later 338

Structural navigation caching 338

Hub site 339

Register as a hub site 339

Hub site association 340

Hub site settings 344

Application of WebParts in the hub site 348

Search in the hub site 350

Targeting news, files, and navigation 352

New Footer Navigation 353

Conclusion 355

Points to remember 355

13. Manage Site Usage 357

Structure 357

Objective 358

Site Usage 358

File Activity Report 361

Site Usage Report 363

Site Activity Webpart 366

Traditional Audit log reports 367

Storage Metrics 369

Conclusion 370

Points to remember 370

CHAPTER 1
Introduction and Site Information

We are living in a revolutionary digital world that is booming unimaginably very fast, and content plays a primary role in it. The use of electronic equipment like computer, mobile, tablet, to access digital content anywhere, anytime, is a part of life now. So, it's essential to manage content effectively, smartly, securely, and make it available at any time, anywhere to the right people. The content management tool comes into the picture as a solution for this. User needs exciting new features and best way to manage content in day to day life with increased speed and quality that can save cost and time. Microsoft SharePoint is the solution for all problems which provide a collaborative platform for content management as well as security of content to make avail content to the right people.

Structure

In this chapter, you will understand:

- Rewind SharePoint content concept
- Scope of power user role
- Templates revised
- Creating sites and subsites using the site template
- Getting started with site settings

- Basic modification in the site
- Selecting the right template

Objective

During the end of the chapter, you will get a clear understanding of:

- Concept of information, site contents, SharePoint sites, site templates.
- Scope of Power user
- New site templates introduced and information about classic templates available
- Creating modern sites and subsites
- Glance on-site settings
- Basic modification of site
- Overview of each site template and its use

Rewind SharePoint Content Concept

Let's rewind very basics about SharePoint, sounds easy, but it's challenging to understand the concept accurately. SharePoint is dealing with all about content. What is the content? Content is all about information. Whatever information we are getting in the form of text, audio, video, or any other format through any medium is called content. What is information? Information is all about data we have. Information or content is vast; how can we organize to make it easy for use? We have to identify and categorize different types of content or information and put a similar type of content into one content type. So, the content type is the actual container of content or information of a similar type. So, we can categorize different types of content into different content types. Then what is site? The site carries all content or information in the form of a content type. We will discuss more about content types in *Chapter 2, Library, and List Smart Management*.

Scope of power user role

Every SharePoint site is owned by a specific group of people, which we call as a site owner. The site owner is the primary person responsible for managing site and has full control, the authority to do all actions at the SharePoint site level. There is another group of people that we call as a site collection administrator. Then it comes into mind who is a site collection administrator. Site collection administrator is responsible for managing the site collection and has full control, the authority to do all actions at the site collection level, and that includes all sites present under that site collection as well. Then you must be thinking, what is the difference between site collection and site? To understand this, you need to understand the hierarchy of the SharePoint site.

SharePoint is based on sites only. For the on-premises environment, when administrators install SharePoint, the first root level site created is the central admin. In central admin, few more sites are created at the next level called **Web Application**. Under each web application administrator, create specific sites which are called **Site Collections**. Under each site collection, we create several sites that we can call as a **Subsite**. Under each subsite, we can create more sites that are subsite of their respective one level higher site. So, the site collection is the top-level site, and rest all sites exist under that site collection. A site itself a subsite of another site, it's just for understanding the level of the hierarchy, but every site maintains its individual set of features and functionalities. Now you must have got a clear understanding of site collection, sites, and subsites.

In SharePoint online, when the administrator creates a site under the `SharePoint Admin Center`, it's a site collection, and we call as the top-level site in SharePoint. This top-level site is owned by site owner/owners who is/are responsible for managing this site collection only. There must be site collection administrator/administrators who has/have full control, authority, in all sites, subsites under that site collection, to manage advanced features apart from the common site management features and functionalities. Normally IT administrators from the technical support operation team are given such site collection administrator permission but for large portals, power users can be assigned such permission to maintain such specific advanced features and functionalities as per business requirements, which we will discuss later. It means Power User has a specific set of permission to act and manage a specific set of advanced tasks similar to an administrator. So, SharePoint administrator will create a site collection and handover to the site collection owner or power user to manage. We will discuss in detail about permission level for each group of people in *Chapter 8, Manage Permission*.

Templates revised

As per the process, the user should request a new site with a detailed business requirement. As an owner, you are the only authorized person to create subsites under site collection, using any one of the site templates, as per your business requirement. How can you decide what type of site is suitable for user requirements? For this, you need to understand what is a template, and what are the different types of site templates available, which you need to select during the process of subsite creation? The template is a schema, or we can say skeleton, which provides a basic structure of site or content type. Template related to the site is called a **site template**, similarly, for a list, library, and other content type called a list template, library template like this. There are predefined templates by Microsoft, based on business requirements, present in SharePoint. You need to understand every site template and its use before creating a site.

Site templates out of box

Here we will discuss different types of site templates available as out of the box, which you need to select during new site creation. The different template has a different layout, features, and purpose of the requirement is different. Let us perform the following steps to create a new site:

1. When users want to create a new site, the user will get an option to select either **Modern Team** site or **Communicate site** or can choose other templates following option **Other options**. Modern **Team site** and **Communication site** are the new site templates introduced to collaborate and communicate better. The following image is a screenshot of default site template options:

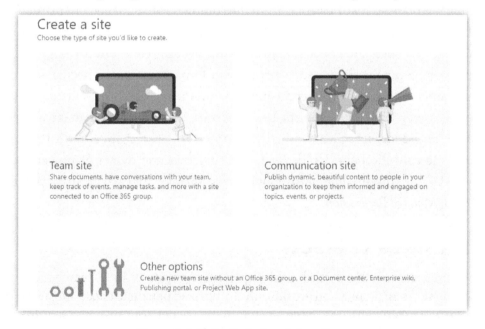

Figure 1.1: Default site template options

2. Proceeding further, click on **Other Options**. You see templates like **Document Center, Enterprise Wiki, Publishing Portal** and option **More templates** to check more default templates available as seen in the following screenshot:

Figure 1.2: Default site template options

3. Click on **More templates**; you see additional templates in the form of categories like **Collaboration, Enterprise, Publishing, Custom**.

4. Click on category **Collaboration** under the option **Create Site Collection | Template Selection**; you see **Team Site (classic experience), Blog, Developer Site, Project Site, Community Site** templates, which are called **Collaboration Templates**.

5. Click on category **Enterprise**; you see **Document Center, eDiscovery Center, Records Center, Team Site – SharePoint Online configuration, Business Intelligence Center, Compliance Policy Center, Enterprise Search Center, My Site Host, Community Portal, Basic Search Center, Visio Process Repository** templates which are called **Enterprise Templates**.

6. Click on category **Publishing;** you see **Publishing Portal, Enterprise Wiki** templates, which are called **Publishing Templates**.

7. Click on **Custom**, where you can find customized templates implemented by developers. All site templates could be seen in the following screenshot:

Figure 1.3: *Default site template options0*

Now you got an idea about default site templates available in SharePoint, out of which you need to select anyone while creating a site. We will discuss the application of site template latter in *Chapter 12, Site Designing and Enhancement*.

Content templates

Inside the site, you will find different contents like **List, Document library, Page, App, Subsite,** which also can be considered as content types. When you create any content, you have options to select a template related to a particular content or content type. Selecting from the drop-down option, **New** will show drop-down option to create a list, library, page, or subsite from respective content type templates available, which can be modified later. The following figure helps in understanding it:

Figure 1.4: *Default Content Templates*

We know, the app model is introduced from the SharePoint 2013 version. So, you see the option **App** while creating content. Click on **App**. You will find a lot of predefined apps based on the type of site templates you selected during site creation. There will be a difference in contents available based on the type of site template selected. Some contents are available after enabling certain site collection features or site features. You should notice these points while creating a site. The following screenshot displays various apps available in SharePoint:

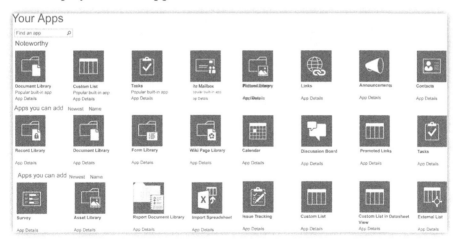

Figure 1.5: *Apps in SharePoint*

Creating sites and subsites using a site template

Now you got a basic idea about the content, content type, site, template, app. Now let's create new modern sites and subsite. As per process, after business approval, a user needs to create a request for site collection with **Name of Site Collection** and **Type of Site** and **Site Owner**. SharePoint administrators are responsible for creating top-level site collection and handover to the site owner, and there will be site collection administrators as well. For large portals, site collection administrator level permission can be given to power users. It all depends on the business requirement. From here, your role comes into the picture. Let's discuss step by step process to create a new modern site. Then we will create subsite using one type of site template available as default.

Modern communication site

My intension is to describe what the newly introduced sites are in SharePoint online and how to create. What is this site for and when to create this type of site is described in the later section **Selecting Right Template**. So, follow the step by step procedure below to create a newly introduced communication site:

1. Sign in to Office 365 portal **http://office365.com**, the user can see all apps present in Office 365, as per the type of subscription you have taken, including **SharePoint**. Click on the **SharePoint** app, as shown in the following screenshot. You will be redirected to the default root site:

Figure 1.6: Apps Launched after sign in Office 365 Portal

2. Click on **Create site** from the top left corner of the site and select **Communication site** template to create a new communication site shown as follows:

Figure 1.7: Communication site template

3. The site creation wizard will open. Select one design from the **Choose a design** option. There are three default designs like **Topic, Showcase, Blank** available shown as follows: Each design provides a different user interface:

Figure 1.8: Communication site designs and fills up all fields during site creation

4. Enter **Site name** as BPB-ModernCommunication, enter user id under **Site owner** who is going to own and manage the site and select the language of the site.

5. Click on **Advanced settings**; you will get additional options like **Time zone** and **Site description**. Enter those details and click on **Finish**. Communication site will be created as per the screenshot below:

Figure 1.9: Communication site home page of design topic

6. You will find images at the top and **News, Events, Documents** below as other contents on the site:

Figure 1.10: *News webparts in communication site home page of design topic*

Modern team site

A modern team site is also newly introduced in SharePoint online. We will discuss its application in the later section **Selecting Right Template**. Currently, just follow the step by step process below to create a **Modern Team Site**:

1. Log in to Office 365; the user can see all apps, including **SharePoint**. Click on **SharePoint**, as shown in the following screenshot. You will be redirected to the default root site.

Figure 1.11: *Apps Launched after sign in Office 365 Portal*

2. Click on **Create site** from the top left corner of the site and select the **Team site** template to create a new modern team site shown in the following screenshot:

Figure 1.12: Team Site Template

3. The site creation wizard will open. Enter **Site name** as `BPB-ModernTeamSite`, enter **Site description**, select **Privacy settings** as **Private – only members can access this site**. One Office 365 group will be created, and the group email address will be the same as the **Site name** (`BPB-ModernTeamSite`) by default, but you can change during the site creation by entering a new email address. Then click **Next** as shown in the following screenshot:

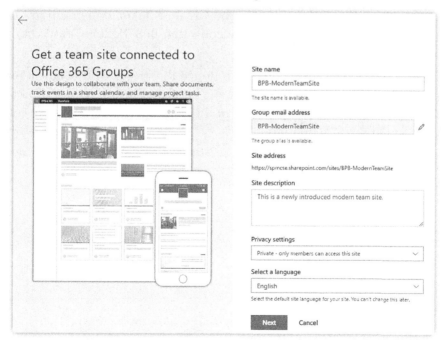

Figure 1.13: Fill up all fields to create a team site

4. Enter additional owner ID, if you want to keep more than one site owner.

5. Add group members under the **Add members** field. It will add members into the Office 365 group and click **Finish** as shown in the following screenshot:

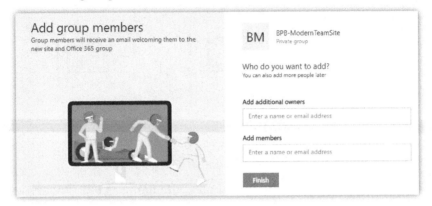

Figure 1.14: *Fill up fields to create a team site*

6. New modern site collection BPB-ModernTeamSite is created, and the URL will be https://spmcse.sharepoint.com/sites/BPB-ModernTeamSite.

7. You will notice, **Create a Team** in the Microsoft Teams option there at the bottom left corner of the site. Click on **Create a Team**, one group in Microsoft Teams, with the same name as site collection BPB-ModernTeamSite, will be created.

8. Log in to Microsoft Teams; you will notice the group **BPB-ModernTeamSite** as seen in the following screenshot. Expand that group; you will notice one folder **General**. The actual location of this folder is inside of the site collection document library **Documents**:

Figure 1.15: *Private Group for Team Site Created in Microsoft Teams*

9. In Site collection Home Page, under left navigation, you will notice one more quick launch **Teams** is added. **General** folder under the document library **Documents**, as seen in the following screenshot:

Figure 1.16: Modern team site home page and folder for storing files by a private group created in Microsoft Teams

SharePoint administrator should create a site collection and provide this to you, but I intend to show you how to create a new modern team site and how it is different from the classic team site. When you create a subsite of template `Team Site (no Office 365 group)`, it will be a new team site only, but no Office 365 group is created.

Now let's create a subsite that can be under your role as per business requirement.

Team site as subsite

In this section, we will discuss how to create subsite under one site collection. Follow the step by step process as below to create a subsite:

1. SharePoint Administrator handover the site collection to the owner. The site collection URL is `https://spmcse.sharepoint.com/sites/BPB-ModernTeam Site`.

2. Access the site collection. Click on **Site contents** from the left navigation menu or the drop-down option after clicking the **Gear** 🔧 button present at the top right corner, as seen in the following screenshot. All site contents will open:

Figure 1.17: Navigate to all site contents in SharePoint site

3. Click on the option **New** from newly introduced command bar and select **Subsite** from drop-down options, as seen in the following screenshot:

Figure 1.18: Navigate to Subsite from drop-down option New

4. Enter **Title** and **Description, URL name, Select a language,** choose one template, for example, **Team Site (no Office 365 group)** keep rest options as default and click on the button **Create** as seen in the following screenshot:

Figure 1.19: Fill up all fields and select the type of subsite template

5. New subsite **BPB-TeamSubSite** of type modern team site with no office 365 group created. Site URL will be `https://spmcse.sharepoint.com/sites/ BPB-ModernTeamSite/BPB-TeamSubSite`, as seen in the following screenshot:

Figure 1.20: Modern Team site with no Office 365 group

6. If you compare this subsite with top-level site collection, you notice both have the same look and feel except two quick launch options under left navigation **Conversations** and **Teams**, which are not present here.

Start page

After sign in to **Office365.com**, users can see all apps, including **SharePoint**. Click on **SharePoint** will redirect to a newly introduced SharePoint modern communication site landing page called **Start Page**. It captures all activity in **Sites, News, Events, Documents** in SharePoint. Which are the sites you frequently visit, sites that you follow, recently visited sites are captured under the category **Frequent, Following, Recent** respectively under section **Site** as seen in the following screenshot:

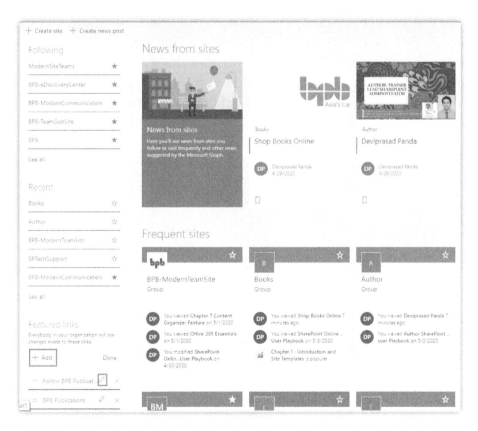

Figure 1.21: Start Page in SharePoint with sections News, Frequent sites visited, sites Following, Recent visited site

There is a section Featured links that give an option to add links that you frequently use Recent documents that capture the files, documents that you visited.

Hub Site

Hub Site is newly introduced in SharePoint by which multiple site collections are associated with one site collection to maintain branding, secure and faster access of site collection for intranet users at any time. Traditionally, the organization creates multiple site collections, subsites, multiple site owners, maintaining branding for site collection was difficult. Also, the organization had to manage at each site collection level. In SharePoint online, thousands of site collections are created. Introduction of hub site feature associates other site collections to the hub site. Let's say one organization BPB Publication has multiple site collections like **BPB-ModernTeamSite, Marketing, HR, Author, Social, Career, News**. So, in total, seven site collections with different URL. Now we can register the **BPB-ModernTeamSite** site collection as a hub site, and then we can associate the rest six site collections to the hub site **BPB-ModernTeamSite** as seen in the following screenshot. Whenever a user accesses any of these six sites, the hub site link will appear at the top of the site collection for quick redirection. Similarly, one organization can create multiple hub sites when the number of a site collection are huge in number and want to collaborate group of site collection for a common purpose. We will discuss more on this in *Chapter 12, Site Designing and Enhancement*:

Figure 1.22: Hub site

Getting started with Site settings

The site is created. Now we need to understand how to manage the site. What are the options available to manage the site? Every site has an option called **Site settings**, where you can control site actions, administer, change the look and feel of the site, manage permission for users and groups, control the site features.

You can open Site settings in multiple ways as below:

- For the modern team site, click on **Site contents** from the left navigation menu. You will find the **Site settings** option under the command bar from all **Site contents**, as seen in *Figure 1.23*.

- For the communication site, classic team site, or any other site, you can find **Settings** under the drop-down option by clicking the **Gear** ⚙ " button present at the top right corner.

- One more smart way is to add `_layouts/15/settings.aspx` after the site URL. For a site collection, the site settings URL will be `https://spmcse.sharepoint.com/sites/BPB-ModernTeamSite/_layouts/15/settings.aspx` and for subsite `https://spmcse.sharepoint.com/sites/BPB-ModernTeamSite/BPB-TeamSubSite/_layouts/15/settings.aspx`. So, adding `_layouts/15/settings. aspx` after the site URL will open site settings of that site:

Figure 1.23: Navigate to Site settings in SharePoint Site

Whether it's site collection or site or any subsite under that hierarchy, the **Site Settings** option and user interface are similar for all. For the new team site, under **Site Settings**, you will find options like **Look and Feel, Web Designer Galleries, Site Administration, Site Actions, Search**. For top-level site collection only, there is an extra option named **Site collection administration**; otherwise, rest all site, subsite has the same options in site setting, as seen in *Figure 1.24*. Except for the new modern team site, rest all site, you will notice an additional option **Users and Permissions** under **Site Settings**:

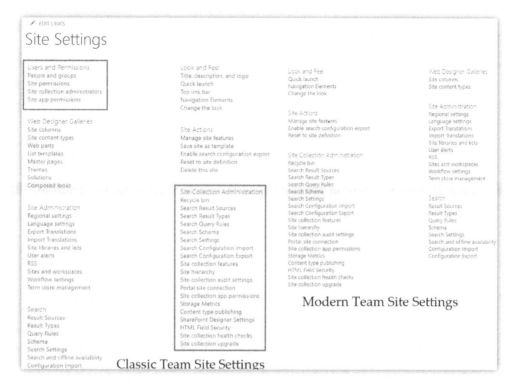

Figure 1.24: Comparing default site settings options between site collection and subsite

Basic modification in Site

Site settings or site page editing are the advanced modes of editing sites. But SharePoint Online provides an option to make some basic changes like theme, layout, background, and logo to maintain branding. Let's discuss how to make some basic changes in the site as per our requirement.

Change the look

In this section, we will discuss how to change basic look and feel and a few site information. Let us perform the following steps to change the look of the site:

1. Click on the **Gear** ⚙ button from the top right corner of the page.

2. Select **Change the look** option from the drop-down, as shown in *Figure 1.25*.

3. You will get another dialog box with options **Theme** and **Header**.

4. Click on **Theme**. You will see another dialog box showing the current theme applied on the homepage. Select any other theme and click on **Save**. You will see the color of the homepage background, button, text changed:

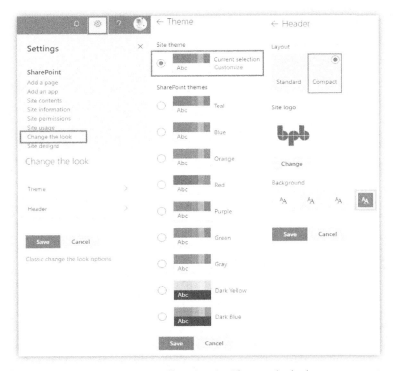

Figure 1.25: All option in Change the look

5. Click on **Header**. You will get additional options like **Layout**, **Site logo**, **Background**. Selecting the option **Compact** from **Layout** will make some space arrangements in the header. You can change the logo of the site following the button **Change** under the **Site logo**. Selecting one option from the next **Background** will change the header background color. After that, you can see the look of the site changed, as shown in *Figure 1.26*:

Figure 1.26: Modern Team site after modifying Theme and Header from Change the look option

6. Once links are there in the **Header**, you will see one more option apart from **Theme**, **Header** is **Navigation**. Click on **Navigation**; you will get options to 2select one **Menu Style** out of the **Mega menu** and **Cascading**. Selecting any one of the options will change the menu option, as shown in the figure below. **Mega menu** is new to SharePoint online that gives a different impression to the site:

Figure 1.27: Navigation header

Modify Site Information

SharePoint online provides options like **Site information** that allows modifying **Site name**, **Site description**, **Privacy settings**, **Delete site**. Follow the step by step process to see how to modify site information:

1. Click on the **Gear** ⚙ button from the top right corner, select the **Site information** option from the drop-down, as shown in *Figure 1.28*.

2. You will get the option to change the **Logo**, **Site name**, **Site description**. You can change the **Privacy settings** from **Private - only members can access the site** to **Public - anyone in the organization can access the site** and click on **Save**.

3. One more option, **Hub site association**, used to associate team site to **Hub Site**. **Hub Site** needs to be configured separately, which we will discuss later:

Figure 1.28: Edit Site Information

Selecting the Right Template

You must have understood what site template is and how to create a site using the site template. We already created a new modern team site, communication site, subsite. Similarly, you can create different sites as per the template available and project requirements. Reminding again, different site templates just provide predefined schema or skeleton for a different site, having specific default content types for each template. Remember, we can edit the site and add apps during need as per our requirement at any time. Now you need to identify the right template which is suitable for user requirements.

Modern Team Site

This site provides a collaborative platform with a brand new template, where users can share documents within team members, organize their activities in the list, share news within a team by creating news post, share news links, create a plan for the team, assign tasks and check the progress of tasks. Integration with OneNote by which users can keep critical notes in the notebook. If the user requirement is limited to this, then you should suggest users for a new modern team site.

Communication site

You can create a communication site with the same step as we did for modern team site creation. You just need to select the **Communication site** template. It is a new template introduced that focus more on representing content with the visually stunning format, widescreen without any left navigational element. Users can create and share news, events, reports, and showcase products with Images. Mainly contents are consumed by and targeted for a large audience but contributed by very few and selected people. This site comes with three design, named **Topic**, **Showcase**, **Blank**. Topic design mostly used for visual contents related to the news, events, reports. Showcase design mostly used to showcase your product during launch and marketing related content that are visually stunning. What are the actions we are taking on this site? We will discuss more on this in a later chapter.

Blog Site (Collaboration)

Blog site allows users to share ideas, experience, observation, announcements in the form of a post. Relate post to any event, ideas, or opinion during the creation of the post. User put their comment, share knowledge and opinion on the post. It is mostly useful for creating knowledge base articles related to company operational support. This classic blog site will be retired soon by the year 2020, and users can create a great blog by using communication sites and news posts further. The following image is a screenshot of the blog site:

Figure 1.29: Default Blog Site template

Developer Site (Collaboration)

If a user is doing development in SharePoint Online, this site provides a platform where user can build their apps, do testing, and finally publish. It is used by developers. The following image is a screenshot of the developer site:

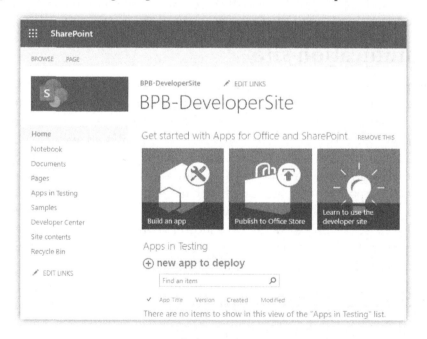

Figure 1.30: Default Developer site template

Project Site (Collaboration)

For a project, we are adding resources to the project, assigning tasks, tracking the progress of tasks assigned to resources. Sharing project documents, news internal to project members. Provide default web part related to the project, which would be helpful for project management. Users can create individual project sites for individual projects. Project Site provides secure integration options to project management tool, Microsoft Project Professional, Microsoft Project Server Application to manage the project to a larger extend, and secure management. The following image is a screenshot of the project site:

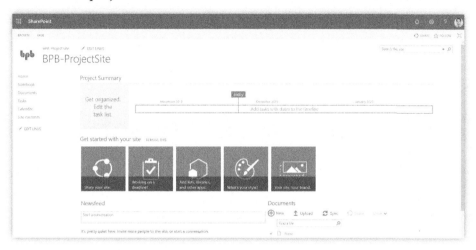

Figure 1.31: Default Project Site template

Community Site (Collaboration)

Community site provides a platform where community members can share their ideas and discuss ideas in common to them. Group of people shares their ideas on a common platform, a kind of social features it provides. The following image is a screenshot of a Community site:

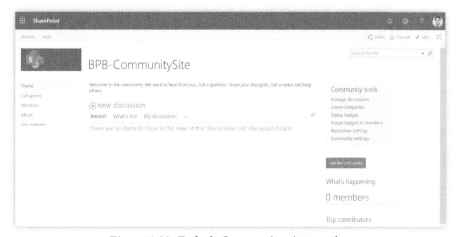

Figure 1.32: Default Community site template

Document Center Site (Enterprise)

Document Center template mostly acts as a dedicated central repository for the documents. When the volume of documents is very high, and user frequently views, contribute or modify the document, this template provides a platform dedicated to documents only with all additional features like metadata navigation, Document ID, Versions, Content types, Content Organizer at one place. It makes better document management. You will find more information related to this site in *Chapter 5, Configure Document ID Service*. The following image is a screenshot of the document center site:

Figure 1.33: Default Document Center Site template

eDiscovery center site (Enterprise)

Process of identifying electronic information like legal documents, financial, litigation, documents related to the investigation, sensitive data across different sources like an exchange, file server, Skype for Business, Teams sites, and delivering information that can act as evidence. eDiscovery Center portal provides a platform to manage the eDiscovery cases, apply the hold, search information by applying query, review information, release the hold, and finally export the information. The following image is a screenshot of the eDiscovery center site:

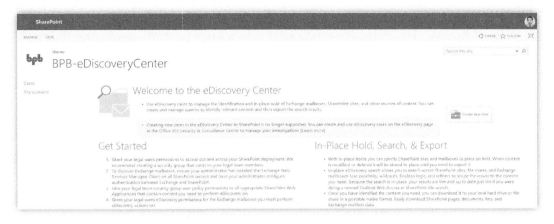

Figure 1.34: Default eDiscovery Site template

Records Center Site (Enterprise)

Record center provides a collaborative platform dedicated to records like company financial document, legal documents and provides specific features related to recording management like security, auditing, policy to information a few more, which we will discuss separately later chapter. If the user requirement is to maintain a record, then this would be the best template. You will find more information related to this in *Chapter 7, Content Organizer Feature*. The following image is a screenshot of the records center site:

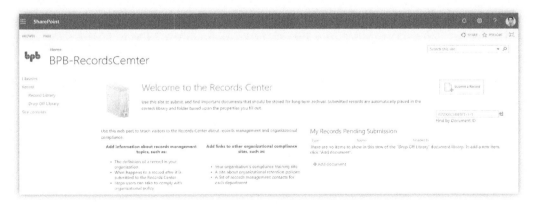

Figure 1.35: Default Record center site template

Business Intelligence Center Site (Enterprise)

Business intelligence Center template mostly used for storing content related to BI like data connection, scorecards, reports, dashboard as well. Facilitates specific contents dedicated to these BI contents, which we will be discussed in the next chapter. The following image is a screenshot of Business intelligence center site:

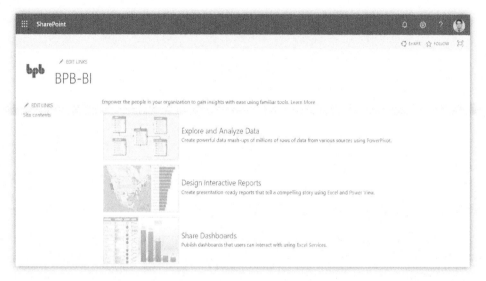

Figure 1.36: Default Business Intelligence Site template

Compliance Policy Center Site (Enterprise)

Using this site can create Policies for content, rules set for document management. You will find more information related to this in *Chapter 4, Configure Information Management Policy*. The following image is a screenshot of the compliance policy center site:

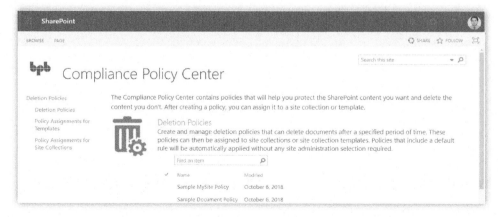

Figure 1.37: Default Compliance Policy Center Site template

Community Portal Site (Enterprise)

Community Portal site acts as a central directory that holds information regarding all community sites present across your organization. It helps users to search and discover topics they are interested in, can follow other community sites, visit topics, and can take active participation in the discussion, which leads to collaborate with your enterprise employees in one place. The following image is a screenshot of the community portal site:

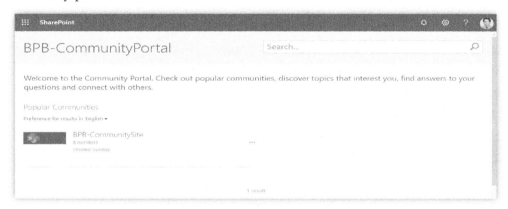

Figure 1.38: Default Community Portal Site template

Visio Process Repository Site (Enterprise)

If a user wants to store, view, share and manage Visio diagrams, this template is the perfect place. The following image is a screenshot of the Visio process repository site:

Figure 1.39: Default Visio Process Repository Site template

Publishing Site (Publishing)

Publishing site provides rich features like additional page layout options as welcome page, customized options available to make your branding site, dynamic sites creation option. Manage workflows and approval centrally, the option to publish content across multiple sites, the option to refine permission and security for content by providing special SharePoint groups and new permission levels. Much more features we will discuss separately in the later *Chapter 10, SharePoint Server Publishing Infrastructure Feature*. It is useful for the sites rich in dynamic content, changing content at one place, and publishing to multiple sites like news, product catalog sites that need a frequent change in content at multiple pages at the same time. The following image is a screenshot of the publishing site:

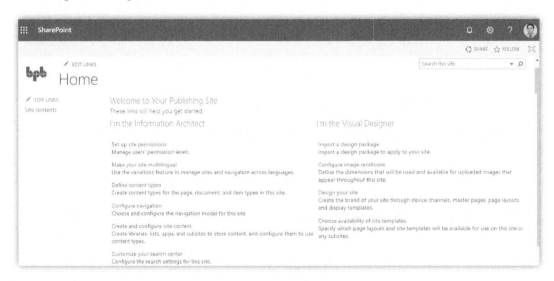

Figure 1.40: Default Publishing Site template

Enterprise Wiki Site (Publishing)

Enterprise wiki is a dedicated site for storing, sharing large volumes of information across the world for an enterprise. It provides an easy way to edit information, add tags and notes, links to make it searchable and quickly find the right information during need. The following image is a screenshot of Enterprise Wiki Site:

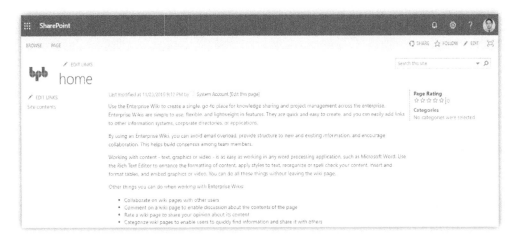

***Figure 1.41:** Default Enterprise Wiki Site template*

Default SharePoint Online Templates

If we want to get all default SharePoint online templates with id, then PowerShell command can help to get this and output will display template **Name**, **Title**, **LocaleId**, **CompatibilityLevel** as seen in the following screenshot:

```
1  Get-SPOWebTemplate
```

```
PS C:\WINDOWS\system32> Get-SPOWebTemplate

Name                       Title                                         LocaleId CompatibilityLevel
----                       -----                                         -------- ------------------
STS#3                      Team site (no Office 365 group)                   1033                 15
STS#0                      Team site (classic experience)                    1033                 15
BLOG#0                     Blog                                              1033                 15
BDR#0                      Document Center                                   1033                 15
DEV#0                      Developer Site                                    1033                 15
OFFILE#1                   Records Center                                    1033                 15
EHS#1                      Team Site - SharePoint Online configuration       1033                 15
BICenterSite#0             Business Intelligence Center                      1033                 15
SRCHCEN#0                  Enterprise Search Center                          1033                 15
BLANKINTERNETCONTAINER#0   Publishing Portal                                 1033                 15
ENTERWIKI#0                Enterprise Wiki                                   1033                 15
PROJECTSITE#0              Project Site                                      1033                 15
PRODUCTCATALOG#0           Product Catalog                                   1033                 15
COMMUNITY#0                Community Site                                    1033                 15
COMMUNITYPORTAL#0          Community Portal                                  1033                 15
SITEPAGEPUBLISHING#0       Communication site                                1033                 15
SRCHCENTERLITE#0           Basic Search Center                               1033                 15
visprus#0                  Visio Process Repository                          1033                 15
```

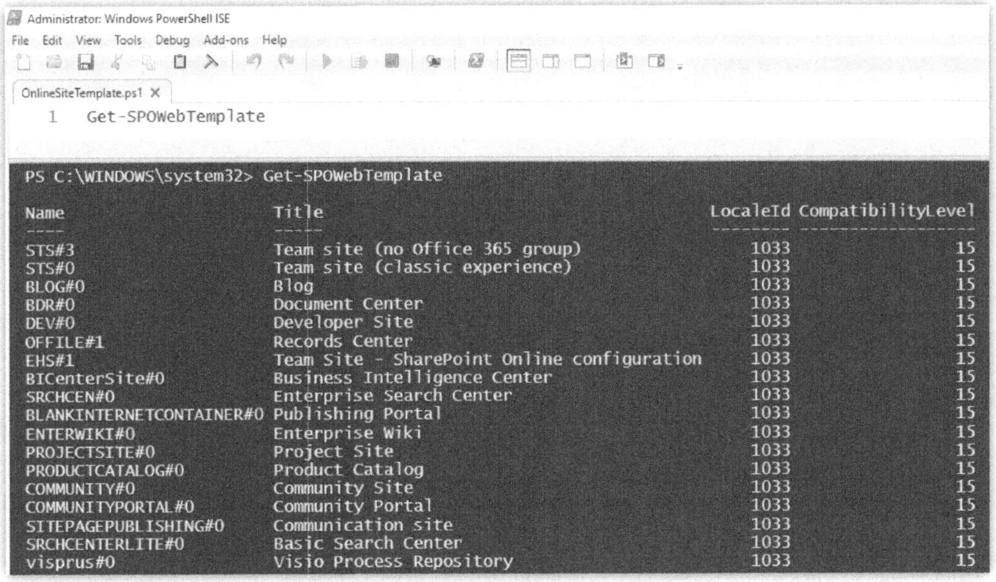

***Figure 1.42:** Default SharePoint Online templates with ID*

Conclusion

In this chapter, we discussed the contents, information, sites. You learned what the default site templates that are available to create sites. We created newly introduced team site, subsites, communication sites, and classic sites as well. We understood the scope of Power-user. We shared information about basic site settings and step by step information to change some basic site information. We also discussed the application of every SharePoint site that we can create. Next chapter, *Chapter 2*, *Library and List Smart Management*, we will discuss default site contents and app available, smart features introduced to manage content, information about apps. Then we will discuss list and library settings, share a glance on site collection features, site features, and its impact on-site content.

Points to remember

- Regular changes are applied in Office 365 and SharePoint Online by which there may be changes happens in the template or some other features.

- This excellent blog site will be retired soon by the year 2020, and the user can create a great blog by using communication sites and news posts further.

CHAPTER 2
Library and List Smart Management

In the previous chapter, we discussed all the SharePoint sites. Let's continue with **Site Content** in this chapter. SharePoint site consists of site contents or content types, which hold the actual content or information on the site. Depending on the type of SharePoint site, you will notice a difference in default contents or content types available on the site. You will notice a few additional contents or content types available or missing for different types of sites. It does not mean you can't add any contents or content types to your current site. You can edit the site to add or remove any content or content type at any moment to manage your site content.

Structure

In this chapter, we will discuss the following topics:

- Default site contents and site features
- Upgraded new features for smart management
- Apps management
- Understand list and library settings is must

Objective

During the end of the chapter, you will get a clear understanding of the following topics:

- Different types of contents available in the site
- Site features or site collection features activated by default
- What are the new features in SharePoint Online?
- Information about apps in SharePoint
- All about the library and list settings

Default Site Contents and Site Features

Here we will discuss the default site contents available in each SharePoint site collection. In the subsite level, you might find few content or content type not there, but site collection you will find more. Also, we will share information about the default site collection features and site features activated, once a site collection is created, for each site collection template. When you access site contents, you will find the contents of the type **List** or **Library**. Now it comes into mind, what is the difference between list and library. Simply can say the library is used to upload and store documents, files whereas list is a type of table where you can save multiple items. Think about one excel file as an example. Each row in an excel file is considered as a list item, so all rows within that excel file constitute one SharePoint **List**. When you upload this excel to a container, that is called the library, which stores this excel file. So multiple excel file stored in a container is called **Library**. Different types of libraries are used to upload and store specific type files each. Similarly, different types of lists are used to store a specific type of item which is pre-identified. Let's discuss what the default site contents available in each type of site template are.

Modern Team Site Contents

Once the site is created, there are specific default contents created on site. Specific contents are created/enabled after activating site collection features or site features. Here we will discuss the default site contents available after site creation.

Let us perform the following steps to check default site contents available and default feature activated for **Modern Team Site**:

1. Access the modern site collection URL (`https://spmcse.sharepoint.com/sites/BPB-ModernTeamSite`) that we created previously.

2. Click on **Site Contents** from left navigation. Alternatively, you can open site content by adding `_layouts/15/viewlsts.aspx` after the site URL (`http://<site url>/_layouts/15/viewlsts.aspx`). Here will be the link for site contents `https://spmcse.sharepoint.com/sites/BPB-Modern TeamSite/_layouts/15/viewlsts.aspx`. You will notice default contents (**Documents**, **Form Templates**, **Site Assets**, **Style Library**, **Site Pages**) of type list or library available, as seen in the following screenshot:

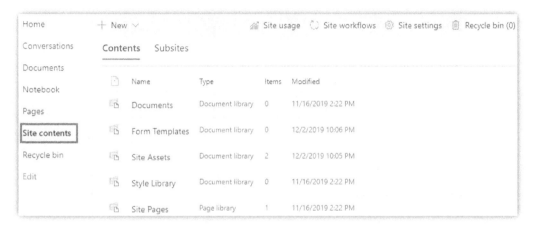

Figure 2.1: *Site contents in the team site default*

3. We already discussed how to open site settings before. So open site settings for site collection (`_layouts/15/settings.aspx`).

4. Click on **Manage Site Features** (`https://<site url>/_layouts/15/Manage Features.aspx`) present under **Site Actions**.

5. You will find below features in **Active** state by default, as shown in *Figure 2.2*, and the feature is limited to site level only.

Site features activated by default:

- Following Content
- SharePoint Recommendations
- Site Notebook
- Site Pages
- Team Collaboration Lists
- Workflow Task Content Type

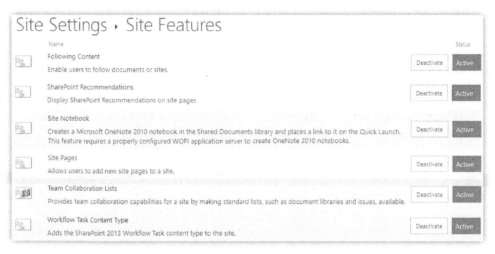

Figure 2.2: Site Features in Active State by default

6. Click on **Site Collection Features** (https://<site url>/_layouts/15/Manage Features.aspx?Scope=Site) present under **Site Collection Administration**, and you will find few features activated by default which are applicable for all subsites present under that site collection.

Site collection feature activated by default as seen in the following screenshot:

- Three-state workflow

Figure 2.3: Site Collection Features in Active State by Default

Modern Communication Site Contents

Similarly, when you open site content (http://<site url>/_layouts/15/viewlsts.aspx) for **Modern Communication Site**, you will find contents **Events, Documents, Style Library, Form Templates, Site Pages** available by default as seen in the following screenshot:

Figure 2.4: Site Contents in Communication Site default

Site Features and Site Collection Features in **Active** state, by default, as seen in the following table below.

Site Features	Site Collection Feature
• Following Content • SharePoint Recommendations • Site Pages • Workflow Task Content Type	• No Feature in Active State

Table 2.1: *Default Site Features and Site Collection Features activated in Communication Site*

Blog Site Contents

Open site content for **Blog Site**, you will find contents **Categories**, **Comments**, **Posts**, **Style Library**, **Form Templates**, **Photos** available by default as seen in the following screenshot:

Name	▼	Type	▼	Description
Lists				
Categories		Lists		Use the Categories list to define the categories available for posts.
Comments		Lists		The Comments list stores comments that have been made on posts.
Posts		Lists		Use the Posts list for posts in this blog.
Document Libraries				
Style Library		Document Libraries		Use the style library to store style sheets, such as CSS or XSL files. The style sheets in this gallery can be used by this site or any of its subsites.
Form Templates		Document Libraries		This library contains administrator-approved form templates that were activated to this site collection.
Photos		Document Libraries		Share a picture with the team by adding it to this picture library.

Figure 2.5: *Site Contents in Blog Site Default*

Site Features and Site Collection Features in **Active** state, by default, as seen in the following table:

Site Features	Site Collection Feature
• Following Content • Minimal Download Strategy • SharePoint Server Enterprise Site features • SharePoint Server Standard Site features • Team Collaboration Lists • Workflow Task Content Type	• Disposition Approval Workflow • Document Sets • Library and Folder Based Retention • Reporting • SharePoint Server Enterprise Site Collection features • SharePoint Server Standard Site Collection features • Site Policy • Three-state Workflow • Video and Rich Media

Table 2.2: Default Site Features and Site Collection Features activated in Blog Site

Developer Site Contents

Open site content for Developer Site, you will find contents MicroFeed, Apps in Testing, App Packages, Documents, Form Templates, Site Assets, Style Library, Site Pages available by default as seen in the following screenshot:

Figure 2.6: Site Contents in Developer Site Default

Site Features and Site Collection Features in **Active** state, by default, as seen in the following table:

Site Features	Site Collection Feature
• Following Content • Getting Started • Minimal Download Strategy • Mobile Browser View • SharePoint Recommendations • SharePoint Server Enterprise Site features • SharePoint Server Standard Site features • Site Feed • Site Notebook • Site Pages • Team Collaboration Lists • Wiki Page Home Page • Workflow Task Content Type	• Disposition Approval Workflow • Document Sets • Library and Folder Based Retention • Reporting • SharePoint Server Enterprise Site Collection features • SharePoint Server Standard Site Collection features • Site Policy • Three-state Workflow • Video and Rich Media

Table 2.3: Default Site Features and Site Collection Features activated in Developer Site

Project Site Contents

Open site content for **Project Site**, you will find contents **Calendar**, **MicroFeed**, **Tasks**, **Documents**, **Form Templates**, **Style Library**, **Site Assets** available by default as seen in the following screenshot:

Name	Type	Description
Lists		
Calendar	Lists	
MicroFeed	Lists	MySite MicroFeed Persistent Storage List
Tasks	Lists	
Document Libraries		
Documents	Document Libraries	
Form Templates	Document Libraries	This library contains administrator-approved form templates that were activated to this site collection.
Style Library	Document Libraries	Use the style library to store style sheets, such as CSS or XSL files. The style sheets in this gallery can be used by this site or any of its subsites.
Site Assets	Document Libraries	Use this library to store files which are included on pages within this site, such as images on Wiki pages.

Figure 2.7: Site Contents in Project Site default

Site Features and Site Collection Features in **Active** state, by default, as seen in the following table:

Site Features	Site Collection Feature
• Following Content • Getting Started • Minimal Download Strategy • Mobile Browser View • Project Functionality • SharePoint Server Enterprise Site features • SharePoint Server Standard Site features • Site Feed • Site Notebook • Team Collaboration Lists • Workflow Task Content Type	• Disposition Approval Workflow • Document Sets • Library and Folder Based Retention • Reporting • SharePoint Server Enterprise Site Collection features • SharePoint Server Standard Site Collection features • Site Policy • Three-state Workflow • Video and Rich Media

Table 2.4: *Default Site Features and Site Collection Features activated in Project Site*

Community Site Contents

Open site content for **Community Site**, you will find contents **Categories**, **Community Members**, **Discussions List**, **Style Library**, **Form Templates**, **Site Assets**, **Site Pages** available by default as seen in the following screenshot:

Name	Type	Description
Lists		
Categories	Lists	Use the Categories list to define the categories available for discussion list posts.
Community Members	Lists	This list keeps a record of ongoing activity by members and reputation they accrue within this community.
Discussions List	Lists	Use the Discussion list to hold forum-style conversations, including question and answer, on topics relevant to your team, project, or community
Document Libraries		
Style Library	Document Libraries	Use the style library to store style sheets, such as CSS or XSL files. The style sheets in this gallery can be used by this site or any of its subsites.
Form Templates	Document Libraries	This library contains administrator-approved form templates that were activated to this site collection.
Site Assets	Document Libraries	Use this library to store files which are included on pages within this site, such as images on Wiki pages.
Site Pages	Document Libraries	

Figure 2.8: *Site Contents in the Community Site default*

Site Features and Site Collection Features in **Active** state, by default, as seen in the following table:

Site Features	Site Collection Feature
• Community Site Feature • Following Content • Minimal Download Strategy • SharePoint Server Enterprise Site features • SharePoint Server Standard Site features • Team Collaboration Lists • Workflow Task Content Type	• Document Sets • SharePoint Server Enterprise Site Collection features • SharePoint Server Standard Site Collection features • Video and Rich Media

Table 2.5: *Default Site Features and Site Collection Features activated in Community Site*

Document Center Site Contents

Open site content for **Document Center Site**, you will find contents **Content and Structure Reports, Reusable Content, Tasks, Workflow Tasks, Documents, Form Templates, Site Collection Documents, Site Collection Images, Style Library** available by default as seen in the following screenshot:

Figure 2.9: Site Contents in Development Center Site default

Site Features and Site Collection Features in **Active** state, by default, as seen in the following table:

Site Features	Site Collection Feature
• Following Content • Metadata Navigation and Filtering • Mobile Browser View • SharePoint Server Enterprise Site features • SharePoint Server Standard Site features • Team Collaboration Lists • Workflow Task Content Type	• Disposition Approval Workflow • Document ID Service • Document Sets • Library and Folder Based Retention • Limited-access user permission lockdown mode • Reporting • SharePoint Server Enterprise Site Collection features • SharePoint Server Standard Site Collection features • Site Policy • Three-state Workflow • Video and Rich Media

Table 2.6: Default Site Features and Site Collection Features activated in Document Center Site

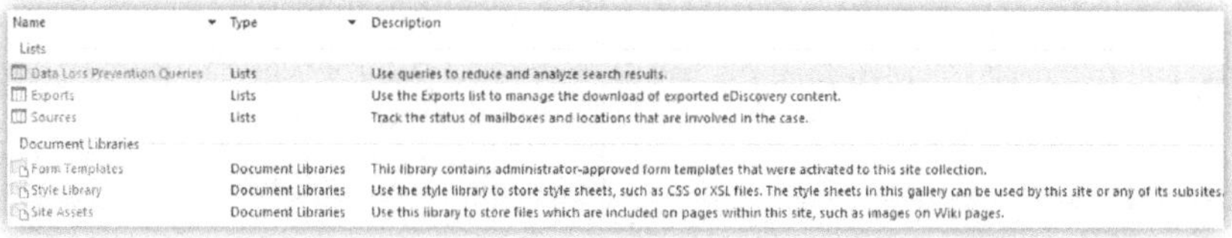

eDiscovery Center Contents

Open site content for **eDiscovery Center Site**, you will find contents **Data Loss Prevention Queries, Exports, Sources, Style Library, Form Templates, Site Assets** available by default as seen in the following screenshot:

Figure 2.10: Site Contents in eDiscovery Center Site default

Site Features and Site Collection Features in **Active** state, by default, as seen in the following table:

Site Features	Site Collection Feature
• Following Content • Metadata Navigation and Filtering • SharePoint Server Enterprise Site features • SharePoint Server Standard Site features • Team Collaboration Lists • Workflow Task Content Type	• Disposition Approval Workflow • Document Sets • Library and Folder Based Retention • Reporting • SharePoint Server Enterprise Site Collection features • SharePoint Server Standard Site Collection features • Site Policy • Video and Rich Media • Workflows

Table 2.7: Default Site Features and Site Collection Features activated in eDiscovery Center Site

Record Center Site Contents

Open site content for **Record Center Site**, you will find contents **Form Templates**, **Record Library**, **Drop Off Library**, **Site Assets**, **Style Library** available by default as seen in the following screenshot:

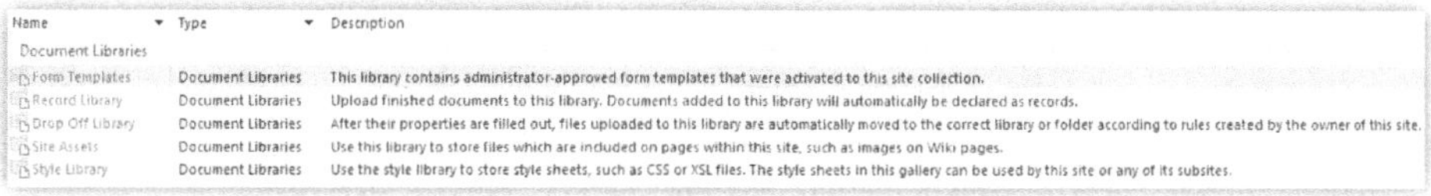

Figure 2.11: Site Contents in Record Center Site default

Site Features and Site Collection Features in **Active** state, by default, as seen in the following table:

Site Features	Site Collection Feature
• Content Organizer • Following Content • Hold • Metadata Navigation and Filtering • SharePoint Server Enterprise Site features • SharePoint Server Standard Site features • Team Collaboration Lists • Workflow Task Content Type	• Disposition Approval Workflow • Document ID Service • Document Sets • In Place Records Management • Library and Folder Based Retention • Reporting • SharePoint Server Enterprise Site Collection features • SharePoint Server Standard Site Collection features • Site Policy • Three-state Workflow • Video and Rich Media

Table 2.8: Default Site Features and Site Collection Features activated in Record Center Site

SharePoint Online Configuration Site Contents

Open site content for **SharePoint Online Configuration Site**, you will find contents **MicroFeed, Style Library, Documents, Site Assets, Form Templates, Site Pages** available by default as seen in the following screenshot:

Figure 2.12: *Site Contents in SharePoint Online Configuration Site default*

Site Features and Site Collection Features in **Active** state, by default, as seen in the following table:

Site Features	Site Collection Feature
• Following Content • Getting Started • Minimal Download Strategy • Mobile Browser View • SharePoint Recommendations • SharePoint Server Enterprise Site features • SharePoint Server Standard Site features • Site Feed • Site Notebook • Site Pages • Team Collaboration Lists • Wiki Page Home Page • Workflow Task Content Type	• Disposition Approval Workflow • Document Sets • Library and Folder Based Retention • Reporting • SharePoint Server Enterprise Site Collection features • SharePoint Server Standard Site Collection features • Site Policy • Video and Rich Media • Workflows

Table 2.9: *Default Site Features and Site Collection Features activated in SharePoint Online Configuration Site*

Business Intelligence Center Site Contents

Open site content for **Business Intelligence Center Site**, you will find contents **Content and Structure Reports, Reusable Content, Workflow Tasks, Images, Site Collection Images, Site Collection Documents, Style Library, Form Templates,**

Dashboards, **Data Connections**, **Documents**, **Pages**, **Site Assets** available by default as seen in the following screenshot:

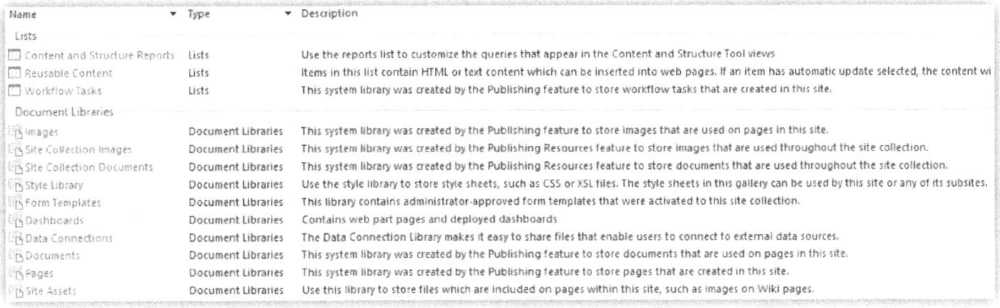

Figure 2.13: Site Contents in Business Intelligence Center Site default

Site Features and Site Collection Features in **Active** state, by default, as seen in the following table:

Site Features	Site Collection Feature
• Following Content	• Document Sets
• SharePoint Server Standard Site features	• Limited-access user permission lockdown mode
• Workflow Task Content Type	• Publishing Approval Workflow
	• SharePoint Server Enterprise Site Collection features
	• SharePoint Server Publishing Infrastructure
	• Video and Rich Media

Table 2.10: Default Site Features and Site Collection Features activated in Business Intelligence Center Site

Compliance Policy Center Site Contents

Open site content for **Compliance Policy Center Site**, you will find contents **Container Settings**, **Dar Tasks**, **Dynamic Scope Binding**, **Policy Assignments**, **Policy Bindings**, **Policy Definitions**, **Policy Events**, **Policy Rules**, **Form Templates**, **Site Assets**, **Style Library** available by default as seen in the following screenshot:

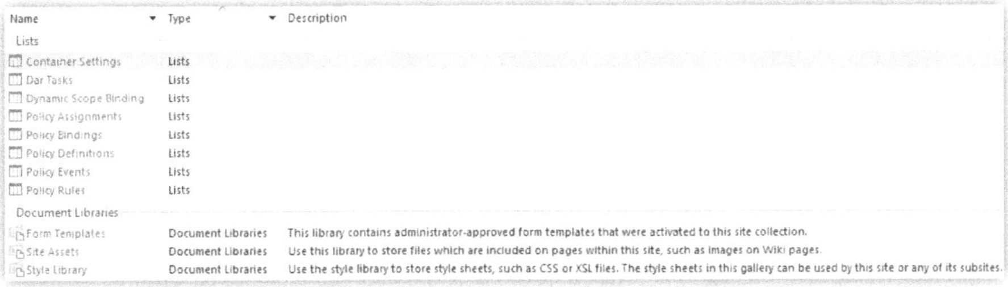

Figure 2.14: Site Contents in Compliance Policy Center Site default

Site features and site collection Features in **Active** state, by default, as seen in the following table:

Site Features	Site Collection Feature
• Following Content • SharePoint Server Enterprise Site features • SharePoint Server Standard Site features • Workflow Task Content Type	• Disposition Approval Workflow • Document Sets • Library and Folder Based Retention • Reporting • SharePoint Server Enterprise Site Collection features • SharePoint Server Standard Site Collection features • Site Policy • Video and Rich Media

Table 2.11: Default Site Features and Site Collection Features activated in Compliance Policy Center Site

Community Portal Site Contents

Open site content for **Community Portal Site**, you will find contents **Style Library**, **Form Templates**, **Site Assets** available by default as seen in the following screenshot:

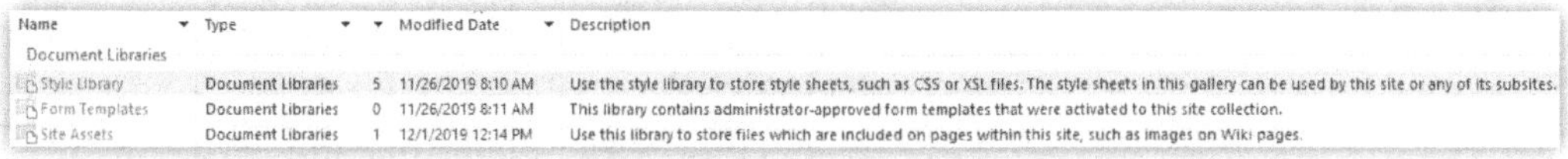

Figure 2.15: Site Contents in Community Portal Site default

Site Features and Site Collection Features in **Active** state, by default, as seen in the following table:

Site Features	Site Collection Feature
• Following Content • Minimal Download Strategy • Team Collaboration Lists • Workflow Task Content Type	• Document Sets • Video and Rich Media

Table 2.12: Default Site Features and Site Collection Features activated in Community Portal Site

Visio Process Repository Contents

Open site content for **Visio Process Repository Site**, you will find contents **Form Templates**, **Style Library**, **Process Diagram**, **Site Assets** available by default as seen in the following screenshot:

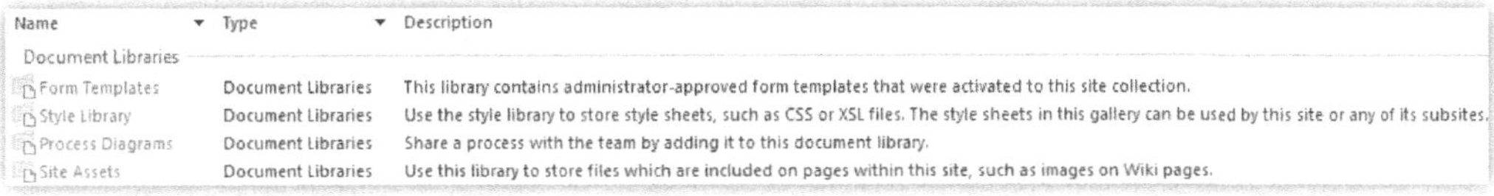

Name ▾	Type ▾	Description
Document Libraries		
Form Templates	Document Libraries	This library contains administrator-approved form templates that were activated to this site collection.
Style Library	Document Libraries	Use the style library to store style sheets, such as CSS or XSL files. The style sheets in this gallery can be used by this site or any of its subsites.
Process Diagrams	Document Libraries	Share a process with the team by adding it to this document library.
Site Assets	Document Libraries	Use this library to store files which are included on pages within this site, such as images on Wiki pages.

Figure 2.16: Site Contents in the Visio Process Repository Site default

Site Features and Site Collection Features in **Active** state, by default, as seen in the following table:

Site Features	Site Collection Feature
• Following Content • Getting Started • Metadata Navigation and Filtering • Minimal Download Strategy • SharePoint Server Enterprise Site features • SharePoint Server Standard Site features • Team Collaboration Lists • Workflow Task Content Type	• Document Sets • Publishing Approval Workflow • SharePoint Server Enterprise Site Collection features • Video and Rich Media

Table 2.13: Default Site Features and Site Collection Features activated in the Visio Process Repository Site

Publishing Portal Site Contents

Open site content for **Publishing Portal Site**, you will find contents **Content and Structure Reports**, **Workflow Tasks**, **Reusable Content**, **Site Collection Documents**, **Documents**, **Form Templates**, **Style Library**, **Images**, **Site Collection Images**, **Pages**, **Site Assets** available by default as seen in the following screenshot:

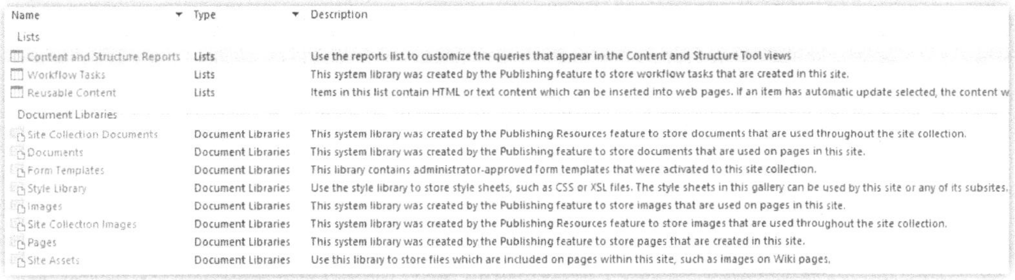

Name ▾	Type ▾	Description
Lists		
Content and Structure Reports	Lists	Use the reports list to customize the queries that appear in the Content and Structure Tool views
Workflow Tasks	Lists	This system library was created by the Publishing feature to store workflow tasks that are created in this site.
Reusable Content	Lists	Items in this list contain HTML or text content which can be inserted into web pages. If an item has automatic update selected, the content w
Document Libraries		
Site Collection Documents	Document Libraries	This system library was created by the Publishing Resources feature to store documents that are used throughout the site collection.
Documents	Document Libraries	This system library was created by the Publishing feature to store documents that are used on pages in this site.
Form Templates	Document Libraries	This library contains administrator-approved form templates that were activated to this site collection.
Style Library	Document Libraries	Use the style library to store style sheets, such as CSS or XSL files. The style sheets in this gallery can be used by this site or any of its subsites.
Images	Document Libraries	This system library was created by the Publishing feature to store images that are used on pages in this site.
Site Collectron Images	Document Libraries	This system library was created by the Publishing Resources feature to store images that are used throughout the site collection.
Pages	Document Libraries	This system library was created by the Publishing feature to store pages that are created in this site.
Site Assets	Document Libraries	Use this library to store files which are included on pages within this site, such as images on Wiki pages.

Figure 2.17: Site Contents in Publishing Portal Site default

Site Features and Site Collection Features in **Active** state, by default, as seen in the following table:

Site Features	Site Collection Features
• Following Content • Metadata Navigation and Filtering • SharePoint Server Publishing • Workflow Task Content Type	• Disposition Approval Workflow • Document Sets • Limited-access user permission lockdown mode • Publishing Approval Workflow • Reporting • SharePoint Server Publishing Infrastructure • Video and Rich Media • Workflows

Table 2.14: *Default Site Features and Site Collection Features activated in the Publishing Portal Site*

Enterprise Wiki Site Contents

Open site content for **Enterprise Wiki Site**, you will find contents **Content and Structure Reports, Workflow Tasks, Reusable Content, Site Collection Documents, Documents, Form Templates, Style Library, Images, Site Collection Images, Pages, Site Assets** available by default as seen in the following screenshot:

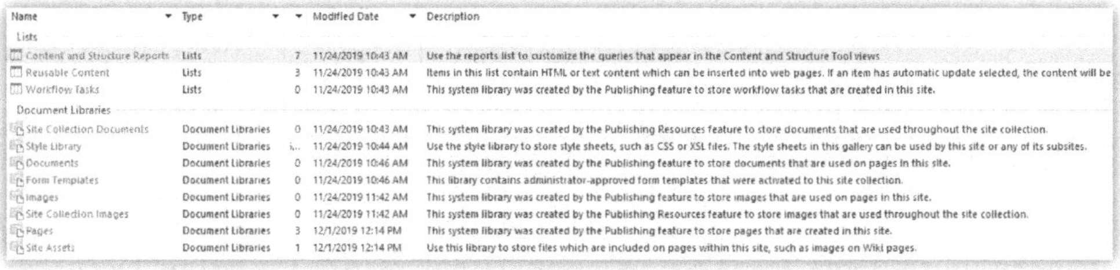

Figure 2.18: *Site Contents in Enterprise Wiki Site default*

Site Features and Site Collection Features in **Active** state, by default, as seen in the following table:

Site Features	Site Collection Feature
• Following Content • Team Collaboration Lists • Workflow Task Content Type	• Disposition Approval Workflow • Document Sets • Limited-access user permission lockdown mode • Publishing Approval Workflow • SharePoint Server Enterprise Site Collection features • SharePoint Server Publishing Infrastructure • SharePoint Server Standard Site Collection features • Video and Rich Media • Workflows

Table 2.15: *Default Site Features and Site Collection Features activated in Enterprise Wiki Site*

Creating a New Document Library

We can create a document library in multiple ways. Follow the step by step process to create a document library:

1. Once a modern site is created, you will find an option **New** in the command bar.

2. Click on **New**. You will see multiple options from which you can click on either **Document library** or **App** to create a document library. If you open **Site contents**, the same two options are available to create a library. You can navigate to these options either way from the home page or site contents, either by clicking **Document library** or by clicking **App**. Click on **Document library** from the site home page.

3. Another dialog box will open. Enter **Name** (`Project Documents 2020`) and **Description** of the document library.

4. Select the checkbox **Show in site navigation** to add this library into site navigation.

5. Click on **Create** will create a document library in site with library URL `https://<site url>/Project Documents 2020` and you see library also added to the left side navigation on site as seen in the following screenshot:

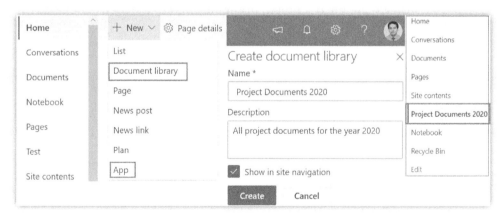

Figure 2.19: Create a Document library from the dropdown option Document library

6. If you are clicking on the **App** instead of the **Document library**, you will be redirected to the app store. Select the app **Document Library**.

7. Another dialog box will open. Enter **Name** (`Project Documents 2020`) of the document library. You can either click on **Create** to create a document library with the rest of the options as default or click on **Advanced Options** to choose other options.

8. Click on **Advanced Options** as seen in the following screenshot:

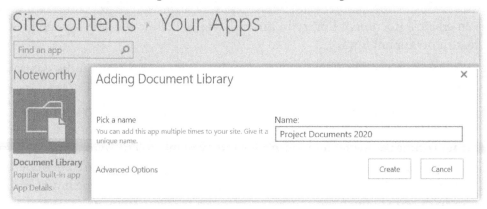

Figure 2.20: Create Document Library from the dropdown option App

9. You will get options to enter **Name, Description**. Choose options from **Create a version each time you edit a file in this document library?** (**Yes** by default) and **Document Template**.

10. You can select any of the document template present under **Document Template** so that when you will create any document in the library, the file of this type template will be created by default.

11. Then click on **Create** the document library as seen in the following screenshot:

Figure 2.21: Document Library Default Document Template

Creating New List

The way we created a document library, we can create a list in multiple ways. Follow the step by step process to create a list:

1. Once a modern site is created, you will find an option **New** in the command bar.

2. Click on **New**. You will see multiple options from which you can click on either **List** or **App** to create a SharePoint list. If you open **Site contents**, the same two

options are available to create a list. You can navigate to these options either way from the home page or site contents, either by clicking **List** or by clicking **App**. Click on **List** from the site home page.

3. Another dialog box will open. Enter **Name** (Custom List) and **Description** of the list.

4. Select the checkbox **Show in site navigation** to add this list into site navigation.

5. Click on **Create** will create SharePoint list in the site and you see list also added to the left side navigation on site as seen in the following screenshot:

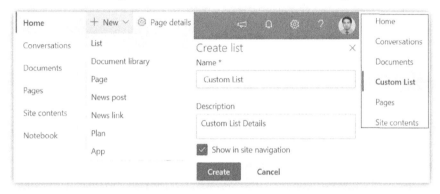

Figure 2.22: Create SharePoint List

6. If you are clicking on **App** instead of **List**, you will be redirected to the app store. Select the app **Custom List**.

7. Another dialog box will open. Enter **Name** (Custom List) of the list. You can either click on **Create** to create a list with the rest of the options as default or click on **Advanced Options** to choose other options.

8. Click on **Advanced Options** will show additional option to enter **Description** of list apart from **Name** as seen in the following screenshot:

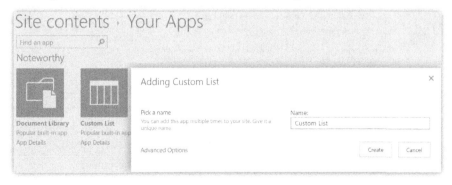

Figure 2.23: Create List from App

9. Navigate to **Site contents** from the left navigation of the site. Click on **New** and select **List** from there will drive you towards the new experience of creating a list, as seen in the following screenshot. Enter name of the list under **Create a list** and click on **Create** as seen in the following screenshot:

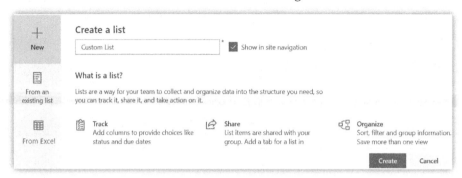

Figure 2.24: Create a list of modern experience

10. We can create a list from an existing list present under any other site. Click on the option **From an existing list**, as shown in *Figure 2.24* above. You notice all sites under the option **Select a site** appears.

11. Select any one of the sites, will make you available all lists present under that site.

12. Select any of the list present under that selected site. Enter **Name** (Customer List) of the list that you want to give under **Create a list** and click on **Create** as seen in the below screenshot.

13. It will create a new list with same template or schema as of that selected list template, but no content of that list is included in the newly created list:

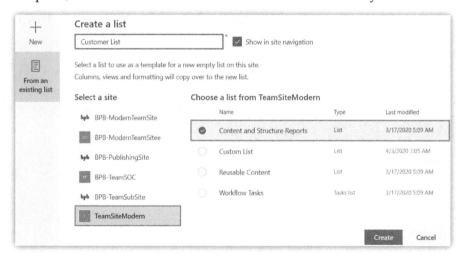

Figure 2.25: Create a list from an existing list

14. If you want, all items should be available under the newly created list while creating a list from an existing list; then, we need to make available another option **Save list as template**. This option can be enabled by PowerShell script only. You can take the help of Microsoft support or administrator to run one PowerShell command as below.

```
Set-SPOSite -Identity <site url> -DenyAddAndCustomizePages 0

Set-SPOSite -Identity https://spmcse.sharepoint.com/sites/BPB-
ModernTeamSite -DenyAddAndCustomizePages 0
```

15. Now open one **List** (contents should be present in it) present in **Site Content**. Click on **Settings** ⚙ from top right corner and select **List settings** from drop down.

16. Identify the category **Permissions and Management** and see the option **Save list as template** available now as seen in below screenshot:

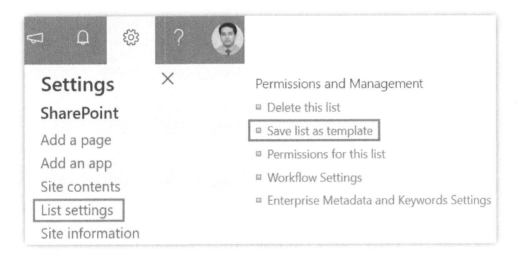

Figure 2.26: Save list as template

17. If you click on that option **Save list as template**, you see options to fill like **File name** (`Custom List Template`), **Template name** (`Custom List Template App`), **Template description**, and a checkbox to select like **Include Content**.

18. Select the checkbox **Include Content** and click on **OK** finally to create a template as seen in below screenshot:

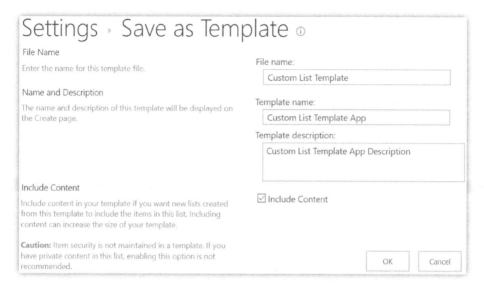

Figure 2.27: Save list as template Include Content

19. You will get a confirmation once the template is created successfully, as seen in the below image. Click on link **list template gallery** as seen in below screenshot:

Figure 2.28: List template gallery

20. You will be redirected to the **list template gallery** where all list templates are stored. URL of that will be of format as below which can enter directly to navigate:

   • https:// <Site URL>/_catalogs/lt/Forms/AllItems.aspx

21. You can also find the list template by navigating to **Site Settings** (https://<site url>/_layouts/15/ settings.aspx) and click the option **List templates** present under **Web Designer Galleries** as seen in below screenshot:

22. You see the created list template including content will be available here as seen in below screenshot:

Figure 2.29: List Template Gallery Under Site Settings

Figure 2.30: List template details

23. Now you can use this template to create a list. If you click on **App** from dropdown option present under **New**, then you can find this template, as seen in the below screenshot, which includes content. Follow the same steps discussed before to create a list:

Figure 2.31: Created List App Details

24. The new feature introduced to create list from Excel. Click on the last option **From Excel**. Enter name of the list under the field **Create a list,** as seen in the below screenshot.

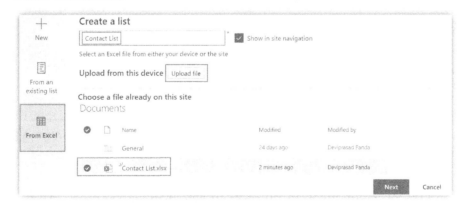

Figure 2.32: Create List From Excel

25. Select any Excel file having table in it, present in the library, which you want to import, or you can upload an Excel file from computer by clicking the button **Upload file** and click on **Next**.

26. From the filed **Select a table from this file**, select table. Items present in the Excel will be populated here. Click on **Create** will create the list in site contents, as seen in the below screenshot:

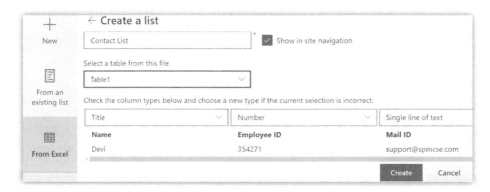

Figure 2.33: List From Excel Created

Upgraded new features for smart management

We discussed default site contents available and features activated, once the site is created as well as discussed a new smart way of creating document library and list. Over time where content grows too fast, representation of the content plays a primary role, storing content securely in the proper category and managing these contents effectively, smartly is very important to get the right content at the right time that ultimately will improve productively, Microsoft keeps on rolling out smart features for end-users. In this section, we will discuss some of the new smart features added to the **SharePoint Library** and **List** that give an ultimate exiting user experience in terms of content management, better collaboration that in turn results in better productive work culture.

Modern Document Library Smart Features

If you compare the document library between the new modern team site and classic SharePoint site, you will find the modern library come up with a fantastic user interface that will make you feel something new, exciting as well. Let's discuss what those new features are and how it helps in better collaboration experience among employees. Let's open a document library:

- Click on **Site Contents** from left navigational menu link or add _layouts/15/ viewlsts.aspx after the site URL to open all site contents.
- Click any one of the document libraries, for example, **Documents**.

Command Bar

Once you opened document library, you will notice, the classic site **Tool Bar** is replaced with a brand new **Command Bar** with options like New ┼, **Upload** ↑, **Quick** edit ✐, **Sync** ⟳, **Export to Excel**, **PowerApps** ⚙, **Automate** ⚙, **Alert me**, **Manage my alerts**, **Switch view options**, **Filters** pane ▽, **Details** pane ⓘ, **Expand** pane ↗ , as seen in the following screenshot. Each option provides new features which we will discuss in detail next:

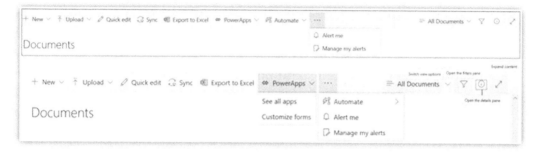

Figure 2.34: Command Bar

New

The first option in command bar you will find as **New** + which is used to create new documents, folders, links, templates. If you remember in the classic site, this option was mentioned as **New Document**. Let us discuss the following steps to see all actions that can be taken under this option:

1. Click on the option **New** + from the modern command bar. You will get drop down with options like **Folder** to create a folder, document templates like **Word document**, **Excel workbook**, **PowerPoint presentation**, **OneNote notebook**, **Forms for Excel** to create respective documents and few more new options like **Link**, **Edit New menu**, **Add template** as seen in the following screenshot:

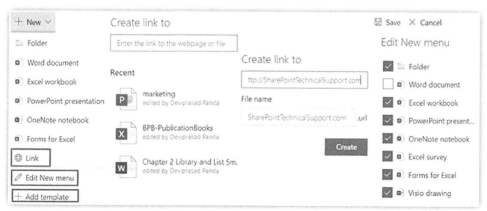

Figure 2.35: Create New

2. Click on **Link**; you will get another dialog box, **Create link to** all documents below that. If you select any one of the documents, that document will be stored in that library as a URL or Link. Clicking on that link will open the document in a new tab. Means link to any document can be stored in the library, and there is no need to uploading the same document in multiple libraries.

3. If you are entering any URL in the box instead of selecting a document, you will get another option below that filed as a **File name** as per the screenshot above, which displays file name with the same name by default (for example, **SharePointTechnicalSupport.com**) as you typed above. You can change the **File name** (for example, **SharePointTechnicalSupport** instead of **SharePointTechnicalSupport.com**) as per your wish and click on **Create** button present below. The link will be saved in the library with a file name ending with **.url**. The **Link** provides an option to add any URL (document URL or list/library URL, site URL) as a link to the library.

4. Next, click on the **Edit New menu** from dropdown **New**. Another window will open with the same templates present under option **New** as seen in the above screenshot *Figure 2.35*. Uncheck any one of the office files or any folder and click on **Save**. Next time when you open dropdown option **New**, you will not find those templates.

5. Next, clicking on **Add template** from dropdown **New**, pop up window opens to select any custom document template from local computer and add to under **New**. It will help to create documents with custom format easily at any time.

6. If **Allow management of content types** is enabled in the document library, and we add any content type (**Link to a Document**) in the library, then that content type will be available under **New** to create the content of that content type template as seen in the following screenshot. How to add content type is described under the section **Content Types** later in this chapter:

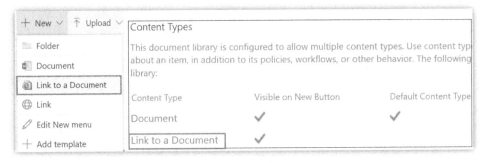

Figure 2.36: Content Type Added Under Drop Down Option New

All document templates under **New** will be replaced by content type **Document**, and selecting this content type template to create content will create a default document template that we discussed in the section Creating New Document Library.

Upload

As the name suggests, the **Upload** ↑ option from the command bar is used to upload files in the document library. It provides options to upload **Files**, **Folder**, **Template**, as seen in the following screenshot. Let us perform the following steps to understand each option:

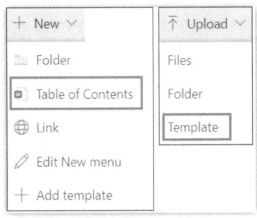

Figure 2.37: *Upload*

1. Selecting the option **Files** from the dropdown option will open a pop-up window to select a single file or multiple files from the local desktop and upload it to the library. Similarly, selecting the option, **Folder** will upload the folder in the library.

2. You can upload files and folders directly by dragging from your local computer into the document library. It depends on which you process you feel comfortable.

3. Next, select the option **Template**, newly introduced, will open a pop-up window to choose one custom template (For example, **Table of Contents**) form local desktop. Once you select and upload that template, this will be added under the dropdown option in **New**. Next time when you need to create a document of type of similar kind (**Table of Contents**), you can just select that template and create.

Note:

*   The limit for a number of list items by default is 30 million, and for the document, the library is also the same 30 million, which includes files and folders.

- The default file upload size limit is increased to 100 GB from 15 GB, and the limit for the file attached in the list is set as 250 MB, OneNote files upload size limit is 2 GB.

- If you are uploading files by drag and drop, limit the file selection as 100 at max.

- The limit for a number of characters, including path and file name length, should not cross 400 characters.

Quick edit

Another option in the command bar is **Quick edit** that displays the library as a datasheet view and allows users to edit multiple items, in the library, from the rows or columns at a time and can save the changes. Select one of the cells from any row or column (for example, **Approval Status**), modify and click on **Exit quick edit**, as seen in the following screenshot. Changes will be reflected:

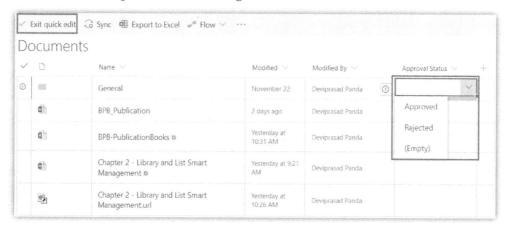

Figure 2.38: Quick edit

Currently you can see 30 items per page in this quick edit mode. New features are rolling out by end of June after which user can see 100 items per page in list or library.

Sync

Option **Sync** in command bar allows users to sync document library with a local computer, to access the file offline, and do the needful from file explorer at any time. It improves the friendly experience for end-users to work offline from the local system and sync at any moment. Let us perform the following steps to configure **Sync**:

1. Click on **Sync** from the command bar. Pop up window will open for **Sign in**. Click on button **Sign in** as seen in the following screenshot:

Figure 2.39: *Configure Sync click on Sync from the command bar*

2. Sign-in will proceed with your account, and **Your OneDrive folder** path under the local system will be displayed where documents will be stored. You can change **Your OneDrive folder** path by clicking the option **Change location**. Click on **Next** once file storage location under the system is set. From next window **Share files and folders** click on **Next** as seen in the following screenshot:

Figure 2.40: *Configure Sync local system file saved location*

3. From the next window, **All your files, ready and on-demand**, click on **Next**. Then you will get confirmation that **Your OneDrive Folder is ready for you** with button **Open my OneDrive folder**. Click on **Open my OneDrive folder** as seen in the following screenshot:

Figure 2.41: *Open OneDrive folder*

4. You will be redirected to the local system document library OneDrive sync folder **SPTechSupport - Documents**, which will be in the format like `<Site Name (SPTechSupport)>` - `<Document Library name (Documents)>` as seen in the following screenshot. Documents will be synced to this local folder which you can access anytime as per requirement:

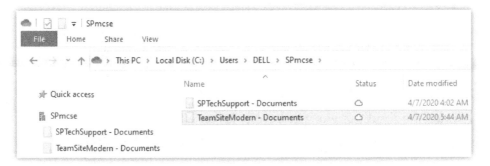

Figure 2.42: Sync folder location

Export to Excel

Clicking the option **Export to Excel** 📴 from command bar will download an Excel file with field columns like **Name**, **Modified** (Date and Time), **Modified By**, **Item Type**, **Path**, and other custom columns if available in detail of the document library as seen in the following screenshot. So, we can export document library inventory as a report in Excel format. Column **Name** in Excel file has a file name with a link to that file. Clicking the link under **Name** will open the file directly in the browser:

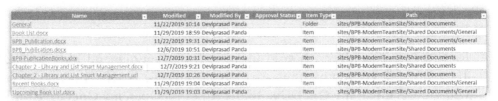

Figure 2.43: Export to Excel

PowerApps

PowerApps ⚙ option from the command bar provides an option to customize the document library form by clicking **Customize forms**. It also used to create an app. PowerApps is the replacement of the InfoPath form, as seen in the following screenshot. We can customize the library form using PowerApps:

Figure 2.44: Customize forms PowerApps

Automate

There is an option **Automate** in the command bar, also called as **Power Automate**, which is newly introduced and used to automate a series of tasks by creating flows connecting multiple services. Previously it was named **Flow** but renamed to **Power Automate** recently. **Power Automate** is integrated with the document library to provide automated tasks. Let us perform the following steps to create a basic flow:

1. Click on **Automate** from the command bar.

2. You get dropdown option **Power Automate** and under that few more options like **Create a flow**, **See your flows**, **Configure flows**. Click on **Create a flow** to start creating flow in the document library as seen in the following screenshot:

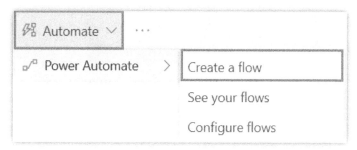

Figure 2.45: Create a flow

3. You will get the option to select the default template of flow creation out of multiple predefined templates. Clicking **Show more** options below that will

display al templates present under power automate for flow creation. Clicking **See your flows** option below that will display all created flows.

4. Click on one template **Send a Customized email when a new file is added**, as per requirement, will redirect you to **Power Automate** window for creating flow based on the template selected as seen in the following screenshot:

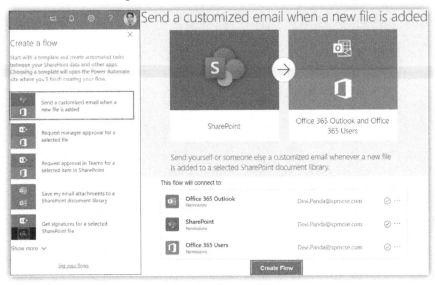

Figure 2.46: Create a flow

5. You will notice services **Office 365 Outlook, SharePoint, Office 365 Users** are involved in the creation of flow for the selected type of template as per the requirement will be available. The side to each service status is showing a **Valid connection**. Click on **Switch account** option to change the account for the connection as seen in the following screenshot:

Figure 2.47: Services involved in the flow

6. Finally, click on **Create Flow** will create a new flow, as seen in the following screenshot. When a new item added to the document library, the user will receive a mail. It is the operation which this flow will complete:

Figure 2.48: Created flow

Switch view options

Switch view options ≡ in command bar provides a way to show the document library contents in a different view. By default, the view is **All Documents** that show all documents. You can create a view to filter show specific contents in that view. Let us perform the following steps to see items in different views:

1. Click on **Switch view options** form the command bar; you will see different views under the dropdown like **List**, **Compact List**, **Tiles**, **All Documents**, **Save view as**, **Edit current view**, **Format Current view** with a view **All Documents** as a default view. The default view (**All Documents**) will be displayed in the command bar for the option **Switch view options**.

2. As shown in the following screenshot, you can notice the contents of the document library in the form of **List**, **Compact List**, **Tiles** respectively:

Figure 2.49: Display content in the form of List, Compact List, Tiles view

3. Newly introduced option **Save view as** provides a way to save the default view (**All Documents**) with another name (**Admin View**), as per your requirement, so that can be used for different business requirements.

4. You will notice the newly created view (**Admin View**) under the dropdown of **Switch view options** with additional option **Set current view as default** to save this view as default as seen in the *Figure 2.50* below, so that next time you access the document library, you will find this new view under command bar as default:

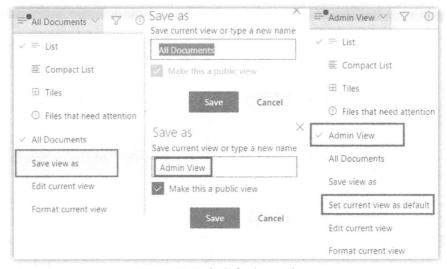

Figure 2.50: Switch view options

5. Option **Edit current view** provides a way to edit the view as per your requirement.

6. Option **Format current view** enables users to add **JSON** codes to make changes in the Document library content view.

7. Another new feature is **Files that need attention**. If you have added any column that is marked as required field and information is not selected/filled for that column or columns, then this option will be marked red error message. Also, the red mark will be available side to default view present in the command bar, as shown in *Figure 2.50*. You need to fill missing properties. The steps for filling this are discussed under the section **Details** pane next.

8. New features are rolling out by end of June after which user can save the quick edit mode of library or list as a view. Just click on Quick edit from ribbon and save that as view following the same procedure as discussed above. Benefits of this is, when user switch to this Quick edit view, items present in library or list will be rendered as quick edit mode for easy and quick editing.

Filters pane

Filter pane ▽ option is newly introduced that includes metadata-based filtering to find content in a modern document library. You must be thinking, what is metadata. If you see *Figure 2.49*, each document library column **Modified** (**November 22, 4 days ago, 3 days ago**), **Modified By** (**Deviprasad Panda, X, Y**) contains information. So, this information in each column is called **metadata**. I mean, metadata is data about data or information about information.

New features in SharePoint Online provides an option to pin library columns to filter pane. Let us perform the following steps to pin library column to filter pane:

1. Click on the library column (**Modified By**).
2. From dropdown option, select **Column settings**.
3. Under column settings, you will find the option to **Pin to filters pane**.
4. You will find this column (**Modified By**) with all information (name of all users Deviprasad Panda, X, Y) present under filter pane. You can filter by selecting any one user. If you **Unpin** this column **Modified By**, it will be removed from filter pane. The following figure helps in understanding it:

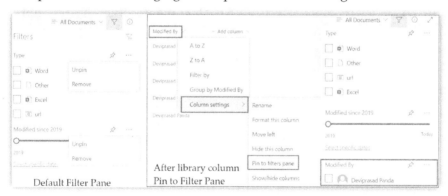

Figure 2.51: Filters pane

Details pane

Details pane ⓘ is a new feature introduced in the command bar that provides an option of inline metadata details for the document in that library. The metadata details include **File Preview** with several views (3) of that file, **Manage access** (users having permission in that file), **Properties** (**Content Type**, **Name**, **Title**), **Activity** (detail actions are taken on that file like editing), **Type** (extension of file), **Modified** (last modified), **Path** (storage location of the file in site), **Size** (size of the file), as seen in the following screenshot:

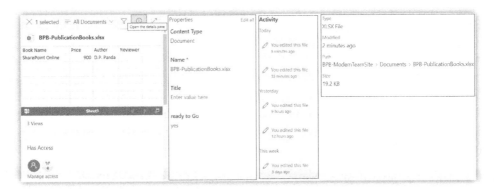

Figure 2.52: Details pane

Users can edit **Properties** of one document by clicking on each of the fields directly one by one else click on **Edit all** to enable all fields under properties in edit mode and edit all the fields at a time.

Similarly, it allows us to edit the properties of multiple documents at a time. Select multiple documents from the library and click on **Details** pane ⓘ. You will find the fields that can be modified, select your changes, and apply changes by clicking **Save**.

As discussed under the above section, **All Documents (Switch view options)** -> **Files that need attention**, when you select **Files that need attention** and click on **Details** pane ⓘ you will get the same options to fill missing details of the document properties. Fill those missing filed properties and save as seen in the following screenshot:

Figure 2.53: Files that need attention

Expand content

If you are mostly working on documents present in the library, then you should try this new option to **Expand content** ✎. Click on **Expand content** from the command bar. You will see command bar and files in the library available, and rest options like left navigation, the header will hide. So, you can focus on documents and their options for work. You can revert the changes by clicking **Collapse content** ⤢ from command bar as seen in the following screenshot:

Figure 2.54: Expand content

Add column simplified

Adding columns to the library is simplified. Click on any one of the columns (For example, **Modified**) in the library, drop down option will appear. Then select **Column settings** will show options to do actions on that selected column like rename, format this column, move right or left, pin or unpin from filters pane, show or hide and at the bottom you will get option to **Add a column**. Clicking on **Add a column** will show type the column you want to create, and selecting one type of column will initiate to create a new column, as seen in *Figure 2.55* below. If you hover between any two columns, you will find a sign **+**, clicking on that will initiate the step for column creation:

Figure 2.55: Add column

Move to/Copy to option

It is one of the newly added options in the modern bar. Selecting one file in the document library will enable multiple options in command bar like **Open**, **Share**, **Copy link**, **Download**, **Delete**, **Move to**, **Copy to**, **Pin to top**, **Version history**, **Check out** as seen in the following screenshot:

Figure 2.56: Options after selection of one file

Click on **Move to** ⊞; you will get an option to choose the destination to move the file, which can be within the same library or folder present in the same library or library present in other sites or folder present in other sites. The user needs to select the destination library or folder and click on **Move here**, which will remove the file from the current location and will save at destination location, as seen in *Figure 2.57* below. During selecting the destination location, the option is there to create a new folder on the spot to move the file:

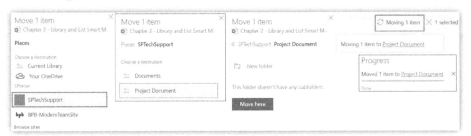

Figure 2.57: Move to

Similarly, if you select **Copy to** ⎘, a copy of the file will be created at the destination location without any impact on the source file.

Pin to top option

Pin to top ⊞ is a newly introduced feature that allows users to add files or folders at the top of the library in **Tiles** format. Users can **Pin** files or folders critical to a business, or they want to highlight. Let us perform the following steps to see various actions taken related to pin:

1. Select any one file or folder from the library that will enable an option **Pin to top** in the command bar. Click on **Pin to top** from the command bar. You see,

the file or folder will be added at the top of the library in **Tiles** view. Currently, it's not supported to Pin multiple files or folders at a time.

2. Select one file from pinned files that will enable an option **Edit pin** in the command bar. Click on **Edit pin** ⚲ will show action like **Unpin** ⚲, **Move left**, **Move right**.

3. Click on **Unpin** to remove from pinned files. Click on **Move left** or **Move right** to rearrange the file place as seen in the following screenshot:

Figure 2.58: Pin to top

Saved for later

Saved for later 🔖 is a type of bookmark in SharePoint, which is introduced to save any page that can be accessed later. Click one news post in the SharePoint site will open that news page. At the bottom of that news page, you will find options to mark that news post as **Saved for later**, as seen in the following screenshot. When you create new site pages at the bottom, you will find this option:

Figure 2.59: Saved for later

Check out/Check in multiple files

Check out multiple files in a single click is supported now, so you don't need to check out each file at a time when there is a requirement of multiple files check out.

Select the files that you want to check out and click the option, **Check out** from the command bar. Once the file is checked out, other users cannot edit that file, so those files need to be check in again. Select multiple files and click on **Check in** will save the changes. Selecting **Discard check out** will not save the modification done in the document as seen in the following screenshot:

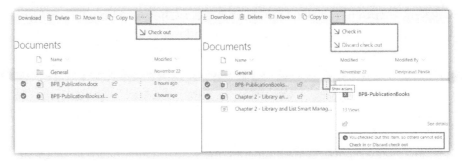

Figure 2.60: Bulk file check out check-in

Submit for approval

Selecting a single document or multiple documents from the library will make enable an option **Submit for approval** 📖 in command bar if **Require content approval for submitted items** is enabled for the library.

Click on **Submit for approval** will send the document for approval, and the status column will be updated as **Pending** from **Draft**. Then you will find the submit for approval as seen in the following screenshot:

Figure 2.61: Submit for approval

Now selecting the file pending for approval will make available another option **Cancel approval** 📖 to cancel the approval process and make the file back to draft again so that you can submit again.

Publish

Navigate to Library **Page**. You may create and save as draft multiple site pages so that can-do future change. In that case, selecting site pages will enable an option

Publish 📖 in the command bar to publish the page directly, which is a new feature in SharePoint. Bulk action like publishing multiple pages is supported by which you can select all draft site pages and click on `Publish` from command bar as seen in the following screenshot:

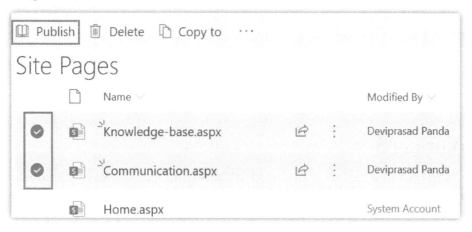

Figure 2.62: Publish documents

New feature is rolling out by end of June after which you will find another option in command bar **Republish**. Also, you will find an icon 📖 side to the page having unpublished changes.

Change the document file group

Users can change the document file group easily by drag and drop. If document library files are in a group, the user can quickly move the file from one group to another by drag and drop. Select the file that you want to change the group. Drag the file and put it over another group, as seen in *Figure 2.63* below. It will update the metadata associated with the file automatically. This action will trigger the flow to change the metadata associated with that. You see below image the metadata **Modified** of the moved file is updated:

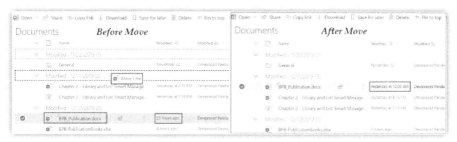

Figure 2.63: *Change in the metadata of the file*

You see below image the metadata **Approval Status** updated once the file is moved to a different group:

Figure 2.64: Change in the metadata of a file

Hover card

Hover card is a new feature introduced in SharePoint that shows quick information about the file details present in the library. If you put your mouse over any document present in the library that we call as hover on file, you will see the properties and actions like the number of **View (1)**, number of **Viewers (1)**, **Time to read (12 min)** under inside look, actions pending underflow under **Your conversations**, and so on, in the form of card which we call as hovercard, as seen in the following screenshot, that gives quick details about usage, traffic, action on the file to analyze and manage better:

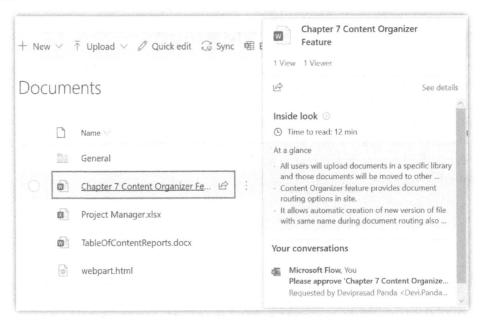

Figure 2.65: File hovercard

Similarly, if you hover over the site name **BPB-ModernTeamSite**, you will see hovercard with site details like site description under **About**, Microsoft Teams group mail ID (BPB-ModernTeamSite@spmcse.com), **Follow in inbox** to get an update with group emails triggered, group **Members**, **Apps**, **Emails**, **Files** as seen in the following screenshot:

Figure 2.66: Hover card site

Modern list smart features

Branding for the SharePoint list is the same as the library. You will get a modern command bar with options like **New**, **Quick edit**, **Export to Excel**, **PowerApps** ⚙, **Automate**, **Alert me**, **Manage my alerts**, **Switch view options**, **Filters** pane, **Details** pane ⓘ, **Expand** pane. Let's discuss a few options next.

Create new item

As we already discussed, SharePoint List gives an experience of the table where you are filling all rows and columns; you will get a similar experience to fill all fields when you create a new list item. Let us perform the following steps to create one list item and will see the new experience in it:

1. Open one **List** (for example, **BPB-Contact**) from site contents.

2. You will notice the branding is the same for both lists and libraries. You will see command bar with similar options that are applicable for list items:

Figure 2.67: List command bar

3. Click on **New** ╇ from command bar; you will get options to fill details for an item like the **Last Name**, **First Name**, **Full Name**, **Email Address**, **Phone Number** like this. Fill all details as per requirement and click on **Save** as seen in the following screenshot:

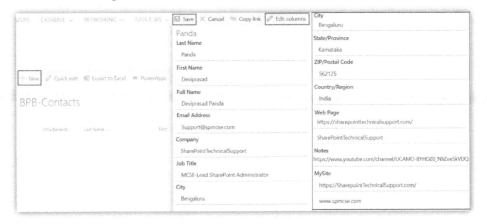

Figure 2.68: Create an item

4. Once the item is created, select the list item and click on **Edit** ✎ from the command bar. Click on **Edit columns** ✎ will display all list columns. Columns with checkbox selected will be displayed in the current view. You can check or uncheck the columns which you want to add or remove from the current view. Columns marked check-in will be displayed in the list:

Figure 2.69: Edit view column new experience

5. Like document library, the list provides an option to edit the metadata details from **Details** pane ⓘ as seen in the following screenshot:

Figure 2.70: Edit properties from Details pane

6. Users can adjust the width of the cell of each filed by dragging right or left. When you hover between two columns, the adjusting option will appear to make it adjust.

Request sign-off

Request sign-off is a new feature introduced that allows quick approval of a single list item or file in the document library and gets sign-off from the approver. It is applicable for both single list item and library file but not supported for folder present library. Previously we were able to create flow for the whole list or library that is applicable for all items present in it but unable to create flow for a single item. Now the new feature introduced that supports creating flow at the item level. There are situations where you need to focus sign-off for critical files or items, whether that is approved or not, and you might not give equal importance for the rest of the files or items, then this would be the best option for those users. Let us perform the following steps to create **Request sign-off** flow for a single list item which also applicable for single files in the library:

1. Open one list **BPB-Contacts** from site contents presents in site **BPB-ModernTeamSite**.

2. Select one item from the list and click on **Automate** from the command bar.

3. Click on option **Request sign-off** from the drop down:

Figure 2.71: Request sign-off

4. Another dialog box **Create a flow** that will appear on the right side. Expand the option, **See details** will display services involved in this flow like **SharePoint**, **Approvals**, **Notifications** as below.

5. Click on **Create flow** will another dialog box. Enter **Approver** name, **Message** and click on **Run flow** will start the flow:

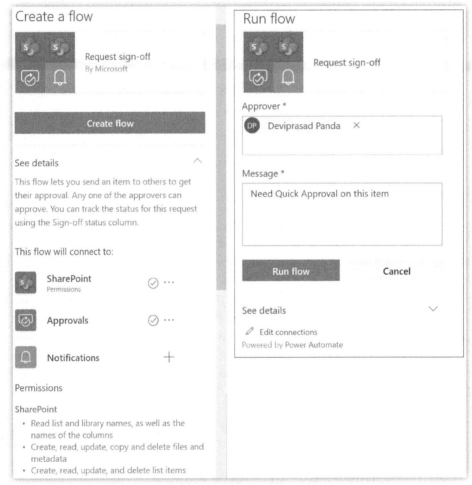

Figure 2.72: Run flow

6. You see an additional column **Sign-off status** column will be added to the list that will show the current status of the item as **Pending**:

Figure 2.73: Sing-off status Pending

7. Approver will receive one mail, which needs to be approved or rejected with the comment:

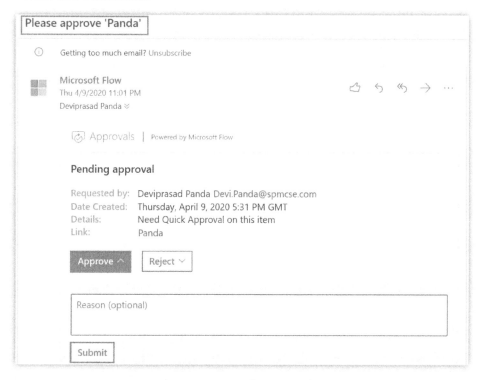

Figure 2.74: *Approve the request from mail*

Once the action is done by the approver, the status will be updated in the list column **Sign-off status**, either **Approve** or **Reject**.

Apps Management

As shown in *Chapter 1, Introduction and Site Information* under *Figure 1.5: Content Templates,* there are multiple content templates in the form of Apps available. We can add Apps by navigating to **Site Contents** and selecting **New | App** from the command bar. Then select the type of App you want to create, fill the details, and click on **Create**. You will get a lot of options to select and create App, but after the creation of, you will get the same settings to manage. As we are going to discuss in the below section.

Understand List and Library Settings is Must

We discussed all actions that can be taken on a document or list item. In this section, we are going to discuss the settings related to the library and list. There is always an option called **Settings**, available for either list or library or site that is used for managing properties of list or library or site. We can control configure actions or features from this setting which we will discuss below:

1. You can open library settings in different ways. Click on **Site contents** (https://<site url>/_layouts/15/viewlsts.aspx) from left navigation, open one document library, click on the **Gear** button 🞮 present at top right corner, you will find **Library settings** (https://<site url>/_layouts/15/ listedit.aspx?List=**) from the drop-down options:

Figure 2.75: Library settings from Settings

2. In another way, open site contents from the site. Click on **Show actions** button of any library and click on **Settings** from the dropdown options, will open the library settings as seen in below:

Figure 2.76: Library settings from show action site contents

3. You will notice multiple options categorized into **General Settings, Permission and Management, Communications, Columns, Views** as shown in the image below:

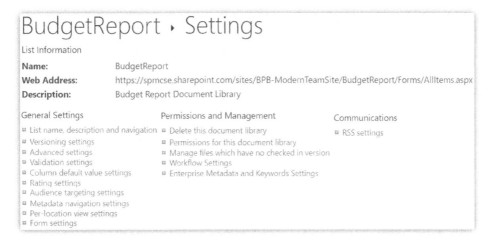

Figure 2.77: Library settings

4. Similarly, when you open **List settings** as seen in *Figure 2.78* below, you will notice similar categories/options under the settings with a slight difference in non-availability of option like **Manage files which have no checked in version** as compared to library settings:

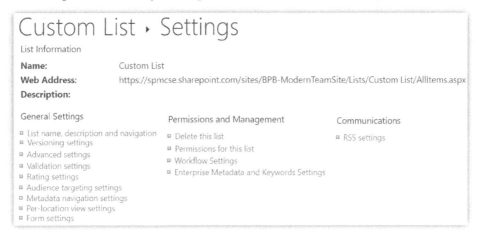

Figure 2.78: List settings

Let's have an overview of all options available under the library or list settings.

General Settings

General setting includes options like **List name, description and navigation, Versioning settings, Advanced settings, Validation settings, Column default value settings, Rating settings, Audience targeting settings, Metadata navigation settings, Pre-location view settings, Form settings**, which we will discuss in details below.

List name, description and navigation

The first option under the **General Settings** category is **List name, description and navigation**. We can change library or list name, description, navigation following the steps below:

1. Click on **List name, description and navigation** (https://<site url>/_ layouts/15/listedit.aspx?List=**) present under category **General Settings**.

2. Another dialog box will open where you can find fields like a library or list **Name**. If you need to change the name of the library, this is where you need to navigate, as seen in *Figure 2.79* below. If you compare this setting between the library and the list, you will not find any difference. Both libraries and lists provide a similar user interface for action.

3. There is an option related to navigation like **Display this document library/ list on the Quick Launch** is available, selecting **Yes** will show this list or library under Quick Launch, and selecting **No** will not show this list or library under Quick Launch.

4. Changing the name of the library or list will not change the URL of the library for your information. I mean, if you change the name of the library from **BudgetReport** to any other name still the library URL remains unchanged:

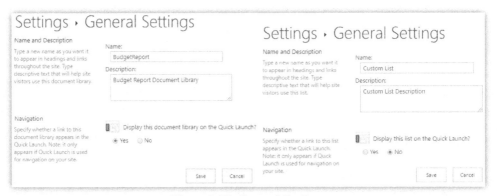

Figure 2.79: General Settings

Versioning settings

Versioning provides an option by which every change in a document is stored as a separate version so that the user can track the changes, view previous version file or item, also can restore any of the file or Item version during need. Follow the step by the information below to get more details on this:

1. When a document is uploaded or created, one version of that file is created. There are some other scenarios when a new version of the file is created like:

   • When a file is edited and saved or when a file with the same name is uploaded again and replaced with existing file

   • If there is any change in document properties and saved

   • If you have auto Save option is enabled then open the file, try some changes but undo the changes and close the document will create a document version

Files checked out once uploaded; the first version is created once checked in, as seen in the following screenshot:

Figure 2.80: *Version history created*

2. Similarly, when an item is created in the list for the first time, one version is created for that item. If any changes in that item happen, that will create a separate version for that item. You can notice the type of changes happened in each version, modified date and time, modified by with person name and the most important the version number as seen in the following screenshot:

Figure 2.81: *Modified properties in the version history*

3. When you open the version settings (`https://<site url>/_layouts /15/ LstSetng.aspx?List=**`), you will find different options like **Content Approval**, **Document Version History**, **Draft Item Security**, **Require Check Out** to control this document versioning. If you compare versioning settings option between library and list, you will find document library versioning settings contains an additional option **Require Check Out** since we upload documents. It needs to check out to lock the file during the edit. Below image you see, left part of the image indicates **Versioning Settings** for library and right part indicates **Versioning Settings** for the list:

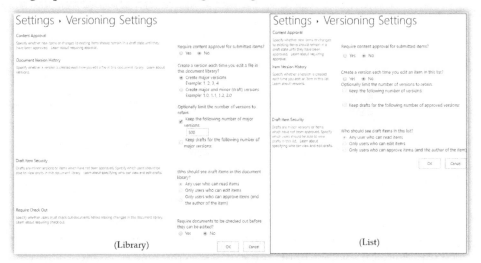

Figure 2.82: Versioning Settings

4. Versioning for document library is enabled by default, whereas for the list, it's disabled. You need to make it enabled from the settings under **Item version history** | **Create a version each time you edit an item in this list** by selecting **Yes**. Versioning numbers are categorized into two types, **Major version**, **Minor version**. So, users can track either **Major versions** or **Major and Minor (draft) versions**.

5. For the **Major version**, document version numbers are created automatically as a whole number like 1.0, 2.0, 3.0, and so on. By default, **Create major versions** are enabled for the library, and the number of document versions to keep is 500 by default, which can be modified to 100 as a minimum. Limit for document library major version ranges from minimum 100 to 50000 maximum.

6. For **Minor version**, document version numbers are created in the decimal format like 1.1, 1.2, 1.3, and so on. Once the document is published as a major version, the version becomes the next whole number 2.0. After that,

the versioning number starts from 2.1, 2.2, and so on. If any file is marked as **Discard checkout**, there is no change in version number, and you will notice the same most recent version number in the version history. Similarly, deleting any one of the minor versions removes that version only and keeps the rest of the version unaffected. Deleted file version moved to **Recycle bin** and option is there to restore that version as well as seen in the following screenshot:

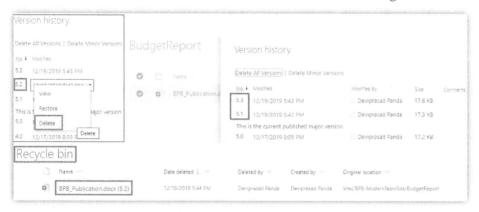

Figure 2.83: Delete version history

7. If you are tracking minor versions by selecting option **Create major and minor (draft) versions** then you will find the option **Keep drafts for the following number of major versions** enabled which stores how many recent major versions (Out of default 500 major versions) will store minor versions as seen in the following screenshot. Default minor version for a single major version is 511:

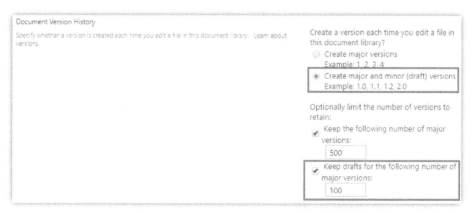

Figure 2.84: Minor version

We will discuss **Content Approval** in detail in the next *Chapter 3, Content Approval Concept*.

Advanced Settings

Advanced Settings (`https://<site url>/_layouts/15/advsetng.aspx? List=**`)
provide multiple advanced options to manage content in library or list as seen in
Figure 2.85 below. Let's discuss different options step by step below:

1. The first option you will find is **Content Types**, and user needs to select
   whether to **Allow management of content types** as **Yes** or **No**:

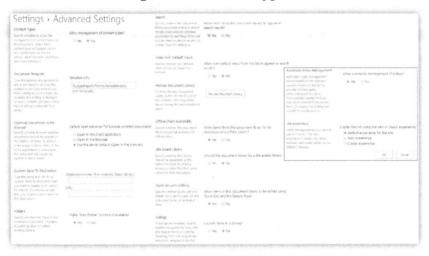

Figure 2.85: Advanced Settings library

2. Selecting **Yes** from **Content Types** -> **Allow management of content types**
   will add another section **Content Types** under **Library Settings** as seen in the
   following screenshot:

Figure 2.86: Content Types

3. The next option under advanced settings is **Document Template** that provides
   an option to edit the default document template for the library. When you
   are adding a document library app, you will find **Advanced Options** in the
   dialog box. Clicking on that, you will get an option **Document Template** at
   the bottom of the page. By default, **Microsoft Word document** is the default
   Document Template if you are creating **Document Library** without clicking
   Advanced Options. So, from option **Library Settings | Advanced Settings |
   Document Template**, when user click on **Edit Template** under **Template URL**

will open the default template (**Microsoft Word document**), which can further be modified. The following figure helps in understanding it:

Figure 2.87: Default document template

4. The next option under advanced settings is **Opening Documents in the Browser** that provides two options like **Open in the client application** and **Open in the browser**. Using this, we can set to open the document in the browser or client application installed in the user system. The default setting is to open the document in the browser on clicking any of the documents present under the library.

5. We will discuss the next option **Custom Send to Destination** in the next *Chapter 7, Content Organizer Feature*.

6. There is an option **Folders** to **Make "New Folder" command available** that is selected **Yes** as default. It enables to create **New Folder** in Document Library from **Command Bar | New**. You can disable the option of creating a folder in the library by selecting **No**.

7. The next option under the **Advanced Settings** is **Search** (**Allow items from this document library to appear in search results**). Whether you want to make documents under this library to be searchable or not can be controlled from here by selecting **Yes** or **No**. Although this library is searchable, but users having no permission to this library cannot see documents in the search results. By default, items under this library are searchable, so the option selected is **Yes**.

8. Next **Index Non-Default Views** provides an option whether to **Allow non-default views from this list to appear in search results** or not by selecting **Yes** or **No**.

9. Next option **Reindex Document Library** provides the option to reindex document library contents on the next crawl schedule. Indexing is a part of the search that is responsible for making content searchable. So, clicking the button, **Reindex Document Library** will recreate index properties for the contents in the document library to make it searchable.

10. Next option **Offline Client Availability** allows document library to enable or disable sync feature with OneDrive and local system by selecting **Yes** or

No. The default option selected is **Yes** means the library is in sync enabled. Configuring sync features can allow users to download files, work offline, and access from a local system file, once connected to the internet. Selecting **No** will disable sync option from the command bar and disable this feature. We already discussed how to configure sync and how it works in the above section **Sync**.

11. **Site Assets Library** is used to store images, media files, or any other digital assets. Option to make the current library as **Site Assets Library** is there. Selecting **Yes** will enable this library as a site asset library. The default selected is **No**.

12. Option **Quick property editing** is selected by default as **Yes**, which enables the option **Quick edit** under document library command bar for bulk editing items. Selecting **No** will disable **Quick edit** options, and you will find missing from the command bar.

13. Option **Dialogs** controls to open the Microsoft form in the form of **Dialog** or **Full page** by selecting **Yes** or **No**. By default, the option selected is **No**.

14. The next option under **Advanced Settings** is **Automatic Index Management** that manages indexing of columns automatically based on the queries to improve performance.

15. Last option **List experience** provides the option to display a library or list in new modern experience or old classic experience. Users can switch from new modern experience to old classic experience and vice versa.

16. Below *Figure 2.88* is the **Advanced Settings** option for **List** that has additional options **Item-level Permissions**, **Attachments** and missing options **Document Template**, **Opening Documents in the Browser**, **Custom Send to Destination** compared to library advanced settings as seen in the following table below:

Library Advanced Settings	List Advanced Settings
Content Types	Content Types
Document Template	Item-level Permissions
Opening Documents in the Browser	Attachments
Custom Send To Destination	
Folders	Folders
Search	Search
Index Non-Default Views	Index Non-Default Views
Reindex Document Library	Reindex List
Offline Client Availability	Offline Client Availability
Site Assets Library	
Quick property editing	Quick property editing
Dialogs	Dialogs
Automatic Index Management	Automatic Index Management
List experience	List experience

Table 2.16: Library Advanced Settings and List Advanced Settings comparison

17. **Item-level Permissions** under list advanced settings are used to set permission for list items. Permission for the list item can be refined by allowing users to **Read all items** or **Read items that were created by the user**. Similarly, editing permissions can be refined by allowing users to **Create and edit all items** or **Create items and edit items that were created by the user**:

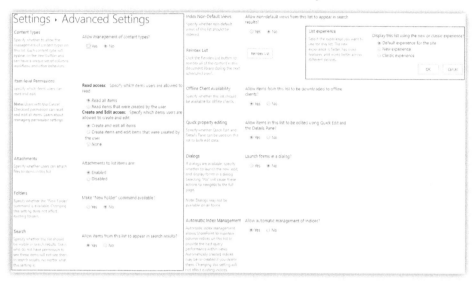

Figure 2.88: Advanced Settings List

Validation Settings

We can apply validation on any column using this option, **Validation Settings**. We have to apply the formula for validation. Let's create an example and will apply validation for a column **DueDate**. We need to set validation so that user should select a due date, a future date greater than today's date else will get the message **Due date Must be greater than today**:

1. Open **Validation Settings** (https://<site url>/_layouts/15/VldSetng.aspx? List=**).

2. Select the column **DueDate** that you want to validate from **Insert Column**.

3. Click on **Add to formula** and then enter >TODAY().

4. Under **User Message**, enter the message you want to display user as **Due date Must be greater than today** and click on **Save**.

5. Finally, opening **Validation Settings** again, you will see the formula as =DueDate>TODAY().

6. Now when you create a new item and choose the **DueDate** field as the current date, you will get validation error **Due date Must be greater than today** and will not allow saving the item as seen in the following screenshot. An only future date will be accepted as per validation settings.

You can find more formulas from the link `https://support.office.com/en-us/article/examples-of-common-formulas-in-sharepoint-lists-d81f5f21-2b4e-45ce-b170-bf7ebf6988b3` **to apply.**

Figure 2.89: Column Validation Settings

Rating Settings

Rating Settings (`https://<site url>/_layouts/15/RatingsSettings.aspx?List=**`) allows to enable or disable ratings in the form of **Star Ratings** or **Likes** for items in library or list as seen in the following screenshot:

Figure 2.90: Rating Settings

Audience Targeting

Audience Targeting (`https://<site url>/_layouts/15/ListEnableTargeting.aspx?List=**`) enables to target specific **File** or specific modern webparts like **News**, **Highlighted content** or classic webparts like **Content Query** relevant to specific groups of users so that contents can only be visible users of those targeted group. The following screenshot displays were to enable Audience Targeting:

Figure 2.91: Audience Targeting

Form Settings

Form Settings (`https://<site url>/_layouts/15/FormSettings.aspx? List=**`) allows to edit the form in **PowerApps** ⚙. In command bar option is there like **Customize Forms**, which redirects to PowerApps for editing form. The following screenshot displays were to enable **Form Settings**:

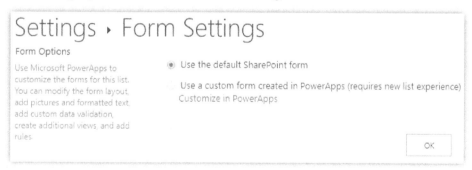

Figure 2.92: Form Settings

Permissions and Management

Next category after **Advanced Settings** is **Permissions and Management** under which you will find options like **Delete this document library**, **Permissions for this document library**, **Manage files which have no checked in version**, **Workflow Settings, Enterprise Metadata and Keywords Settings**. Let's discuss each option one by one.

Delete this document library

Click on **Delete this document library** will generate one dialog box with a message like **All files will be deleted and will be moved to recycle bin**. Once you confirm, the library will be deleted and moved to the recycle bin. The document library can be restored by navigating to the recycle bin and clicking **Restore** from the command bar as well, if required. Same actions applicable for **List**, the user can delete the list following the same process as the library.

There will be a new feature **File Delete Lockout override** will be rolled out. If the user is deleting any document file from the library, which is already in an open state at another location by other users, then the user will get a message like **It looks like someone has the file open. Delete Anyway? with delete button below**. If you click on the **Delete** button, it will override, and the file will be deleted.

We could restore the library to the previous time if any unwanted actions happened by mistake, following the new way. Let's follow the steps below to do the same:

1. Click on **Settings (Gear** icon) ⚙ from the top right corner of the site. Click on **Restore this library** from the dropdown.

2. Select **Custom date and time** from dropdown field **Select a date**.

3. There will be a slider below that, which you can slide to change the number of days for keeping library file versions.

4. Select the files you want to restore for library and click on **Restore** will back the library to the previous state:

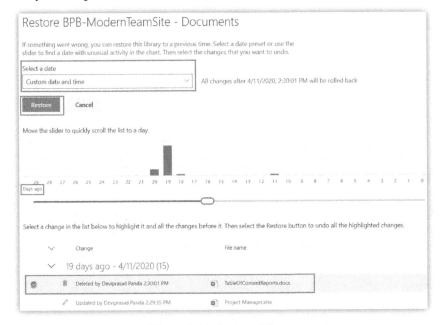

Figure 2.93: Restore Library

Note: Library **Documents** is a default library for the modern team site. Remember, we discussed in Chapter 1 that one Microsoft Teams Group is created in every Modern Team Site. Many services are dependent on this default library. So, this library **Documents** should not be deleted, and that is why there is no option to **Delete this document library** under **Library Settings** for this library.

Permissions for this document library

Permission for the library can be managed by following the option **Permissions for this document library** (`https://<site url>/_layouts/15/user.aspx?obj =**,doclib&List=**`) as seen in the following screenshot. Permission can be managed from the library level as well that is limited to this library only. We will discuss this in *Chapter 8, Manage Permission*:

Figure 2.94: Permission for a document library

Manage files which have no checked in version

If you have set the option, `Require documents to be checked out before they can be edited?` Under `Versioning Settings` is selected `Yes`, then you will find the document uploaded to the document library is `Checked Out To` you. You need to check in the file after your upload or modifying completed. If the file is not Check-in, you will find that file under this option `Manage files which have no checked in version` (`https://<site url>/_layouts/15/ManageCheckedOutFiles.aspx?List=**`) as seen in the following screenshot:

Figure 2.95: Manage files which have no checked-in version

Someone having permission needs to take ownership of this file, then only it will be moved out of this location.

Workflow Settings

Using this option **Workflow Settings** (https://<site url>/_layouts/15/WrkSetng.aspx?List=**), the user can create or remove workflows applicable to document library and items under the library, check the status of the workflow as seen in the following screenshot. What is a workflow and how to create other actions related to this will discuss in *Chapter 3, Content Approval Concept:*

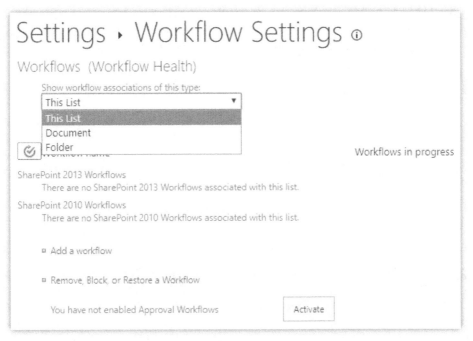

Figure 2.96: Workflow Settings

Enterprise Metadata and Keywords Settings

This option enables the library to **Add Enterprise Keywords** and **Enterprise Keywords** column to the library. Similarly, list settings also have this option to apply keywords and **Enterprise Keywords** column on the list. The following screenshot displays where to enable **Enterprise Metadata and Keywords Settings** (https://<site url>/_layouts/15/metadatacolsettings.aspx?List={**}). We will discuss this more in *Chapter 9, Managed Metadata Concept:*

Figure 2.97: *Enterprise Metadata and Keywords Settings*

Communications

Under this category, you will find an option **RSS Settings** (`https://<site url>/_layouts/15/listsyndication.aspx?List=**`) by which we can subscribe RSS feed as seen in the following screenshot:

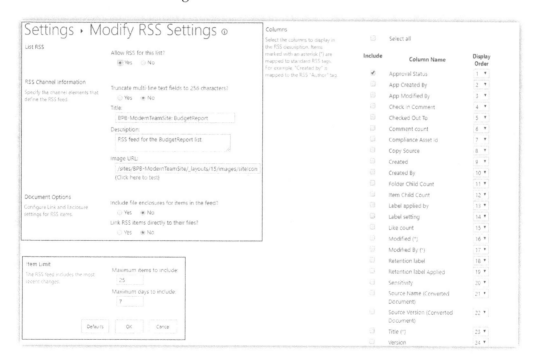

Figure 2.98: *RSS Settings*

Columns

Column stores properties or information of document items. When the library created, you will find default columns of different types except **Column ordering**. **Column Ordering** is present in list **Columns** as seen in the following screenshot:

Columns

A column stores information about each document in the document library. The following columns are currently available in this document library:

Column (click to edit)	Type	Required
Title	Single line of text	
Created	Date and Time	
Modified	Date and Time	
Enterprise Keywords	Managed Metadata	
Created By	Person or Group	
Modified By	Person or Group	
Checked Out To	Person or Group	

▫ Create column

▫ Add from existing site columns

▫ Column ordering

▫ Indexed columns

Figure 2.99: Columns

Create column

We already discussed creating a column from the command bar option before. You can create new columns from hereunder list or library settings as well by following the steps below:

1. Clicking on the option **Create Column** (`https://<site url>/_layouts/15/fldNew.aspx?List=**`), you will be redirected to select the type of column you want to create with other options related to that as seen in the *Figure 2.100* below.

2. Let's say you need to create a column of type **Choice**, select that option, then enter the **Description** of that column.

3. Next from the option **Require that this column contains information**, select **Yes** or **No**. If selected, **Yes**, this column must contain information and cannot be left blank.

4. Next option to **Enforce unique values** allows to select unique value each time or can contain the same information. By default, it's selected as **No**. You can keep the same information for all items.

5. Then for the option **Type each choice on a separate line**, you need to enter choice values like **Approved, Rejected**:

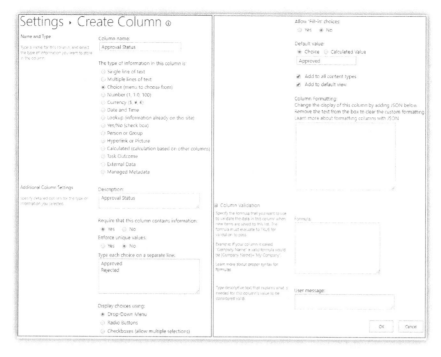

Figure 2.100: *Create Column*

6. The next option provides an option to choose the type of display for your choice option, whether it should be **Drop-Down Menu** or **Radio Buttons** or **Checkboxes (allow multiple selections)**.

7. Selecting **Yes** from option **Allow 'Fill-in' choices** provide an additional option to **Specify your own value** instead of the dropdown choice as seen in the following screenshot:

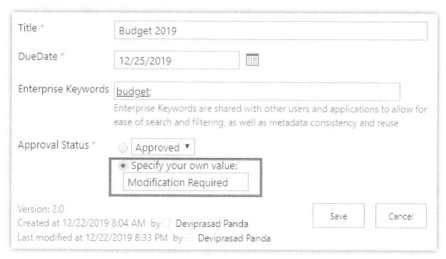

Figure 2.101: *Allow 'Fill-in' choices*

1. Select the **Default Value** for the column out of the choice values you entered. The default value will be selected automatically when you create an item in the library. You can modify different values apart from the default value during the creation of the item. If you are setting any default value for the column, then this column will be added to **Column default value settings** present under **Library Settings | General Settings**.

2. The next option is adding this column to **Add to all content types**, **Add to default view**. Selecting the checkbox will add the column. By default, it's selected.

3. Validation for the column can be set by applying formulae, as discussed before, from the next option, **Column Validation**.

Similarly, we can create columns of other types as well.

Add from existing site columns

You can add columns from existing site columns from the option **Add from existing site columns**. Let us perform the following steps to create a column from existing site columns:

1. Clicking on the option **Add from existing site columns** (https://<site url>/_layouts/15/AddFieldFromTemplate.aspx?List=**) will open another page where you have to select one category (for example, **All Groups**) from **Select site columns from** option.

2. Then select one column (for example, **DueDate**) from **Available site columns** and click on **Add** present side to that.

3. Next, select the checkbox **Add to default view**, **Add to all content types** to add this column to the default view, content types and click **OK** as seen in the following screenshot:

Figure 2.102: Add from existing site columns

Column ordering

Order of the columns which is displayed in library can be changed by the option **Column ordering** (https://<site url>/_layouts/15/formEdt.aspx?List=**). Form the option **Position from Top** change the numbering you want to set and click on **OK** as seen in the following screenshot:

Figure 2.103: Column ordering

Indexed columns

Option **Indexed Columns** (https://<site url>/_layouts/15/Indexed Columns.aspx?List=**) shows the number of columns that are indexed. When the number of items in the library or list crossing 5000, then Automatic index created up to items 20000. If the item is more than that, you can create an *index column* manually following the steps below. Indexing is created to improve items query and performance. Let us perform the following steps to create an index column:

1. Click on **Indexed Columns** (https://<site url>/_layouts/15/Indexed Columns.aspx?List=**).
2. Click in **Create a new index**.
3. Select one column under the option. **Select the primary column for this index** from the dropdown and click **Create** as seen in the following screenshot:

Figure 2.104: Indexed Columns

4. Supported Column Types for indexing are **Single line of text, Choice (single value), Number, Currency, Date and Time, Person or Group (single value) (Lookup), Managed Metadata (Lookup), Yes/No, Lookup (Lookup)**.
5. Unsupported Column Types are **Multiple lines of text, Choice (multi-valued), Calculated, Hyperlink or Picture, Custom Columns, Person or Group (multi-valued) (Lookup), External data**.

Views

The next option under **Library settings** is **Views**. When you open the library or list, you see an item, columns that are under default view (**All Documents**), as seen in *Figure 2.105* below. So, the view represents how to show information, what is the information you want to show, and how to show information based on the requirement of people. Let us perform the following steps to see the options present in **View**:

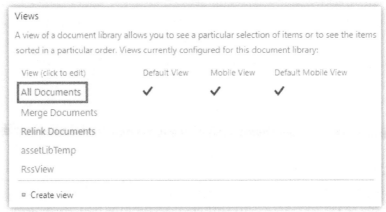

Figure 2.105: Views

1. Click on the view **All Documents**; another page will open, which has multiple options like **Name, Columns, Sort, Filter, Tabular View, Group By, Totals, Style, Folders, Item Limit, Mobile**.

2. You will see the **Name** of the file as **All Documents**. Next, you will see a few **Columns**, but only six columns are selected, as seen in *Figure 2.106* below. It is where you can control what columns you want to show in the library. So only selected columns will be seen in the library view, and rest will be hidden. You can change the numbering of columns also to change the order of display:

Figure 2.106: Edit View

3. Next option **Sort** by which we can set conditions for the column to show the order in which items will be displayed. The following figure helps in understanding it:

Figure 2.107: Sort

4. You can apply filtering to show items based on condition. If the condition is satisfied, then only items will be displayed. The following figure helps in understanding it:

Figure 2.108: Filter

5. We can enable or disable the checkbox for each item in the library by the option, **Allow individual item checkboxes** under **Tabular View**.

6. Grouping of items can be done by following the option **Group By**. Same way, we need to select the **Filter group by the column** based on which items will be displayed in the group.

7. We can select the default option of showing items, whether in the form of **Collapsed** or **Expanded**.

8. By default, the **Number of groups to display per page** is **30**, which can be modified as well. The following figure helps in understanding it:

Figure 2.109: Group By

9. Option to display item count by changing any column option **Total** to **Count** as seen in the following screenshot:

Figure 2.110: Total Count

10. Users can set the **Style** of view, can **Show items inside folders**, or **Show all items without folders** by selecting radio buttons as per requirement.

11. **Number of items to display** in view is **30** by default shown as batches, which can be modified as per requirement.

12. Option to **Adjust mobile settings for this view** is there. We can **Enable this view for mobile access** and **Make this view the default view for mobile access. Number of items to display in list view web part for this view** is there by default **3**, which can be modified. One column is selected for **Field to display in mobile list simple view** as seen in the following screenshot:

Figure 2.111: Style, Folder, Item Limit, Mobile Settings

13. There are five types of views like **Standard View, Datasheet View, Calendar View, Gantt View, Access View**, which user can create following the option **Create view** (`https://<site url>/_layouts/15/ViewType.aspx?List=**`) and selecting the type of view user want to create out of those five view templates.

Content Types

Content Types are a reusable collection of columns or metadata. Once you enable **Allow management of content types** under the settings under **Advanced Settings**, you will notice the **Content Type** option added under **Library settings**, as seen in the following screenshot.

Figure 2.112: Content Types

Click on the **Content Type** (**Document**) you will see few columns as seen in the following screenshot:

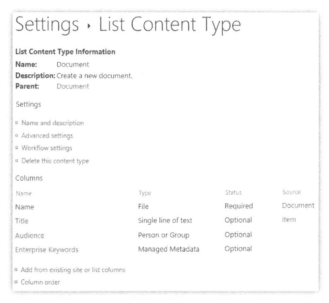

Figure 2.113: Content Type Settings

You will see some columns are added under **Columns** in **Library settings**, as seen in *Figure 2.114* below, which are due to the content type, which is added. That's why we call this content type as reusable columns or metadata. If you add any column in content type, then the same column will be added to library columns:

Figure 2.114: Columns

Navigate to the **Site Settings** (`https://<site url>/_layouts/15/settings .aspx`) and click on **Site Content Types** (`https://<site url>/_layouts/15/mngctype.aspx`) present under **Web Designer Galleries**, you will see all content types available at the site level which can be reused. Option to **Create** (`https://<site url>/_layouts/15/ctypenew.aspx`) new content type is also there to create as per your requirement as seen in the following screenshot:

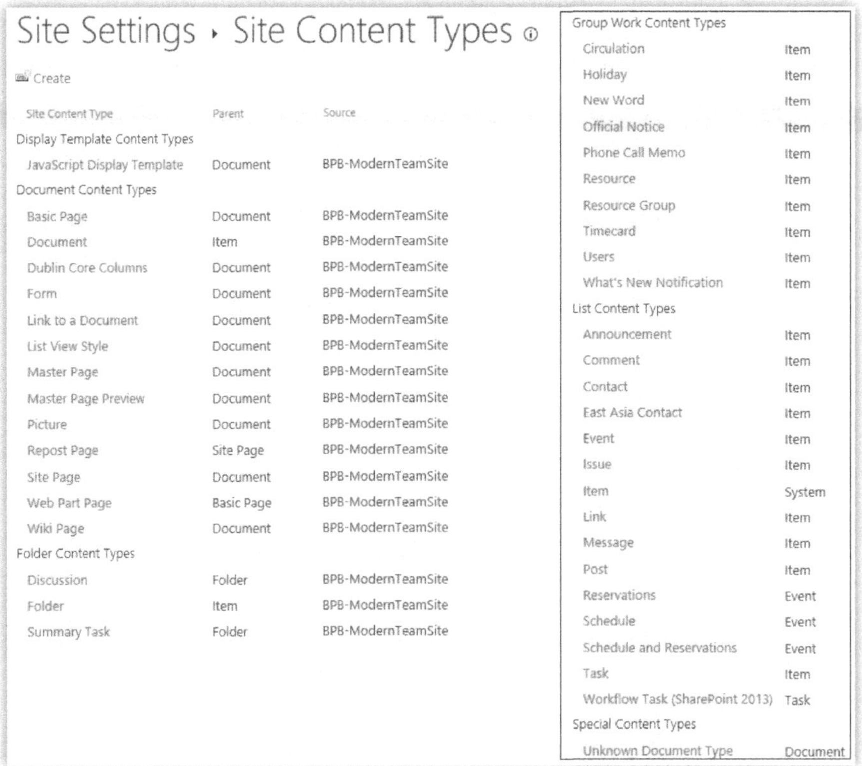

Figure 2.115: Site Content Types

Enhanced Features in Quick Edit Mode

New features are rolling out by which user can edit properties of documents and list items once in the default form that's too multiple items at a time. There will be an option **Properties** user will find in command bar.

Another feature will be rolled out after which user can open document library or list items within the view form under quick edit mode.

Another feature rolling out after which there will be an option **New** available in command bar to create a new list item in Quick Edit mode via the default form

Traditional column creation is replaced with an enhanced mode of column creation. Clicking on the plus sign during hover between two columns and selecting one type of column will display a dialog box at the right side to fill details for site column as shown in figure below.

During quick edit mode, selecting any column will add column in the list or library as shown in figure below.

Traditional hyper link column, date time column is replaced with an enhanced field in quick mode as shown in figure below.

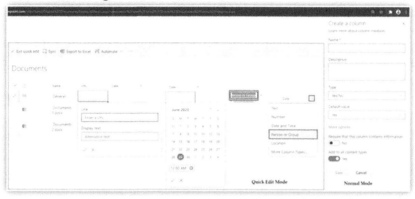

Figure 2.116: *Enhanced Column Rolled out*

New features rolling out by which row height can be adjusted to either **Fixed height**, **Autofit height**. There will be some visual update which user will notice during hover of mouse also during selecting rows.

Conclusion

In this chapter, we discussed default contents in SharePoint once a site is created. Site features and site collection features activated by default after site creation based on the type of site user creating. We discussed the new smart features introduced for site content management and each option present under the library and list settings and its application. Next, in *Chapter 3, Content Approval Concept* will discuss what content approval is and how it works in SharePoint.

Points to Remember

- Limit for a number of list items by default is 30 million, and for the document, the library is also the same 30 million, which includes files and folders.
- The default file upload size limit is increased to 100 GB from 15 GB, and the limit for the file attached in the list is set as 250 MB; OneNote files upload size limit is 2 GB.
- If you are uploading files by drag and drop, limit the file selection as 100 at max.
- The limit for a number of characters, including path and file name length, should not cross 400 characters.
- Activating Site or Site Collection Features, add templates, more functionalities, and content types.

- There is no option **Delete this document library** under **Library settings** for the library **Documents** in the modern team site since it's the default library, and many services are dependent on this.
- In this chapter, wherever its mentioned like this format `_layouts/15/****.aspx`, means this section is added after the site URL `http://<site url>/_layouts/15/****.aspx`.
- Regular changes are applied in Office 365 and SharePoint Online by which there may be changes happening in the template or some other features.

CHAPTER 3
Content Approval Concept

In the previous chapter, we discussed site contents and settings to manage the site content. In this chapter, we will discuss a specific setting related to site content, which we call content approval. This setting related to content is present under list or library settings, but we have not discussed it at that moment since we have planned to discuss that separately. It is an essential feature and mostly used, which needs special attention.

Structure

In this chapter, we will discuss:

- Content approval overview
- Enable content approval process
- How content approval works
- Approval workflow in the content approval process
- Approval workflow using Power Automate

Objective

During the end of the chapter, you will get a clear understanding of:

- What is content approval?
- Settings responsible for content approval.
- How content approval works?
- How can we automate content approval and its benefits over the manual approval process?

Content approval overview

Most of the cases, we need business documents or contents to be reviewed and approved by managers or dedicated users before making it available to intranet users to finalize content. It is when the content approval process comes into the picture. Secure documents like policy, budget, finance, legal documents pass through either single-level approval or multiple levels of approval process before finalizing. So, it's a good practice to keep documents pass through approval to keep under, monitor, updated. Content approval can be applied to content types, library, and lists which carry actual content.

Enable content approval process first

Once you are ready to use the **Content Approval** feature, then the first step to proceed in the content approval process is to activate one sitting from the library or list settings. Let us perform the following steps to enable the content approval process in a library:

1. Navigate to the **Library settings** (https://<site   url>/_layouts/15/ listedit.aspx?List=**) in site.

2. Click on **Versioning settings** (https://<site   url>/_layouts/15/ LstSetng.aspx?List=**) present under category **General settings**.

3. You will find an option **Content Approval** (**Require content approval for submitted items?**), where you need to choose **Yes** or **No**. Change the selection to **Yes** from the default selection **No** as seen in the following screenshot:

Figure 3.1: Enable Content Approval

4. Changing the above setting will enable additional security in the library. You will notice option **Draft Item Security (Who should see draft items in this document library?)** is enabled for library and default selected option is **Only users who can approve items (and the author of the item)**, which means documents or items uploaded or added are visible to only approvers and the user who submitted the document or item. Although other users have permission in the library, they cannot see the documents or items till it's not approved (**Document in draft**), which enables additional security to the user to make the content visible once finalized and approved. You can change the settings to make it visible if required as seen in the following screenshot:

- **Any user who can read items**: All users having permission to the library can see library items.

- **Only users who can edit items**: Users having **Edit** permission can see the documents.

- **Only users who can approve items (and the author of the item)**: Approver of the document and user who submitted the item (**Author**) only can see the documents submitted:

Figure 3.2: Draft Item Security Setting

5. Click on **OK** to apply the changes.

6. Additionally, you can change the **Document Version History** to **Create major and minor (draft) versions** from the default selected option **Create major versions** as seen in the following screenshot:

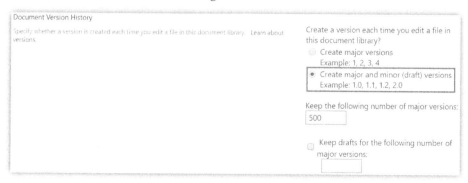

Figure 3.3: Major and minor version

7. The same steps are applicable to enable the content approval process for the list as well.

How Content Approval works

Once settings are applied, you can start using the feature. Let's perform the following steps to check and understand how content approval works in the library.

1. Open the **Document** library in which you enabled content approval.

- You will notice one additional column **Approval Status** added to the library view.

- Once you open **Views** from library settings or open **Switch View Options** from command bar, you will see two additional views named **Approve/reject Items** and **My submissions** as seen in the following screenshot:

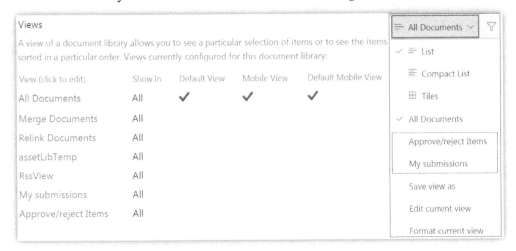

Figure 3.4: Impact of the feature on Views

2. Upload one document in the library, you will notice the status of the document under the newly added column **Approval Status** as **Pending** means, the document already submitted for approval, when option **Document Version History** is selected as default **Create major versions**.

3. If you configured the option **Document Version History** to **Create major and minor (draft) versions** from the default selected option **Create major versions**, you will notice the status of the column **Approval Status** as **Draft** and need an additional step to submit for approval.

4. Select the file; you will see a newly added option **Submit for approval** in the command bar. You can click on this option else; you can click on **Ellipses**

button ⋮ present side to document, then click on **More**, then click on **Publish** to send the document for approval, as seen in the following screenshot:

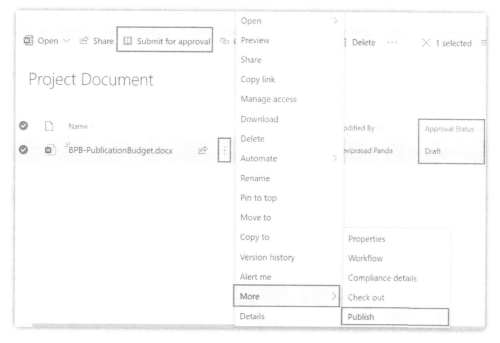

Figure 3.5: Document Approval Status

5. Once the document submitted for approval, the status of the column **Approval Status** will change to **Pending**.

6. The submitted document needs to be approved by the approver (user having full control in the library). The Approver needs to navigate to the library.

7. Select the document that needs to be approved, click on **Ellipses** button ⋮ present side to document, then click on **More**, then click on **Approve/Reject**.

8. Alternatively, this can be approved by clicking the **Ellipses** button ••• from the command bar and then select **Approve/Reject** from the drop-down option, as seen in the following screenshot.

9. Bulk files/multiple files approval at a time is supported. Approver might require approving multiple documents as per their suitable time. In that case, the approver can select the newly created view **Approve/reject items** from **Switch view options** present in the command bar. Documents that need approval will only be displayed in the library. Select all files and click on **Approve/reject items** as seen in the following screenshot:

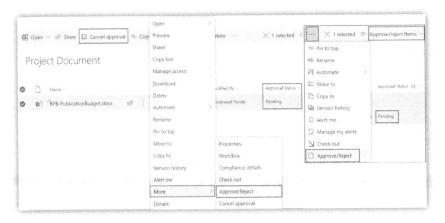

Figure 3.6: Approve or reject

10. One dialog window will open with options like **Approved, Rejected, Pending** so to take appropriate action on the same as seen in the following screenshot:

Figure 3.7: Approve or reject the request

11. Select **Approved**, enter a comment, and click on **OK**.

12. Once approved, the status of the document under the column **Approval Status** is changed to **Approved** from **Pending**, as seen in the following screenshot. Now the document is available for all users having permission in the library.

13. We discussed the manual process of approval, where approver needs to open the library and follow the process of approval. But how approvers will know if anyone uploaded document and its pending for approval. For this, approver needs to set an alert on the library so that approver will receive alert mail if the document is added and then need to access the library manually for approval. It is tough to manage, time taking also, so its not a good process for approval.

Approval Workflow in the content approval process

The approval process can be made simple and easy by implementing workflow in the library or list that ultimately saves time and drive people to do productive work. When we are automating a series of the task then it's called workflow. Let's perform the following steps to create and apply a workflow to see how it is helpful in the content approval process.

Activate a feature first

You need to activate a feature first to enable the approval workflow. Let's perform the following steps to activate the feature:

1. Navigate to **Site settings** (`https://<site url>/_layouts/15/settings. aspx`) as seen in the following screenshot:

Figure 3.8: Site settings

2. Click on **Site collection features** (`https://<site url>/_layouts/15/Manage Features.aspx?Scope=Site`) present under **Site Collection Administration** as seen in the following screenshot:

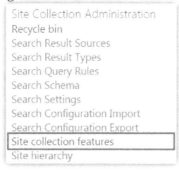

Figure 3.9: Site collection features

3. Identify the feature **Workflows** at the bottom and click on **Active** then the feature will change to state **Active** as seen in the following screenshot:

Figure 3.10: Activate feature Workflows

4. It will make the workflow templates **Approval – SharePoint 2010** available under **Select a workflow template** as seen in the following screenshot:

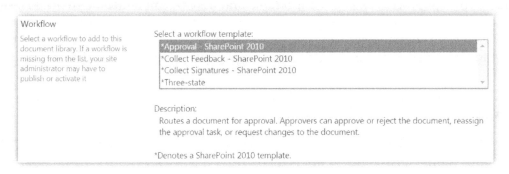

Figure 3.11: Approval – SharePoint 2010 template

5. You will find more features related to workflow other than **Workflows** like **Disposition Approval Workflow**, **Publishing Approval Workflow**, **Sample Proposal**, **SharePoint 2007 Workflows**, **Three-state workflow** under site collection feature as seen in the following screenshot:

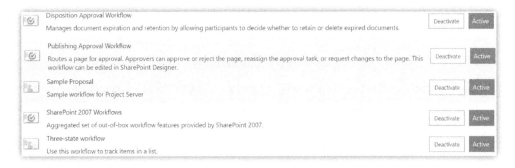

Figure 3.12: Workflow features in Site Collection

6. You can activate those feature to get more templates like **Disposition Approval**, **Publishing Approval** as seen in the screenshot below and create another type of workflows:

Figure 3.13: Workflow templates

Create Approval Workflow

Once the feature is active, you can start proceeding to create a workflow. Let's perform the following steps to create a workflow.

1. Navigate to **Site contents** (`https://<site url>/_layouts/15/viewlsts.aspx`), open one document library (for example, **BudgetReport**), click on the **Gear** Button ⚙ present at top right corner, you will find **Library settings** from the drop-down options. In another way, open site contents from the site. Navigate to `Site contents`, right click your mouse on any one library or click on **Ellipses** button ⋮ present side to document library and click on **Settings** from the drop-down options, will open the library settings (`https://<site url>/_layouts/15/listedit.aspx?List=**`) as seen in the following screenshot:

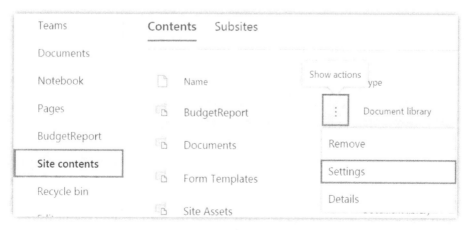

Figure 3.14: Library settings

2. Click on **Workflow Settings** (`https://<site url>/_layouts/15/WrkSetng.aspx?List=**`) present under **Permissions and Management** as seen in the following screenshot:

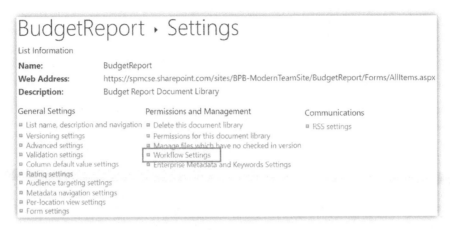

Figure 3.15: Workflow settings

3. Click on **Add a workflow** (`https://<site url>/AddWrkfl.aspx?List={**}`) under **Workflow Settings** as seen in the following screenshot:

Figure 3.16: Add a workflow

4. Select template **Approval – SharePoint 2010** from **Select a workflow template**.

5. Enter **Name (Enter a unique name for this workflow)** as **Budget Approval Workflow**.

6. The next option you will find is **Start Options**, which defines the workflow triggering settings. You see the option selected by default as **Allow this workflow to be manually started by an authenticated user with Edit Item permissions**, which means the user needs to start the workflow manually. This setting is selected because when there is an error in workflow triggering, it may require running the workflow manually. We can still restrict the manual running workflow by selecting the setting **Require Manage Lists Permissions to start the workflow**, which means users who have permission to manage the list can only start this workflow manually, no other users can.

7. Select the checkbox **Creating a new item will start this workflow** present under **Start Options** at the bottom so that when a new item is created, or document is added to the library, then the workflow will be triggered automatically.

8. Keep rest options as it is and click **Next** as seen in the following screenshot:

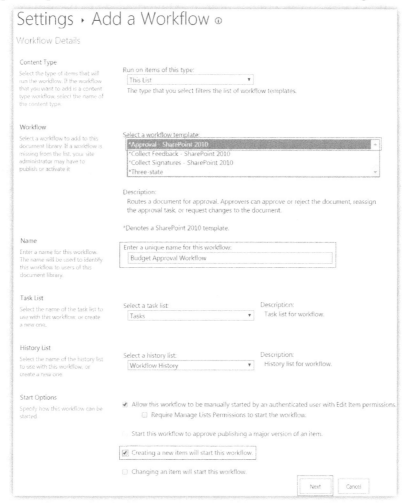

Figure 3.17: Approval workflow template

9. Enter Approvers ID under the filed **Approvers**, which can be one user or multiple users.

10. Describe the message that should go to the approver in the mail once a request is created under the field **Request**.

11. Enter a due date for the request for approval under the field **Due Date for All Tasks**.

12. Under **Duration Per Task**, you can enter 1 or 2 or 3, and so on, and under **Duration Units** select unit as **Day(s)**, **Week**, **Month**, which mean duration is 1 month or 1 week or 1 month. No need to select anything at this moment. Keep as default.

13. In option **CC**, you can enter any user ID who needs to be updated regarding the start and end of the approval process without being part of the approver list.

14. If you select the option **End on First Rejection**, then the approval request will be rejected if any one of the approvers rejects the request.

15. If you select the option **End on Document Change**, then workflow requests will be rejected if there is any modification done in between the workflow under the approval process.

16. Select the box present under **Enable Content Approval** to **Update the approval status after the workflow is completed** and click **Save** as seen in the following screenshot:

Figure 3.18: Approval workflow saved

17. Workflow is created now. You will find the workflow name **Budget Approval Workflow** and **Workflows in progress** status (**0** workflows running now) under **Workflow Settings** as seen in the following screenshot:

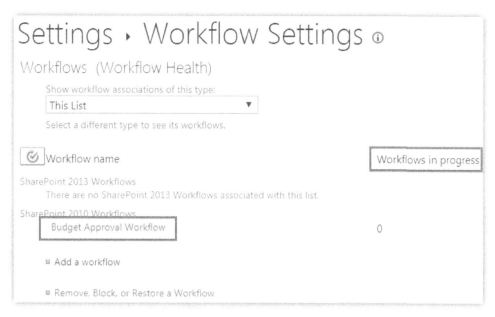

Figure 3.19: Workflow created

How the approval workflow works

The approval workflow is created now. Let's see how it works and how it is different from the manual approval process. Let's perform the following steps to check what happens precisely:

1. Now upload one document in library **BudgetReport** where we created the workflow.

2. You will notice one additional column **Budget Approval Workflow** is added in library, and reflecting the current status of the document as **In Progress** as seen in the following screenshot:

Figure 3.20: Upload document in the library

3. Approver will receive one mail with subject as **Approval has started on <uploaded file name>**. Click on the **File Name with link** for a review of the document. Once the review of the document is done, click on the link **View the status of this workflow** present at the bottom as seen in the following screenshot:

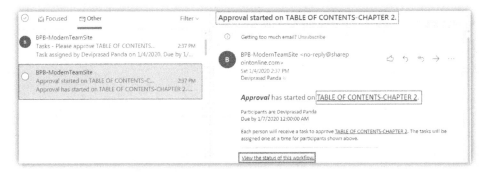

Figure 3.21: Approval Started Mail to Approver

4. Workflow Status page will open where we can see the current status of the workflow. It holds information about the **Initiator, Started** date and time, **Document** name, **Status** of the document, **Workflow Visualization**, as seen in the following screenshot:

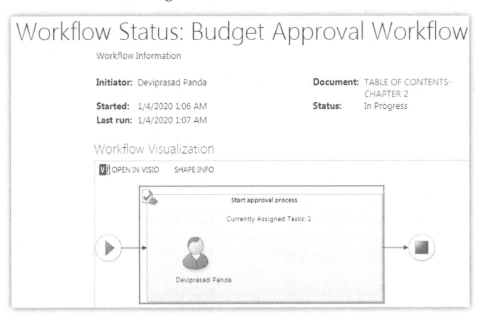

Figure 3.22: Workflow information

5. The approver can see the **Workflow History** at the bottom. Under **Event Type** can see as **Workflow Initiated** and **Task Created**. Under **Description** can see **Task created for Deviprasad Panda. Due by: 1/7/2020 12:00:00 AM**.

6. Approver needs to click on the **Link with file name (Please approve TABLE OF CONTENTS-CHAPTER 2)** present under field **Title** and category **Tasks** as seen in the following screenshot:

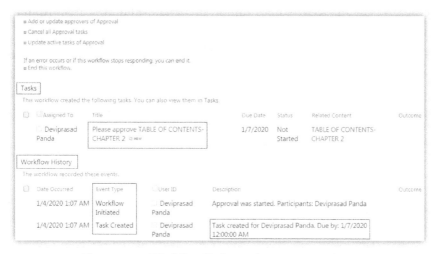

Figure 3.23: Workflow Tasks needs approver action

7. Another window will open from where approver need do the needful. Enter comment under the field **Comments** and click **Approve** as seen in the following screenshot:

Figure 3.24: Workflow Task action window

8. Now go back to the library and you will notice the status of document as **Approved**. Click on the status **Approved** that will redirect you to the **Workflow Status** page as seen in the following screenshot:

Figure 3.25: Workflow completed and Status updated

9. Now you see the **Status** field under **Tasks** is updated as **Completed**, and the **Outcome** field is updated as **Approved**.

10. Under **Workflow History** you see under **Event Type** status updated as **Task Completed** and **Workflow Completed**. **Description** its showing task is assigned to whom and approved by whom with the comment put by the approver. The **Outcome** is updated that **Approval was completed** as seen in the following screenshot:

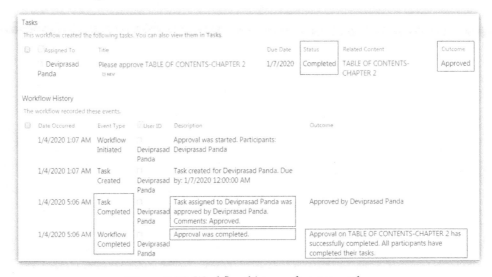

Figure 3.26: Workflow history after approval

Benefits of Approval Workflow

You must have noticed the process of workflow compared to the manual process. The benefits of the workflow, as mentioned below:

1. There is a reduction in the manual effort that, in turn, saves time and improves productivity.

2. The user gets a mail with all details and links. Gets task reminders as well.

3. The link to the document is there in the mail. Users can download that file directly from the link instead of opening manually from the library.

4. Link to check the status of the workflow directly is there, and the user can do needful.

5. Every event type is tracked, and so that from workflow history, you can get all specific actions taken on that document.

Approval flow using Power Automate

We can create a flow to automate the approval process using Power Automate, which is going to be the future to automate task. In the future, the workflow will be replaced by power automate. Let's perform the following steps to create a basic approval flow:

1. Access the library and click on **Automate** from the command bar, then click on **Power Automate** from the drop-down and select **Create a flow**.

2. You will get flow templates to select. Scroll down and click on **See more templates** as seen in the following screenshot:

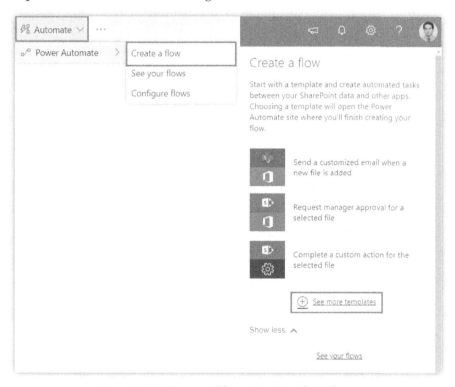

Figure 3.27: Command bar option to select Flow

3. You will be redirected to the **Power Automate** page where you can see more templates in for of categories like **Featured**, **Shared with me**, **Approval**, **Button**, **Data collection**, **Visio**, **Email**, **Events**, and **calendar**, **Mobile**, **Notifications**, **Productivity**, **Social Media**, **Sync**. Click on category **Approval** and select the template **Start approval when a new item is added** as seen in the following screenshot:

Figure 3.28: Template Start approval when a new item is added

4. Another window will appear where you can see the services (**Office 365 Outlook**, **SharePoint**, **Approvals**, **Office 365 Users**) involved in approval flow. Click on **Continue**:

Figure 3.29: Services involved in Approval Flow

5. You will be redirected to the flow page wherein the first block named **When a new item is created**, you need to select **Site Address** and **List Name**. Under **Site Address** select site from the drop down option or can enter a custom value, selecting the option **Enter custom value** at the bottom, if site id not found under the drop-down as seen in the following screenshot:

Figure 3.30: Enter Site Address and List Name

6. The next block underflow is **Start an approval**, which configures settings for the approval mail to the approver. Keep it as it is for the moment, as seen in the following screenshot:

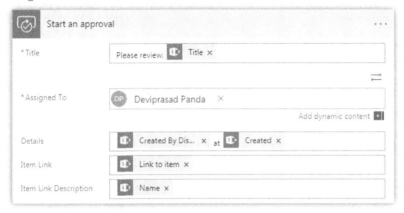

Figure 3.31: Start an Approval

7. The approval mail that approver will receive as seen in the following screenshot below. You can compare both above *Figure 3.28* and *Figure 3.29* you will get a clear idea:

Figure 3.32: Approval mail to Approver

8. Another block for configuration is **Condition** where we need to configure the **Response** as seen in the following screenshot:

Figure 3.33: Condition

9. If the **Response** is **Yes** the configuration for **Approved** mail of format as below under the block **If yes** as seen in the following screenshot:

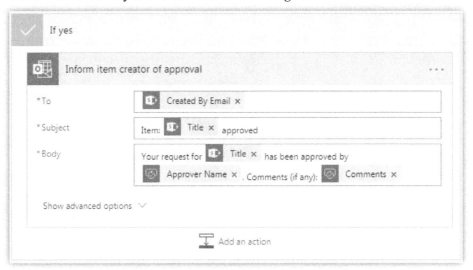

Figure 3.34: Action on condition satisfied

10. The example of the approved mail is as seen in the following screenshot:

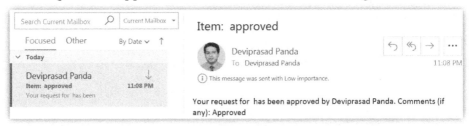

Figure 3.35: Task Approved

11. If the **Response** is **No** the configuration for **Rejected** mail of format as below under the block **If no** as seen in the following screenshot:

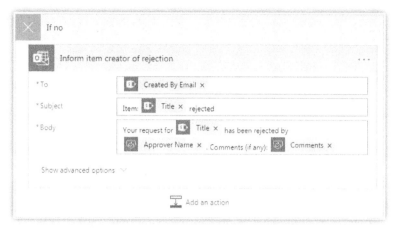

Figure 3.36: Action on condition not satisfied

12. Other blocks represent the error configuration which keeps as it is for the moment as seen in the following screenshot below, but it can be customized at any moment:

Figure 3.37: Action on error

13. Finally, click on the **Save** button present at the bottom.

14. Now when any document is added in library, the approver will receive mail to do the needful as seen in the following screenshot:

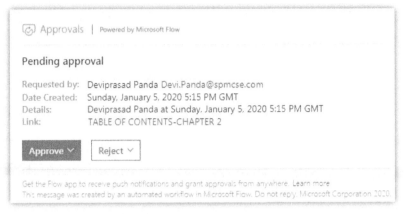

Figure 3.38: Approval mail to Approver

15. Approver needs to do the needful. Approver needs to click in **Approve** the request with **Comment** and click **Submit**, as seen in the following screenshot.

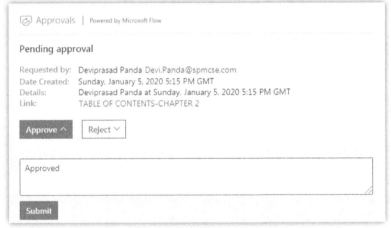

Figure 3.39: Approve or Reject from mail

16. After the request is approved, the requestor will receive mail finally, as seen in the following screenshot:

Figure 3.40: Task Approved

17. You can check the history on flow completed and can check the steps completed for the item. Under **My flows** click on the flow **Start approval when a new item is added** as seen in the following screenshot:

Figure 3.41: *History of My flows*

18. You will see under **Runs** flow showing status as **Succeeded**. Click on the link (**Jan 6, 10:32 AM (21 min ago)**) present under **Start** as seen in the following screenshot:

Figure 3.42: *Flow status*

19. Then opening in each block will show you the series of actions taken under that block. If you open the block **Start an approval**, then you will see the details as seen in the screenshot below. The green mark at top right corner indicated in executed blocks as seen in the following screenshot:

Figure 3.43: *History of Start an approval*

20. Similarly, expanding other blocks, you can see the series of actions taken under that. Block marked cross are skipped (Block If no), as seen in the following screenshot:

Figure 3.44: Condition Satisfied and Block "If yes" executed

Conclusion

In this chapter, we had a glance at the content approval concept. We discussed the steps to enable the content approval process in the library or list. Understood how manually approve content and how it works. Then we discussed step by step how to automate the content approval process by applying workflow and automate. We understood how automating the approval process works and how it's different from the manual process with all benefits. Next, in *Chapter 4, Configure Information Management Policy*, we will discuss information management policy and how to apply it in SharePoint.

Points to Remember

- The focus is to share the approval concept instead of mentioning multiple examples.
- Workflow and Power Automate can be used to automate tasks to a new level.
- Content can be approved by a single user or multiple users. We can add additional users' same way the first user is added.
- Bulk Approval can be made possible for approvers.
- Approvers can be users having Full Control permission or Design permission or any Custom Permission group having Approve Items permission.
- In this chapter, wherever its mentioned like this format _layouts/15/****. aspx, means this section is added after the site URL `http://<site url>/_ layouts/15/****.aspx`.
- Regular changes are applied in Office 365 and SharePoint Online by which there may be changes happening in the template or some other features.

CHAPTER 4

Configure Information Management Policy

In the previous chapter, we discussed content approval and how to automate the content approval process using workflow or power automate. It's essential to maintain security and compliance with information, regulations, and business process internal to the organization. We can track the content access for employees, duration of access, apply specific actions for unused contents like delete, move to a location, and so on, by applying policies. So, in this chapter, we will discuss how to configure and apply information management policies to complete specific actions like retention, audit events related to the content present in the site, apply security by implementing barcodes and labels.

Structure

In this chapter, we will discuss the following topics:

- Introduction to Information Management Policies
- Activate Dependent Feature
- Apply Site Policies
- Content Type Policy Templates Creation
- Enable Retention, Auditing, Barcodes, Labels Policies
- Applying Policy in Content Types, Library, Folder, List
- Timer Job Action

Objective

During the end of the chapter, you will get a clear understanding of:

- Information Management Policy overview
- Dependent Features for Information Management Policies
- How to create and apply Site Policies
- How to create a Content Type Policy Template
- How to enable and setup Retention, Auditing, Barcodes, Labels Policies
- How to apply policies in Content Types, Library, Folder, List
- Responsible Timer Jobs for retention action

Activate Feature First

To apply policies, we need to activate one dependent site collection feature that will enable Information Management Policy and allow retention schedules applicable for site, contents. Let's perform the following steps to activate the feature:

1.   Navigate to `Site settings (https://<site url>/_layouts/15/settings.aspx)` as seen in the following screenshot:

Figure 4.1: Site settings

2. Click on `Site collection features (https://<site url>/_layouts/15/Manage Features.aspx?Scope=Site)` present under `Site Collection Administration` as seen in the following screenshot.

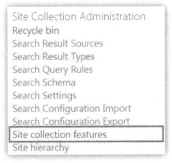

Figure 4.2: Site collection features

3. Identify the site collection feature **Site Policy** at the bottom and click on Active, as seen in the following screenshot:

Figure 4.3: *Activate feature Site Policy*

Apply Site Policies

We can apply site policies for deletion from option Site Closure and Deletion. Let's perform the following steps to create site policy.

1. Navigate to Site settings (`https://<site url>/_layouts/15/settings.aspx`).

2. Click on `Site Policies` (`https://<site url>/_layouts/15/ProjectPolicies.aspx`) present under `Site Collection Administration` as seen in the following screenshot:

Figure 4.4: *Site Policies*

3. Click on `Create` (`https://<site url>/_layouts/15/projectpolicy config.aspx`) under `Site Policies` settings as seen in the following screenshot:

Figure 4.5: *Create Site Policies*

4. Enter **Name** and **Description** for the new `Site Policy` (For example, `Delete BPB-ModernTeamSite Policy`).

5. Next, under **Site Closure and Deletion**, you will find three options like **Do not close or delete site automatically, Delete sites automatically, Close and delete sites automatically**. Select the second option **Delete sites automatically**, as seen in the following screenshot:

Figure 4.6: *New Site Policy*

6. You can set **Deletion Event** as either **Site closed date** or **Site created date**. Select **Site closed date**. We also need to mention after how many days or months (**3 months**) or **year** from the closed date, the site will be deleted automatically.

7. Select checkbox **Send an email notification to site owners this far in advance of deletion** and set one value (**2 months**) so that owners will start receiving mail before (**2 months**) that date of site deletion.

8. Select checkbox **Send follow-up notifications every** and set one value (**14 days**) so that owners will get follow up mail in that frequency (**14 days**).

9. Select the checkbox **Owners can postpone imminent deletion for:** and enter one value (**1 months**) so the site will not be deleted automatically for that duration and will be on hold.

10. Finally, click on **OK** to apply the changes.

11. Since we have chosen **Delete sites automatically** and **Deletion Event** as **Site closed date**, the policy will be applied when the site is manually marked, **Close this site now**.

12. Let's perform the following steps to mark the site as **Close this site now**.

13. Navigate to **Site Settings** (`<_layouts/15/settings.aspx>`).

14. Click on **Site Closure and Deletion** (`https://<site url>/_layouts/15/ Project PolicyAndLifecycle.aspx`) present under **Site Administration** as seen in the following screenshot:

Figure 4.7: Site Closure and Deletion

15. You will notice the option **Close this site now** options under **Site Closure** is greyed out. Click on the drop-down option from **Site Policy**, select the policy **Delete BPB-ModernTeamSite Policy** that we created below and click on **OK** as seen in the following screenshot:

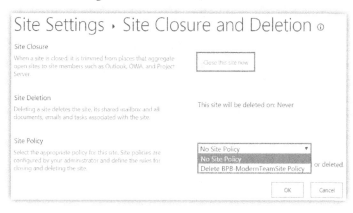

Figure 4.8: Apply Site Policy

16. Now again, open **Site Closure and Deletion** present under **Site Administration**. This time you will find **Close this site now** is enabled, so click on that. Then click on, **OK**.

17. You notice the status of **Site Closure** changed to **Open this site** with the site closed date **This site was closed on: 1/8/2020 12:16 AM**, and field **Site Deletion** changed to **Postpone deletion of this site for 1 month**. The site owner can postpone deleting if feel to extend 1 month following this option.

18. At the top of the site above the banner, you will find a message like **This site will be deleted on Wednesday, April 8, 2020**. Also, **This site is read only at the site collection administrator's request** as seen in the following screenshot so that no contents can be added to keep the latest data and migrate user to other site or location as per business requirement:

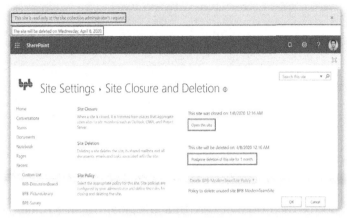

Figure 4.9: *Site Deletion Policy Applied*

19. If you are selecting the option **Close and delete sites automatically**, there is no requirement of manually setting the option **Close this site now**, since you are setting here directly. Enter a value (**1 years**) for **Site created date**. Enter value (**3 months**) for **Site closed date**. It means after a 1-year, the site will be marked as closed, and after **3 months** site will be deleted automatically. Settings **Send an email notification to site owners this far in advance of deletion** and **Send follow-up notifications every** will send notifications and follow up emails the same way as we discussed before, as seen in the following screenshot. Rest all steps same, the site will be deleted automatically as scheduled, and the user can message above the banner:

Figure 4.10: *Close and Delete sites automatically*

Content Type Policy Templates Creation

Let's perform the following steps to create a content type policy template:

1. Navigate to **Site Settings** (`<_layouts/15/settings.aspx>`).

2. Click on **Content Type Policy Templates** (`https://<site url>/_layouts/15/Policylist.aspx`) present under **Site Collection Administration** as seen in the following screenshot:

Figure 4.11: *Content Type Policy Templates*

3. Enter **Name** and **Administrative Description**; as seen in the following screenshot:

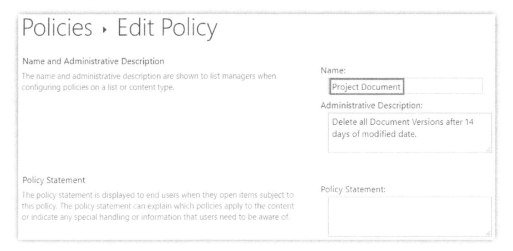

Figure 4.12: *Content Type Policy Templates Name and Administrative Description*

4. You will find four categories of Information policy named **Enable Retention**, **Enable Auditing**, **Enable Barcodes**, **Enable Labels**, as seen in the following screenshot:

Retention

Schedule how content is managed and disposed by specifying a sequence of
retention stages. If you specify multiple stages, each stage will occur one after
the other in the order they appear on this page.

Note: If the Library and Folder Based Retention feature is active, list
administrators can override content type policies with their own retention
schedules. To prevent this, deactivate the feature on the site collection.

☐ Enable Retention

Auditing

Specify the events that should be audited for documents and items subject to
this policy.

☐ Enable Auditing

Barcodes

Assigns a barcode to each document or item. Optionally, Microsoft Office
applications can require users to insert these barcodes into documents.

☐ Enable Barcodes

Labels

You can add a label to a document to ensure that important information about
the document is included when it is printed. To specify the label, type the text
you want to use in the "Label format" box. You can use any combination of fixed
text or document properties, except calculated or built-in properties such as
GUID or CreatedBy. To start a new line, use the \n character sequence.

☐ Enable Labels

Figure 4.13: Information policy categories

4. Click on **OK** for the moment; you will see the **Content Type Policy Templates**
   is created as seen in the following screenshot, but there is no policy applied in
   this template. We will discuss each category separately in the next section:

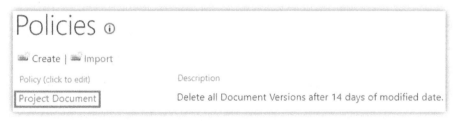

Figure 4.14: Content Type Policy Template created

Enable Retention

Let's perform the following steps to configure retention policy in the Content Type
Policy Templates that we created above:

1. Click on the policy **Project Document** that we just created.

2. Click on the checkbox **Enable Retention**; you will see another option **Add a
   retention stage…** enabled, as seen in the following screenshot. Click on **Add a
   retention stage…** as seen in the following screenshot:

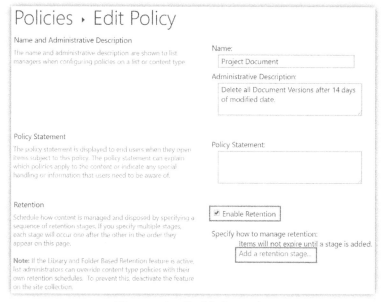

Figure 4.15: Enable Retention

3. Another dialog box will open where you will find three categories, **Event**, **Action**, **Recurrence**.

4. From the **Event** category, select **Time Period** as **Last Modified** with the number of days (**14 days**) present under **This stage is based off a date property on the item**, as seen in the following screenshot.

Under **Time Period** we can find three options to choose as below:

- Created date
- Last Modified
- Declared Record

Figure 4.16: Event types and Action types

5. From **Action**, select **Delete all previous versions** and finally click on **OK**, as seen in the following screenshot.

Different options under **Action** to choose as below:

- `Move to Recycle Bin`
- `Permanently Delete`
- `Transfer to another location`
- `Start a workflow`
- `Skip to next stage`
- `Declare record`
- `Delete previous drafts`
- `Delete all previous versions`

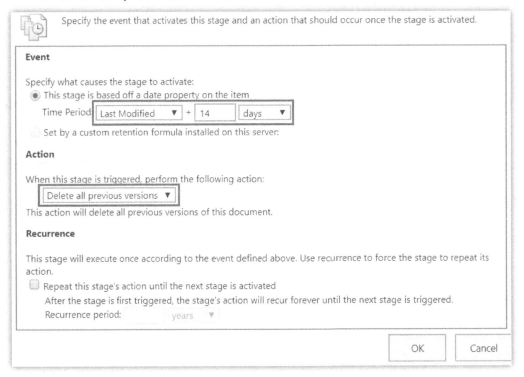

Figure 4.17: Events and Actions selected

6. You will see the retention policy is applied in the **Content Type Policy Templates**, which is ready to apply now, as seen in the following screenshot. Click on **OK** from **Edit Policy** again to save the template:

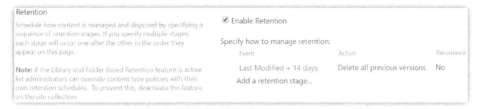

Figure 4.18: *Retention policy created*

7. Applying this policy will delete all previous versions of the document, after 14 days of the last modified date of that document, automatically.

Enable Auditing

The next category under information policy is **Auditing** that captures events like **Editing items**, **Checking out or checking in items**, **Moving or copying items to another location in the site**, **Deleting or restoring items**. Click on the checkbox **Enable Auditing** and select the events that you want to log for audit and click **OK** finally to apply changes as seen in the following screenshot:

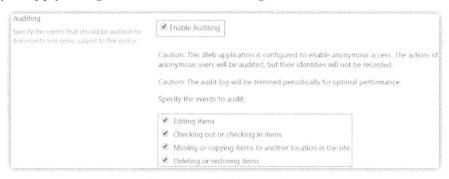

Figure 4.19: *Enable Auditing*

The events log due to this setting can be found in **Audit log reports** present under **Site Collection Administration**, as seen in the following screenshot:

Figure 4.20: *Audit log Reports*

Enable Barcodes

The next category under information policy is **Barcodes**. Click on the checkbox **Enable Barcodes** to enable barcodes. Next, you will get another option **Prompt**

users to insert a barcode before saving or printing enabled which you can select for additional security as seen in the following screenshot:

Figure 4.21: Enable Barcodes

After enabling this and applying the policy template in the library, upload one document library that will generate **Barcode**, as seen in the following screenshot:

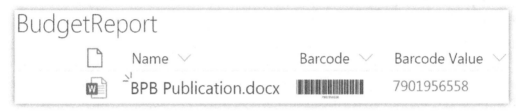

Figure 4.22: Enable Barcode

Enable Labels

Like Barcode, you can insert **Labels** in office documents by enabling the feature. Select the checkbox **Enable Labels** and **Prompt users to insert a label before saving or printing**. Enter document property, for example, **{Version}** the field **Label format** and click **OK** finally to apply changes as seen in the following screenshot:

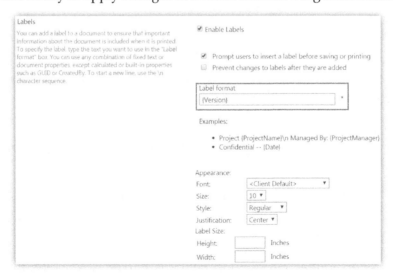

Figure 4.23: Enable Levels

Applying Information Management Policy

We discussed how to create and apply site policies. Also, I discussed how to configure different policies and created a custom content type policy template. Now, will discuss how to apply those Information Management policies. We can apply policies in the library, list, and content types, which will be discussed next.

Applying Policy in Content Types

Let's perform the following steps to apply Information Management policies in content types:

1. Navigate to **Site contents** (<_layouts/15/viewlsts.aspx>), right click your mouse on any one library or click on **Ellipses** button ⋮ present side to document library and click on **Settings** from the drop-down options, will open the **Library Settings** (<_layouts/15/listedit.aspx?List=****>) as seen in the following screenshot:

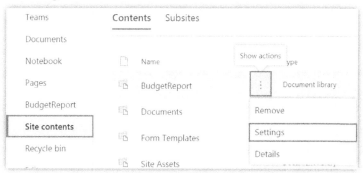

Figure 4.24: Library Settings

2. Click on **Information management policy settings** (https://<site url>/_layouts/15/policycts.aspx?List={**}) present under **Permissions and Management** from **Library Settings** as seen in the following screenshot:

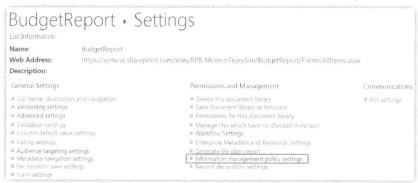

Figure 4.25: Library Settings

3. Policy settings page (`<_layouts/15/policycts.aspx?List={*****}>`) will open where you can see the source **Source of retention for this library** is selected as **Content Type**. Click on the `content type` **Document** as seen in the following screenshot:

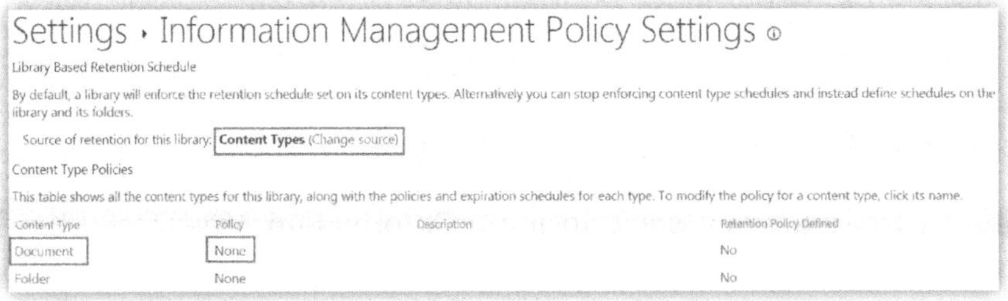

Figure 4.26: Information management policy settings

4. Select **Define a policy** from **Information Management Policy Settings: Document** and click on **OK**, as seen in the following screenshot:

Information Management Policy Settings: Document

Specify the Policy

Specify the information management policy for this content type. If you would like to use one of this site's predefined policies then select "Use a site policy". Alternatively, you can directly create or edit the policy settings.

Specify the policy:
- None
- Define a policy...
- Use a site collection policy:
  Project Document ▾

[OK] [Cancel]

Figure 4.27: Define a policy

5. You will be redirected to the **Edit Policy** (`<_layouts/15/policyconfig.aspx?ctype=*>`) the page where you can apply **Enable Retention**, **Enable Auditing**, **Enable Barcodes**, **Enable Labels**, as discussed before under the section **Content Type Policy Templates Creation** in this chapter above. Follow the process to apply policies to apply any policies from 4 categories and click **OK**.

6. Now you will see in **Information Management Policy Settings** (`<_layouts/15/policycts.aspx?List={***}>`) under **Content Type Document**, **Policy** is showing as **Custom Policy** and **Retention Policy Defined** is showing **Yes** as seen in the following screenshot. So the custom policy is applied to document content type:

Figure 4.28: Custom Policy applied

7. If you select **Use a site collection policy** from **Information Management Policy Settings: Document** instead of **Define a policy** as mentioned in Step 4 above, you will get an option to select a custom policy template **Project Document** that we created under **Content Type Policy Templates** (`https://<site url>/_layouts/15/Policylist.aspx`) present under **Site Collection Administration** as seen in the following screenshot. Policies configured in that custom policy template will be applied to the library:

Figure 4.29: Use a site collection policy

8. Now you will see in **Information Management Policy Settings** (`<_layouts/15/policycts.aspx?List={*****}>`) under **Content Type Document**, **Policy** is showing as **Project Document** and **Retention Policy Defined** is showing **Yes** as seen in the following screenshot. So, policies under the custom content type policy template are applied to document content type:

Figure 4.30: Custom content type policy template applied

9. We can apply policies in content type present in **Site content types** also so that when these content types are added in the library, policies are applied automatically. Since site content types are reusable, applying policies at site content level makes policies also reusable once the content type is added. Let's perform the following steps to apply policies in the content type.

10. Navigate to **Site Settings** (`<_layouts/15/settings.aspx>`).

11. Click on **Site content types** (`https://<site url>/_layouts/15/mngctype.aspx`) present under **Web Designer Galleries** as seen in the following screenshot:

Figure 4.31: Site content types

12. Click on **Picture** present under **Document Content Types**, as seen in the following screenshot:

Figure 4.32: Document Content Types

13. You will be redirected to the content type settings page. Click on **Information management policy settings** (`https://<site url>/_layouts/15/policy.aspx?ctype=0x0**`) present under that as seen in the following screenshot:

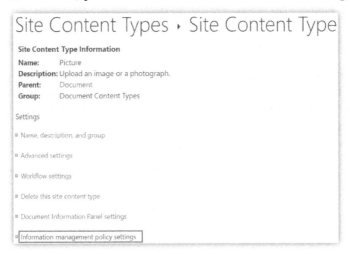

Figure 4.33: Content Type information management policy settings

14. Select **Use a site collection policy** from **Information Management Policy Settings** and select the custom policy template **Project Document** that we created before. Click on **OK**, as seen in the following screenshot:

Figure 4.34: Use a site collection policy

15. Now open **Library Settings** (`https://<site url>/_layouts/15/listedit.aspx?List=**`). Click on **Add from existing site content types** (`https://<site url>/_layouts/15/AddContentTypeToList.aspx?List=**`) present under **Content Type** as seen in the following screenshot:

Figure 4.35: Add from existing site content types

16. Under **Select Content Types**, select **Picture** from **Available Site Content Types**, click on **Add >** and click **OK** as seen in the following screenshot:

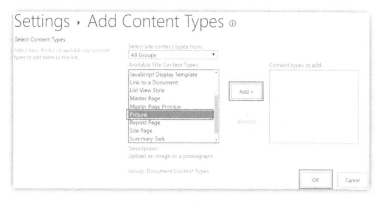

Figure 4.36: Add content types

17. If you now open the **Information Management Policy Settings** (https://<site url>/_layouts/15/policycts.aspx?List={**}) from **Library Settings**, you will see policy applied to the content type can be reused in the library as seen in the following screenshot:

Figure 4.37: Custom Content Type Policy Template Reusable

18. When you apply the content type **Picture**, this policy is applied to that library.

Applying Policy in Library

Let's perform the following steps to apply Information Management policies in the Library:

1. Navigate to **Library Settings** and click on **Information management policy settings** (https://<site url>/_layouts/15/policycts.aspx?List={**}) present under **Permissions and Management**.

2. The source type is selected as **Content Types**. Click on **Change source** (https://<site url>/_layouts/15/expirationconfig.aspx?List=***) as seen in the following screenshot:

Figure 4.38: Change Source

3. From the next window, click on **Library and Folders**. One message dialog box will open, click on **OK** as seen in the following screenshot:

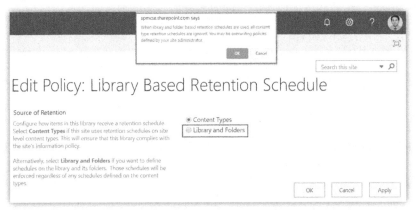

Figure 4.39: Select Library and Folders

4. Now **Library and Folders** option is selected, and **Add a retention stage...** is enabled as seen in the following screenshot. You apply the retention policy as discuss before and click on **Apply** finally:

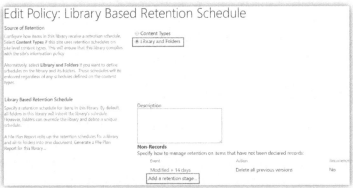

Figure 4.40: Add a retention stage

5. After applying, you will see a **Note** like **Since this library is using library and folder retention, all documents will use those schedules. Content type retention policies are ignored**, as seen in the following screenshot. So, policies applied at the library and folder will override policies applied to content type:

Figure 4.41: Library and Folder policy applied

Applying Policy in Folder

Folders present in the library inherits the policy applied in library level policy. You can apply policy at the **Folder** level, which will override the policy applied at the library level.

Let's perform the following steps to apply **Information Management policies** in **Folder**:

1. Follow the same *Step 1* to *Step 3*, as discussed under the section **Applying Policy in Library**.

2. Next, you select the folder present at the left navigation and then select **Define retention stages**. It will enable another option, **Add a retention stage...**, to apply. You can apply the same policy way we discussed before and click **OK** finally to apply changes, as seen in the following screenshot:

Figure 4.42: Folder Level policy applied

Applying Policy in List

You can follow the same process as described under the section **Applying Policy in Library**.

Timer Job Action

We discussed retention policies and how it works. But let me share; you might feel like the policy is not active or showing any result for a few days. You need to understand; all retention policy depends on the timer jobs Information Management Policy and Expiration Policy that are scheduled weekly by default that cannot be modified. So, although you scheduled policy for someday, that action will not complete or effective unless the time jobs are running successfully weekly. For the on-premises environment, it can be changed manually, but for SharePoint Online, the schedule for the timer job cannot be modified; you may contact the SharePoint support team for help.

Conclusion

In this chapter, we had a glance at the Information Management Policy. What are these policies, where to apply it, what is the dependent feature related to policy to make the options available related to information management policy? Discussed step by step how to create and apply site policy, content type policy template. Understood how to enable and setup retention, auditing, barcodes, labels policies also its application in content types, library, folder, list. Also, we covered the timer job responsible for this retention policy, and it's useful to complete the action. Next, in *Chapter 5, Configure Document ID Service* will discuss document id service in SharePoint.

Points to remember

- Activate the feature **Site Policy** makes the option **Information Management Policy** available.

- All retention policy depends on the timer jobs **Information Management Policy** and **Expiration Policy** that are scheduled weekly by default that cannot be modified. So, although you configure a retention policy for a particular date, action will be executed as per the scheduled timer jobs.

- In this chapter wherever its mentioned like this format _layouts/15/****. aspx, means this section is added after the site URL http:// <site url> /_layouts/15/****.aspx.

- Regular changes are applied in Office 365 and SharePoint Online by which there may be changes happening in the template or some other features.

CHAPTER 5

Configure Document ID Service

Introduction

In the previous chapter, we discussed all information policy. In this chapter, we will discuss the document id service. The **Document ID** is a system-generated unique ID assigned to each document once uploaded in the library. There is a unique **Document ID URL link** associated with each document ID that is in the format `https://<Site URL>/_layouts/15/DocIdRedir.aspx?<Document ID>`. Benefits of document ID are like; it's very helpful to manage record or document. Documents can also be easily tracked irrespective of the location where it is stored. Let's discuss in detail and see its application in the site and its behavior.

Structure

In this chapter, we will discuss:

- Introduction to the Document ID
- Activate Dependent Feature
- Edit Document Library View
- Document ID Settings Configuration
- Testing Scenarios

Objective

During the end of the chapter, you will get a clear understanding of:

- Document ID overview
- Dependent feature for Document ID service
- How to add dependent column to the library
- Modify Document ID Settings
- Document ID Service Test Case

Activate feature first

To apply document ID service, we need to activate one dependent site collection feature first that will enable this service and will apply system-generated document ID to contents. Let's perform the following steps to activate the site collection feature.

1. Navigate to **Site settings** (https://<site url>/_layouts/15/settings. aspx) as seen in the following screenshot:

Figure 5.1: Site Settings

2. Click on **Site collection features** (<_layouts/15/ManageFeatures. aspx?Scope =Site>) present under **Site Collection Administration** as seen in the following screenshot:

Figure 5.2: Site Collection Feature

3. Identify the feature **Document ID Service** at the bottom and click on **Active** then the feature will change to state **Active** as seen in the following screenshot:

Figure 5.3: *Document ID Service Feature*

Edit View to Add Column

Once the feature is activated, there will be few changes in the site collection. You will find an additional column in view **Document ID** (linked to document), which needs to be added in the document library default view. Let's perform the following steps to edit the view and add a column to the library:

1. Navigate to **Library Settings** (`https://<site url>/_layouts/15/ listedit.aspx?List=**`) and click on the default view **All Documents** present under category **Views** as seen in the following screenshot:

Figure 5.4: *Document Library Views*

2. Identify the column **Document ID (linked to document)** presently under option **Columns** from the **Edit View** page and select the checkbox as seen in the following screenshot:

Figure 5.5: *Add Column To View*

3. Now upload one document in the library; you will find a **Document ID** linked to the document, as seen in the following screenshot:

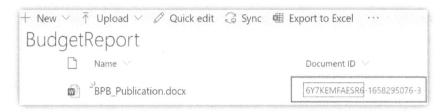

Figure 5.6: Document ID

Document ID settings configuration

You notice the document id generated stars with **6Y7KEMFAESR6**, which we call as **Prefix** of **Document ID**. We can set a customized prefix as per our requirement. Let's perform the following steps to create a customized prefix for Document ID:

1. Navigate to **Site Settings** (`<_layouts/15/settings.aspx>`).

2. Click on **Document ID settings** (`https://<site url>/_layouts/15/DocIdSettings.aspx`) present under **Site Collection Administration** as seen in the following screenshot:

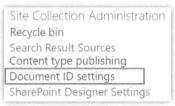

Figure 5.7: Document ID Settings.

3. On the **Document ID Settings** page, you will notice the option **Assign Document IDs** is selected by default, under the option **Begin IDs with the following characters**; you will find the default prefix ID (**6Y7KEMFAESR6**) as seen in the following screenshot:

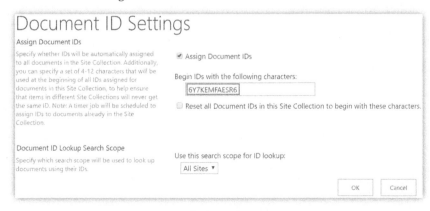

Figure 5.8: Default Prefix Document ID

4. Under the option **Begin IDs with the following characters**, enter a customized ID (**SPMCSE**) of your choice and click on **OK**.

5. If you have documents already uploaded in the library and then configuring this option, then you can select the checkbox **Reset all Document IDs in this Site Collection to begin with these characters** that will reset the default prefix ID to this customized one **SPMCSE**. Once you click **OK**, you will see a message **Configuration of the Document ID feature is scheduled to be completed by an automated process**, as seen in the following screenshot.

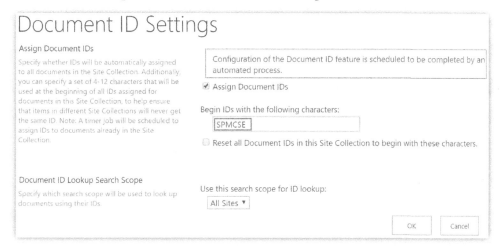

Figure 5.9: Customized Document ID

6. If you upload any document now, you will not see any change in **Document ID** immediately. There are two timer jobs **Document ID assignment job**, **Document ID enable/disable job**, scheduled **Daily**. Once these jobs run, then only this change will be effective. After that, you will see the document ID of the uploaded document, as seen in the following screenshot:

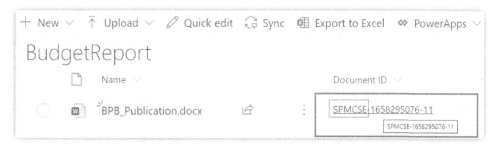

Figure 5.10: Customized Document ID applied

Different testing scenarios

Let's check different testing scenarios and will see the changes in document ID once the file is moved or copied to a different location within a site collection or outside site collection. We will check the four scenarios as below and will see Document ID Changes or not:

- Move the file to a folder present in the same library
- Move the file to a different library in the same site collection
- Move the file to different Site Collection
- Copy file to a folder

Move file to folder in the same library

In this section, we will discuss the change in document ID when the file is moved to a folder present in the same library. Create one file in the library and move this file to a folder present in the same document library and observe the Document ID. Let's perform the following steps to check:

1. Create one folder in the same library first.

2. Now select one file present in the same library.

3. Click on **Details Pane**, right click on **Document ID**, and click on **Copy link address**.

4. You see, the link address has the **Document ID** at the end. Now click on **Move to** from the command bar, as seen in the following screenshot:

Figure 5.11: *Move the file in the same folder*

5. Choose the destination as the **Current Library**. Select the folder present in the same library. And click on **Move here** as seen in the following screenshot:

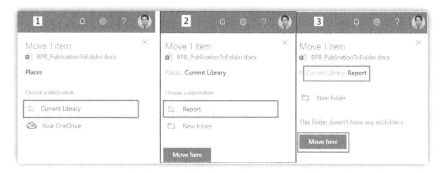

Figure 5.12: Move the file to the folder step by step

6. The file will be moved to a new folder. You will see the **Document ID** as it was in the source location. There is no change in **Document ID**, as seen in the following screenshot. Now select the file moved to the folder. Click on **Details Pane**, right click on **Document ID**, and click on **Copy link address**. If you compare both source and destination URL, you see there is no change in **Document ID URL link**; both are same:

Figure 5.13: Document ID of the file after file moved

Move the file to a different library in the same site collection

Now you upload documents in two different libraries and move the document from one library to another library following the same process as we did before except the destination location as a different library in the same site collection. If you notice, there is no change in **Document ID** and **Document ID URL link** after file moved, as seen in the following screenshot:

Figure 5.14: Move the file to a different library in same site collection

Move the file to a different site collection

Now move one document from one site collection to another site collection. Considering the situation with destination site collection, the **Document ID** feature not activated. Let's perform the following steps to check:

1. Follow the same steps for moving the file in a different site collection. You will get a message like **The file or folder contains properties that will be lost at the new destination**, as seen in the following screenshot. If you click on the button **Move anyway**, the document ID properties present at the source site will be lost at the destination site collection:

Figure 5.15: Move the file to different site collection without activating the feature

2. Now follow the same process as discussed in the above sections *Activate feature first*, Edit View to Add Column, Document ID Settings Configuration one by one to set custom **Document ID Prefix** in another site collection as seen in the following screenshot:

Figure 5.16: Custom Document ID prefix

3. Now upload one document in a library present in the destination site collection, you will see **Document ID** starting with the new prefix **PROJECT**.

4. Now try to move the document again to this site collection as a destination. Since the Document ID feature is activated in this site collection. You will

notice after the file is moved to this new site collection, there is no change in **Document ID** and **Document ID URL link** as seen in the following screenshot:

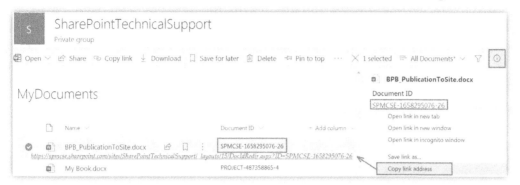

Figure 5.17: Move the file to different site collection after activating the feature

5. If you select the checkbox **Reset all Document IDs in this Site Collection, to begin with these characters** present in **Document ID Settings** and apply changes, the Document ID of all documents will be updated as per the current prefix (**SPMCSE** to **PROJECT**) of the site collection. Changes will be reflected once these two timer jobs, **Document ID assignment job**, **Document ID enable/disable job** scheduled **Daily** will run successfully.

Copy to folder or library

We see the Document ID properties while moving to a different location within one site collection or outside side collection. Let's see the behavior while copying a file within one site collection or outside side collection:

1. Now copy the file selecting the option **Copy To** from the command bar in the library and select destination one folder in the same library. You see, both **Document ID** and **Document ID URL link** changed.

2. Now copy a file to different library present in the same site collection, you see both **Document ID** and **Document ID URL link** changed as seen in the following screenshot:

Figure 5.18: Copy to folder or library

Copy to a different site collection

Now copy the file selecting the option **Copy To** from the command bar in the library and select destination library present in another site collection. After copied, you see both **Document ID** and **Document ID URL link** changed. **Document ID Prefix** also changed as per the configuration of that site collection, as seen in the following screenshot:

Figure 5.19: Copy to a different site collection

Find by Document ID Webpart

Since **Document ID** is not changing, we can find the document directly by entering document id in the search bar, irrespective of the document location. In the Classic SharePoint site, we can add one webpart **Find by Document ID** to search documents specific based on **Document ID**, as seen in the following screenshot. We will discuss how to add a webpart latter chapter but showing the webpart available related to this for understanding:

Figure 5.20: Find by Document ID Webpart

Once you added this webpart in the SharePoint site, you will see an option of search, as seen in the following screenshot:

Figure 5.21: *Find by Document ID Webpart added*

You can enter the Document ID; pressing *Enter* will open the document directly.

Document ID Value Document property

You can add **Document ID Value** to document present in the library, which would be helpful to share and identify during need. by following the process as mentioned below:

1. Open the document present in the library in a desktop application.

2. Click in **Insert** from the ribbon. Click on **Quick Parts** under the section **Text**.

3. Under the dropdown, select **Document Property** and under that select **Document ID Value**. You will notice the **Document ID** property will be added in the document, as seen in the following screenshot:

Figure 5.22: *Document ID Value Document property*

Conclusion

In this chapter, we had a glance at document id all about, why it's used, what is the purpose of using this? Understood the dependent features for document ID. Discussed step by step to edit library view and configuration of document ID settings for custom documents ID prefix. Did testing and understood the behavior of document ID in different scenarios of moving the document to a different location. Next, *Chapter 6, Document Sets Feature*, will discuss the document set feature and its application.

Points to remember

- **Document ID Service** Site Collection Feature activation is a must.

- There are two timer jobs **Document ID assignment job, Document ID enable/ disable job** scheduled **Daily**. Once these jobs run successfully, then only change in **Documents ID Prefix** and **Reset all Document IDs in this Site Collection, to begin with these characters** will be effective.

- In this chapter, wherever its mentioned like this format `_layouts/15/****. aspx`, means this section is added after the site URL `http:// <site url> /_layouts/15/****.aspx`.

- Regular changes are applied in Office 365 and SharePoint Online by which there may be changes happenings in the template or some other features.

CHAPTER 6

Document Sets Feature

In the previous chapter, we discussed how to configure document ID Service and how it works. In this chapter, we will discuss all the document sets feature. The document set is an advanced version of a folder that holds a specific set of common documents that will be available to all newly created document sets. Means once you create a new document set, there are few default contents which will be created which are common to all document set. The document set is a content type that share metadata and metadata columns, provides options to manage content in the document set by applying workflow. Let's proceed to discuss in detail about document set.

Structure

In this chapter, we will discuss the following:

- Introduction to the document set
- Activate dependent feature
- Creating a site content type
- Adding content type to the library
- Creating a modern document set

Objective

During the end of the chapter, you will get a clear understanding of:

- Document set overview
- Dependent feature for the document set
- Creating site content type, content type columns, edit document set settings
- Creating library, views, and adding content type to the library
- Creating a modern document set and how it is different from the classic document set

Activate feature first

To apply document set service, we need to activate one dependent site collection feature first that will enable this service. Let's perform the following steps to activate the site collection feature:

1. Navigate to **Site Settings** (`<_layouts/15/settings.aspx>`) as seen in the following screenshot:

Figure 6.1: Site Settings

2. Click on **Site Collection Features** (`<_layouts/15/ManageFeatures.aspx?Scope =Site>`) present under **Site Collection Administration** as seen in the following screenshot:

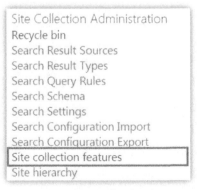

Figure 6.2: *Site Collection Feature*

3. Identify the feature **Document Sets** at the bottom and click on `Activate` as seen in the following screenshot:

Figure 6.3: Document Sets Site Collection Feature

Creating a new content type of type document set

Let's perform the following steps to create a new site content-type:

1. Navigate to **Site Settings** (`<_layouts/15/settings.aspx>`).

2. Click on `Site Content Types` (`<_layouts/15/mngctype.aspx>`) present under **Web Designer Galleries** as seen in the following screenshot:

Figure 6.4: Site Content Types

3. Under **Site Content Types** click on **Create** (`<_layouts/15/ctypenew.aspx>`) to create a new content type as seen in the following screenshot:

Figure 6.5: Create Site Content Types

4. Enter details like **Name** (`BPB Publication`) of content type, **Description**.

5. Select **Document Set Content Types** from the dropdown option **Select Parent Content Type From**. Option **Parent Content Type** will be selected as **Document Set** by default automatically as seen in the following screenshot:

Figure 6.6: Fill Details for New Site Content Type

6. Next, under the option **Group** select checkbox **New Group** and enter group name BPB Publication Group. Keep rest options as default as it is and click on **OK**. The new content type will be created as seen in the following screenshot, and you can see in **Site Content Types**:

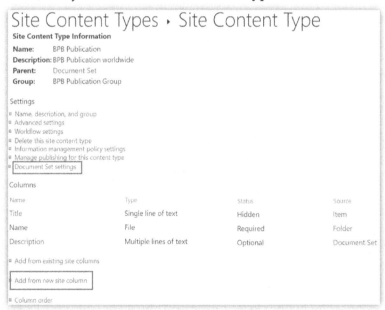

Figure 6.7: Content Type Settings

Creating site columns

The next step is to create site columns in the content type. Let's perform the following steps to create the document set content column:

1. Click on **Add from new site column** from the content type settings page that we created just.

2. Select the column type as **Choice**, enter **Column Name** as seen in the following screenshot:

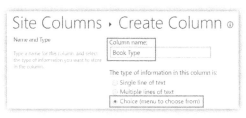

Figure 6.8: Enter Column Name during Creating Column

3. Enter column **Description**.

4. Select **Yes** from the option **Require that this column contains information**, which will make the column to fill details mandatory and cannot be left blank.

5. Enter choice details (PDF Book, Kindle Book, Paper Book) under the option **Type each choice on a separate line**.

6. From option **Display choice using**, select **Checkboxes (allow multiple selections)**.

7. From **Allow 'Fill-in' choices**, select **No**. Selecting **Yes** will allow you to enter your custom details apart from choices, you entered, which we don't need here.

8. From the option **Default Value**, select one choice value (Paper Book) that we created and finally click on **OK** to create the column as seen in the following screenshot:

Figure 6.9: Fill Details for creating the column

9. You see column **Book Type** added to content type columns. Similarly, add more columns **Book Category** to content type with choice details **Computer Science, Information Technology, Computing, Application Development, Big Data and Business Intelligence, Business, Networking and Servers, Virtualization and Cloud, Web Development** as seen screenshot below:

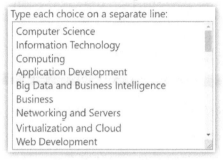

Figure 6.10: Create another column

10. Now you see both columns **Book Type** and **Book Category** are added to content type columns as seen in the following screenshot:

Columns			
Name	Type	Status	Source
Title	Single line of text	Hidden	Item
Name	File	Required	Folder
Description	Multiple lines of text	Optional	Document Set
Book Type	Choice	Required	BPB Publication
Book Category	Choice	Required	BPB Publication

▫ Add from existing site or list columns
▫ Column order

Figure 6.11: Document set columns crated

The next step is to change settings in the document set content type.

Document set settings

Let's perform the following steps to change a few settings under **Document Set Settings**:

1. Navigate to option **Content Types** present under **Library Settings** and click on content type **BPB Publication**.

2. From manage content type page, under **Content Type Settings** click on **Document Set settings**.

3. Identify the option **Default Content** and upload a few common content templates that would be available in all document sets by clicking **Choose File** as seen in the following screenshot:

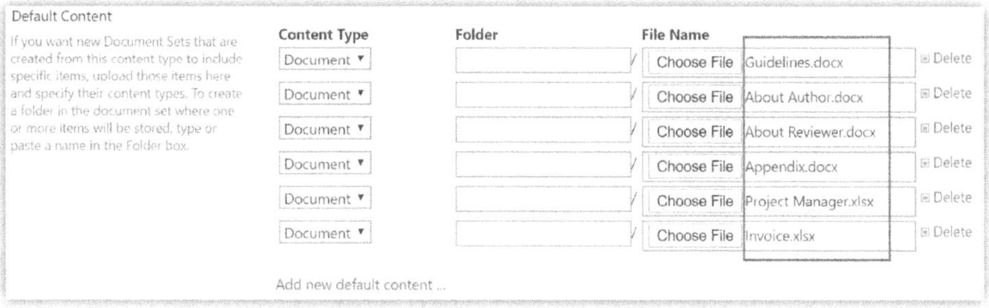

Figure 6.12: Default Contents in Document Set

4. Identify the option **Shared Columns** and click on checkbox **Shared** for the columns **Book Type** and **Book Category** that we created as seen in the following screenshot:

Figure 6.13: Shared Column

5. Under the option **Select View**, keep the default view **All Documents** for the moment. But when you created a new view **Document Set** which is mentioned next section, you need to update that view here latter as seen in the following screenshot:

Figure 6.14: Document Set View

6. Once all changes are done then click on **OK** to apply changes.

Create a document library

Let's perform the following steps to create one document library:

1. Navigate to **Site Contents** (`<_layouts/15/viewlsts.aspx?view=14>`) in the site and click on **New** command bar and select **App** from the dropdown as seen in the following screenshot:

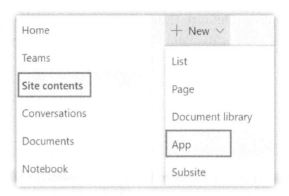

Figure 6.15: Add App to Site

2. You will be redirected to the **Add Apps** page where you can select any app that you want to add. Click on the app **Document Library**, another dialog box will open.

3. Enter document library **Name** (BPB Project) from option **Pick a name** and click on **Create** as seen in the following screenshot:

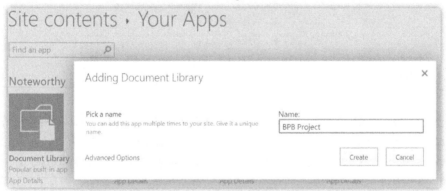

Figure 6.16: Create a Document Library App

Document library BPB Project is created now. The next step is to add document set content type BPB Publication in this document library.

Allow management of content types

Before adding document set content type BPB Publication in the library, you need to enable **Allow management of content types**. Let's perform the following steps to enable **Allow management of content types**:

1. Navigate to **Library Settings** and click on **Advanced Settings** under the category **General Settings** as seen in the following screenshot:

Figure 6.17: *Advanced Settings in the document library*

2. Enable **Content Types** by selecting checkbox **Allow management of content types** and apply changes as seen in the following screenshot:

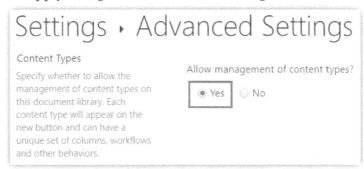

Figure 6.18: *Allow Management of Content Types*

3. You will see **Document** as default content type added to **Library Settings** with added new category **Content Types**. Now we can proceed for adding content type BPB Publication in the library BPB Project.

Adding content type to the library

Let's follow step by step procedure to add content type BPB Publication in the library BPB Project:

1. Navigate to option **Content Types** present under **Library Settings** and click on **Add from existing site content types** (https://<site url>/_layouts/15/AddContentTypeToList.aspx?List=**) as seen in the following screenshot:

Figure 6.19: *Add from existing site content types*

2. From the **Add Content Types** page, under dropdown option **Select site content types from** select the group **BPB Publication Group** that we created while creating content type.

3. Content-type `BPB Publication` related to that group **BPB Publication Group** will appear in the next box. Select the content type and click on **Add** present side to that box. Content-type `BPB Publication` will be added to another box **Content types to add** then click on **OK** finally to apply changes as seen in the following screenshot:

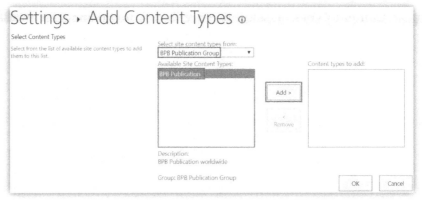

Figure 6.20: Add Content Types

4. Now content type `BPB Publication` is added to the library, but this content type is not the default content type.

Change the default content type

We need to make content type `BPB Publication` as default content type. Let's follow step by step procedure to change the default content-type:

1. Navigate to option **Content Types** present under **Library Settings** and click on **Change new button order and default content type** (`https://<site url>/_layouts/15/ChangeContentTypeOrder.aspx?List=**`) as seen in the following screenshot:

Figure 6.21: Change new button order and default content type

2. From change content type order page, uncheck **Document** content type **Visible** checkbox and click on **OK** to apply the change as seen in the following screenshot:

Figure 6.22: *Change the Default Content Type*

3. You see in the **Content Type** category, content type BPB Publication is set as default content type as seen in the following screenshot:

Figure 6.23: *Content Type Added*

4. We can delete the library content type **Document** now from the **Content Type** category since we need the only document set content type BPB Publication.

Delete content type from the library

Let's follow the step-by-step procedure to delete the content type from the library:

1. Navigate to option Content Types present under Library Settings and click on content type Document.

2. From manage content type page, under Content Type Settings click on Delete this content type as seen in the following screenshot:

Figure 6.24: *Delete Content Type*

3. This change will remove the **Document** content type from the library, and we can proceed with default content type BPB Publication now.

Creating a document set view

In this section we will create a view for the document set. Let's follow the step-by-step procedure to create a document library view:

1. Navigate to option **Views** present under **Library Settings**, you see the view **All Documents** as the default view. Click on **Create View** as seen in the following screenshot:

Figure 6.25: Create View

2. There are 4 types of view template **Standard View**, **Datasheet View**, **Calendar View**, **Gantt View** present from which we can select. Click on **Standard View** as seen in the following screenshot:

Figure 6.26: View Templates

3. Enter **View Name** (Document Set) and select the checkbox **Make this the default view** as seen in the following screenshot:

Figure 6.27: Enter View Name

4. Select the checkbox under column **Display** for the columns **Book Type**, and **Book Category** to display the columns in the library as seen in the following screenshot:

Figure 6.28: Display Column Name in View

5. Scroll down and identify the category **Folders** and select **In folders of content type** and select content type BPB Publication from the dropdown.

6. Expand the category **Mobile** and select the checkboxes **Enable this view for mobile access** and **Make this view the default view for mobile access** and click on **OK** to apply as seen in the following screenshot:

Figure 6.29: In folders of the content type

7. New view **Document Set** created as seen in the following screenshot:

Figure 6.30: View Created

Create a modern document set

Let's follow the step-by-step procedure to create a modern document set:

1. Now open the library BPB Project and click on **New** from the command bar.

2. You will see the content type BPB Publication is added to this menu

3. Click on **Edit New Menu** from the dropdown.

4. Uncheck the box **Folder** and click on **Save**. Now only document set content type BPB Publication is present under the option **New** in the command bar.

5. Click on the document set content type BPB Publication as seen in the following screenshot:

Figure 6.31: Edit New Menu

6. You will find all content type columns which you need to fill. Enter details **Name** (Project 1904), **Description** (Project 1904: SharePoint Online Power User Playbook), **Book Type** (PDF Book, Kindle Book, Paper Book), **Book Category** (Information Technology) and click on **Save** as seen in the following screenshot:

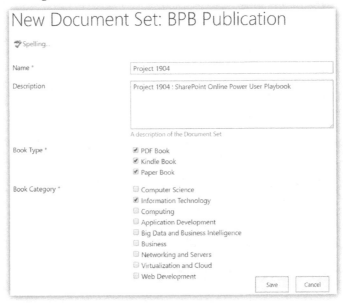

Figure 6.32: Create a Document Set

7. The document set `Project 1904` is created and you will see the default contents, which we have uploaded before, present in the document set created. Users can start uploading their content in this document set now.

8. You see the default view inside the document set is set as a **Document set** view. Also, columns **Book Type** and **Book Category** inheriting details as seen in the following screenshot:

Figure 6.33: *Document Set Default Contents*

9. Open the document library `BPB Project` and can see the document set `Project 1904`. Click on the view **All Documents**, select the view **Document Set**.

10. Click again the view **Document Set** and select **Set current view as default** from the dropdown which will make this view as default for the library as seen in the following screenshot:

Figure 6.34: *Document Set View*

11. Select document set `Project 1904` again and click on **Details Pane** from the command bar. You can see all properties of the documents set. This is how the **Modern Document Set** looks like same as the new modern library as seen in the following screenshot:

Figure 6.35: Document Set Properties

12. If we want to see the **Classic Document Set**, click on the option **Return to classic SharePoint** present at the bottom of the left navigation menu as seen in the following screenshot:

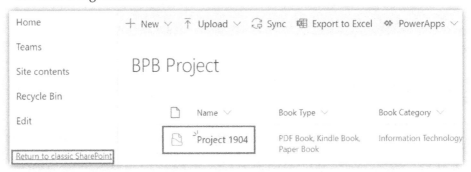

Figure 6.36: Return to classic SharePoint Document Set

13. You will be redirected to the classic document library with the document set Project 1904. Click on the documents set, you will be redirected to another page which is called the document set **Welcome Page**:

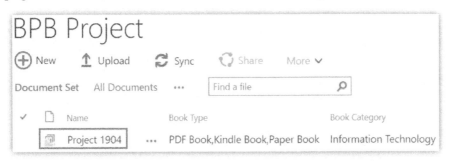

Figure 6.37: Classic Document Set in Library

14. This is the **Welcome Page** of the document set, which shows document set properties at the top and contents below as seen in the following screenshot below. Click on **View All Properties** to see the document set properties:

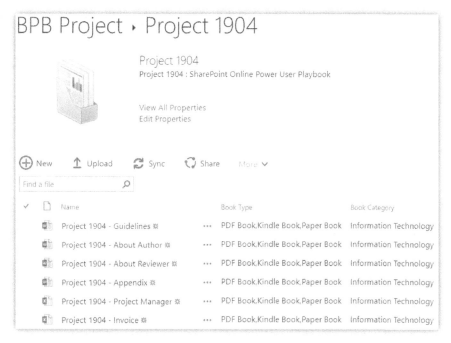

Figure 6.38: Classic Site Document Set Welcome Page

15. This is the document set properties which you will find in classic site document set as seen in the following screenshot:

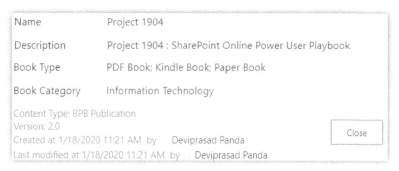

Figure 6.39: Classic site Document Set Properties

We created one document set for publication project related to the book SharePoint Online Power User Playbook that has specific documents which are common to all book project and required for book publication. Similarly, we can create a separate document set for each project for each book for better organization of book publication project. This is just an example to show how it works, you can categorize your own to get its benefit of the document set and its use as seen in the following screenshot:

Figure 6.40: Multiple Document Sets for Different Book Project

If you have **Document ID** feature active you see, each document set has its document ID assigned as seen in the following screenshot:

Figure 6.41: Document ID Assigned to Each Document Set

If you search document ID, you will get the document set as a result as seen in the following screenshot:

Figure 6.42: Search Document Set

Conclusion

In this chapter we had a glance on the document set all about, what is the purpose of using this. Understood the dependent features for the document set. Discussed step by step to create site content type, adding columns to the content type. How to configure document set settings. How to add document library from the app, how to create library view, add the content type to library. The created modern document set and discussed how it's different from the classic site document set. Next in *Chapter 7: Content Organizer Feature* will discuss how content organizer feature works.

Points to remember

- The document sets site collection feature activation is a must.

- The modern document set interface is similar to the modern library. You will not see the document set on the welcome page that you were getting in the classic site document set.

- In this chapter wherever its mentioned like this format `_layouts/15/****. aspx`, means this section is added after the site URL `http://<site url>/_ layouts /15/****.aspx`.

- Regular changes are applied in Office 365 and SharePoint Online by which there may be changes happen in the template or some other features.

CHAPTER 7
Content Organizer Feature

In the previous chapter, we discussed document sets feature, how to configure, and its application. In this chapter, we will discuss the content organizer feature. The content organizer feature provides document routing options on the site. All users will upload documents in a specific library and those documents will be moved to other libraries or sites based on the rules, conditions match for that upload. It allows automatic creation of a new version of the file with the same name during document routing also auto-create new folders when the number of items in a folder crosses the limit.

Structure

- In this chapter, we will discuss the following:
- Introduction to the content organizer
- Activate dependent feature
- Configuring content organizer settings
- Creating content organizer rules
- How content organizer works

Objective

During the end of the chapter, you will get a clear understanding of:

- Content organizer overview
- What is the dependent feature for the content organizer
- How to configure content organizer settings
- How to create content organizer rules
- How documents are routing based on rules and conditions

Activate feature first

To apply the content organizer feature, we need to activate one dependent site feature first that will enable this service. Let's perform the following steps to activate the site feature:

1. Navigate to **Site settings** (`<_layouts/15/settings.aspx>`) as seen in the following screenshot:

Figure 7.1: Site Settings

2. Click on **Manage site features** (`<_layouts/15/ManageFeatures.aspx>`) present under **Site Actions** as seen in the following screenshot:

Figure 7.2: Manage Site Features

3. Identify the feature **Content Organizer** and click on **Activate** as seen in the following screenshot:

Figure 7.3: Activate Site Feature

4. You might get an error as seen in the following screenshot if the dependent feature is not active related to this:

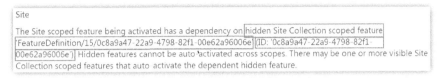

Figure 7.4: *Error While Activating Feature*

5. This error is due to a hidden feature **Document Routing Resources** with feature ID **0C8A9A47-22A9-4798-82F1-00E62A96006E** which depends on site collection features **SharePoint Server Publishing Infrastructure**, **SharePoint Server Enterprise Site Collection features**, **SharePoint Server Standard Site Collection features**. If anyone of these site collection features is active, you will not receive this error while activating the **Content Organizer**.

6. What you can do is, activate the site collection feature **SharePoint Server Standard Site Collection features** first as seen in the below screenshot, following the same step that we discussed in *Chapter 6*, *Document Sets* section *Activate feature first*:

Figure 7.5: *Site Collection Dependent Feature*

7. Now proceed to activate the site feature **Content Organizer** following the steps 1 to 3 above.

8. Once the **Content Organizer** feature is activated, navigate to **Site Settings** (`<_layouts/15/settings.aspx>`) and you will find 2 additional options **Content Organizer Settings**, **Content Organizer Rules** under **Site Administration**. Under **Site Contents**, you will find additional library **Drop Off Library**.

Content organizer settings

We need to configure some settings related to content organizer which can be done in Content Organizer Settings. Let's perform the following steps to configure Content Organizer Settings:

1. Navigate to **Site Settings** (`<_layouts/15/settings.aspx>`).

2. Click on **Content Organizer Settings** (`<_layouts/15/Document Router Settings.aspx>`) present under **Site Administration** as seen in the following screenshot:

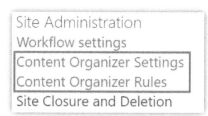

Figure 7.6: New Settings Added in Site Administration

3. You will be redirected to the **Document Router Settings** page where you will find many options to configure. The first option is to **Redirect Users to the Drop Off Library**. You will find the checkbox **Require users to use the organizer when submitting new content to libraries with one or more organizer rules pointing to them** is enabled default since it enables routing as seen in the following screenshot. As I already shared there will be one new document library **Drop Off Library** will be created after the site feature **Content Organizer** is activated. Users need to upload create documents here and as per content organizer rule documents will be routed to different libraries or sites as the target location.

Figure 7.7: Redirect Users to the Drop Off Library Option under Content Organizer Settings

4. The next option is **Sending to Another Site**. If there is a requirement of moving the document to a different site, select the checkbox **Allow rules to specify another site as a target location**. Currently no need to select this checkbox. Keep it as default unchecked, as seen in the following screenshot:

Figure 7.8: Sending to Another Site Option under Content Organizer Settings

5. Select the checkbox **Create subfolders after a target location has too many items Number of items in a single folder** present under **Folder Partitioning** as seen in the following screenshot. When the number of items in a folder is more than 2500 then the new folder will be created and documents will be routed to the new folder, by enabling this option. There is a threshold limit for the number of items in a folder for better performance that's why this option is provided:

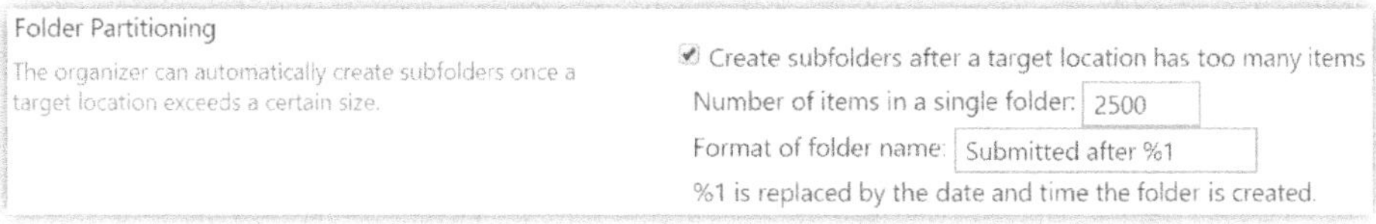

Folder Partitioning
The organizer can automatically create subfolders once a target location exceeds a certain size.

☑ Create subfolders after a target location has too many items
Number of items in a single folder: 2500
Format of folder name: Submitted after %1
%1 is replaced by the date and time the folder is created.

Figure 7.9: Folder Partitioning Option under Content Organizer Settings

6. Next **Duplicate Submissions** provides an option to handle duplicate files routed to the target location. Select the option **Use SharePoint versioning** which will create a new version of the file at the target location when a file with the same name created at **Drop Off Library** and routed to target location as seen in the following screenshot. Option **Append unique characters to the end of duplicate filenames** will create new file name at the target location:

Duplicate Submissions
Specify what should occur when a file with the same name already exists in a target location. If versioning is not enabled in a target library, the organizer will append unique characters to duplicate submissions regardless of the setting selected here.

● Use SharePoint versioning
○ Append unique characters to the end of duplicate filenames

Figure 7.10: Duplicate Submissions Option under Content Organizer Settings

7. Option **Preserving Context** enables us to save the audit log and properties of the submitted document. Keep this option as default and not select at the moment as seen in the following screenshot:

Preserving Context
The organizer can save the original audit logs and properties if they are included with submissions. The saved logs and properties are stored in an audit entry on the submitted document.

☐ Save the original audit log and properties of submitted content

Figure 7.11: Preserving Context Option under Content Organizer Settings

8. Next option **Rule Managers** enables to send mail for certain conditions like **when submissions do not match a rule** and **when content has been left in the Drop Off Library**. Both options are selected by default. Enter **users or group** who will receive mails as seen in the following screenshot:

Rule Managers
Specify the users who manage the rules and can respond when incoming content doesn't match any rule.

Rule Managers must have the Manage Web Site permission to access the content organizer rules list from the site settings page.

☑ E-mail rule managers when submissions do not match a rule
☑ E-mail rule managers when content has been left in the Drop Off Library
Enter users or groups separated by semicolons:

Deviprasad Panda;

Number of days to wait before sending an e-mail: 3

Figure 7.12: Rule Managers Option under Content Organizer Settings

9. **Submission Points** shows the web service URL `https://spmcse.share point.com/sites/BPB-ModernTeamSite/_vti_bin/OfficialFile.asmx` that needs no action from our end now as seen in the following screenshot:

Figure 7.13: *Submission Points Option under Content Organizer Settings*

Create a new site content type

We need to create a new content type and add it to a specific library. Let's perform the following steps to create a new site content-type:

1. Navigate to **Site Settings** (`<_layouts/15/settings.aspx>`).

2. Click on **Site Content Types** (`<_layouts/15/mngctype.aspx>`) present under **Web Designer Galleries** as seen in the following screenshot:

Figure 7.14: *Site Content Type*

3. Under **Site Content Types** click on **Create** (`<_layouts/15/ctypenew.aspx>`) to create a new content type as seen in the following screenshot.

Figure 7.15: *Create Site Content Type*

4. Enter details like **Name** of content type as **Project** and **Description** as **Project Details Documents**.

5. Select **Document Content Types** from the dropdown option **Select Parent Content Type From**. Option **Parent Content Type** will be selected as a **Document**.

6. Next under the option **Group** from **Existing Group** select group name BPB Publication Group and click on **OK** as seen in the following screenshot. A new content type will be created, and you can see in **Site Content Types**.

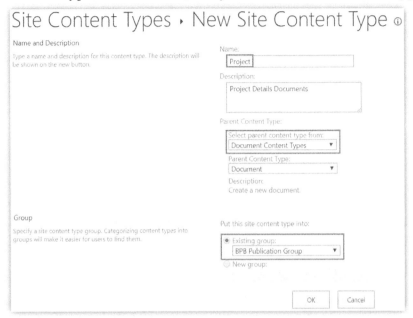

Figure 7.16: New Content Type Details

7. Click on **Advanced settings** (<_layouts/15/ChangeContentTypeOptional Settings.aspx?ctype=***>) from manage content type page as seen in the following screenshot:

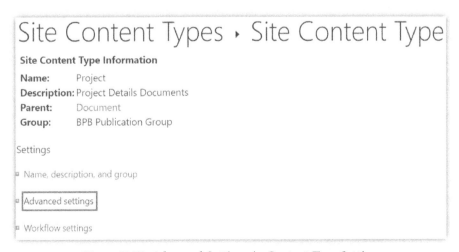

Figure 7.17: Advanced Settings in Content Type Settings

8. You will get the **Change Content Type Optional Settings** page. Select the option **Upload a new document template** select Project.xlsx from your local system as a template as seen in the following screenshot:

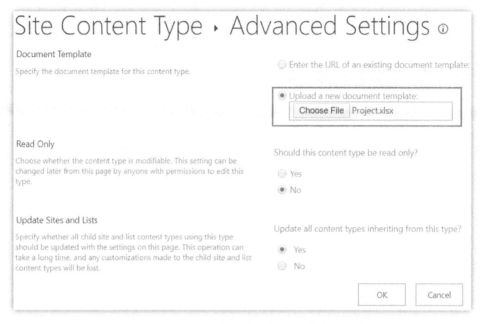

Figure 7.18: *Custom Template in Site Content Type*

9. Keep rest option as default and click on **OK**.

10. A new content type **Project** is created.

11. Similarly create 4 more content types **Tables of Contents**, **Author**, **Project Manager**, **Invoice** with custom templates Tables of Contents.docx, Author.docx, Project Manager.xlsx, Invoice.xlsx respectively.

Create a document library

Create a new document library with the name Project. Let's perform the following steps to create a new document library:

1. Navigate to **Site Contents** (<_layouts/15/viewlsts.aspx?view=14>).

2. Click on **New** from the command bar. Select **Document Library** from the dropdown menu.

3. Enter **Name** of the library Project and **Description** and click on **Create** as seen in the following screenshot:

Figure 7.19: *Create a Document Library*

4. Similarly create 4 more libraries named **Tables of Contents, Author, Project Manager, Invoice**.

Allow management of content types

The next configuration is to enable **Allow management of content types** in the library. Let's perform the following steps to enable **Allow management of content types**:

1. Navigate to **Library Settings** (`<_layouts/15/listedit.aspx?List=%7B24****>`) and click on **Advanced Settings** (`<_layouts/15/advsetng.aspx?List=%7B24***>`) under the category **General Settings** as seen in the following screenshot:

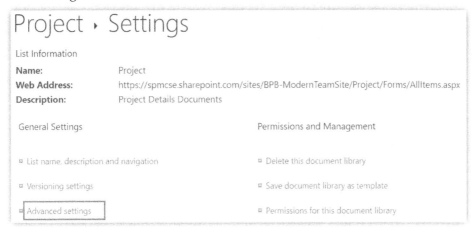

Figure 7.20: *Advanced Settings in Library Settings*

2. Enable **Content Types** by selecting checkbox **Allow management of content types** and apply changes as seen in the following screenshot:

Figure 7.21: Allow Management of Content Type

3. You will see **Document** as default content type added to **Library Settings** with added new category **Content Types**. Now we should proceed for adding content type **Project** in the library **Project**.

Adding content type to the library

We need to add the content type in the newly created document library. Let's perform the following steps to add content type **Project** in the library **Project**:

1. Navigate to option **Content Types** present under **Library Settings** and click on **Add from existing site content types** as seen in the following screenshot:

Figure 7.22: Add from Existing Site Content Types

2. From the **Add Content Types** page, under dropdown option **Select site content types from** select the group BPB Publication Group.

3. Content type **Project** related to that group BPB Publication Group will appear in the next box. Select the content type **Project** and click on **Add** present side to that box. Content type **Project** will be added to another box **Content types to add** then click on **OK** finally to apply changes as seen in the following screenshot:

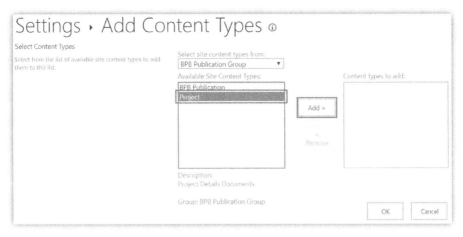

Figure 7.23: Add Content Type

4. Now content type **Project** is added to the library.

5. Follow the same steps to add content types **Tables of Contents**, **Author**, **Project Manager**, **Invoice** to respective libraries **Tables of Contents**, **Author**, **Project Manager**, **Invoice**.

6 The reason being we are adding this content type to the library because, when we will create **Content Organizer Rules** and will select **Target Location** then will get an error if the selected content type is not present in target library as seen in the following screenshot:

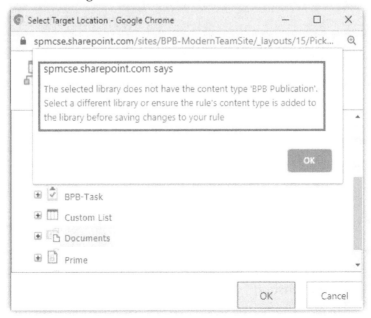

Figure 7.24: Notification If Content Type Not Added In Library

Content organizer rules

Now we are good to go for the creation of **Content Organizer Rules** which is responsible to route documents to different library or site based on content types and metadata. Let's perform the following steps to create **Content Organizer Rules**:

1. Navigate to **Site Settings** (<_layouts/15/settings.aspx>). Click on **Content Organizer Rules** (<RoutingRules/Group%20by%20Content%20 Type.aspx>) present under **Site Administration**.

2. Click on **New** from command bar as seen in the following screenshot:

Figure 7.25: Content Organizer Rules

3. Enter **Name** (Project) of the rule.

4. Next option **Rule Status And Priority** is selected as **Active** with **Priority – 5** (Medium) as seen in the following screenshot. You can change the priority from **Priority 1** (Highest) to **Priority 9** (Lowest). When there are multiple rules present and multiple rules match once you upload documents then high priority rule will run first and rules with a priority less will run late:

Figure 7.26: Rule Status and Priority

5. From option **Submission's Content Type**, select the **Group** that we created before BPB Publication Group and content type select as **Project** as seen in the following screenshot:

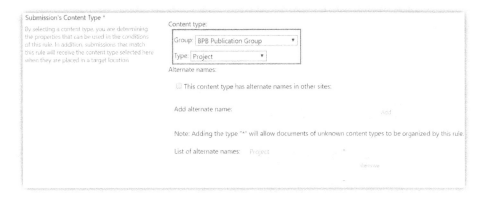

Figure 7.27: Submission's Content Type

6. The next option is **Conditions**. We can set conditions **Property** as **Content Type** and **Operator** as **is equal to** as seen in the following screenshot. We can select the option **Add another condition** below to add more than one condition:

Figure 7.28: Conditions

7. Then we need to select **Target Location** to which the documents will be routed to once condition satisfied. Click on **Browse**. Another window will open, where you need to choose the document library **Project** that we create before as target location for the content type **Project** and click on **OK** once library selected as seen in the following screenshot:

Figure 7.29: Target Location Selected

8. Similarly create 4 more content organizer rules for content types **Tables of Contents**, **Author**, **Project Manager**, **Invoice** as seen in the following screenshot:

Figure 7.30: Content Organizer Rules Created

How do the content organizer rules work?

We configured the **Content Organizer Settings** and created **Content Organizer Rules**. Let's perform the following steps to understand how it works:

1. Navigate to the **Drop Off Library** present under **Site Contents**.

2. Click on **New** from the command bar.

3. Select the content type template **Project** and create a file named `ProjectReport`. Similarly create files `TablesOfContentReports`, `AuthorReports`, `ProjectManagerReports`, `InvoiceReports` using content-type templates **Tables of Contents**, **Author**, **Project Manager**, **Invoice** respectively as seen in the following screenshot.

4. Now upload files with name **Project**, **Tables of Contents**, **Author**, **Project Manager**, **Invoice** in the **Drop Off Library** as seen in the following screenshot:

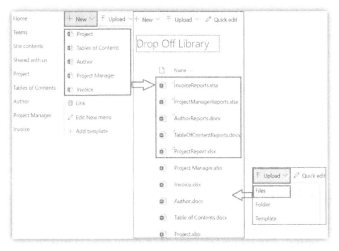

Figure 7.31: *Documents Created Using Content Type and Documents Uploaded*

5. As per the **Content Organizer Rules**, documents created using content type template should be moved to respective libraries **Project**, **Tables of Contents**, **Author**, **Project Manager**, **Invoice** but it will not happen immediately.

6. There is a timer job **Content Organizer Processing** scheduled **Daily** is responsible for this as seen in the following screenshot. Means every day, at a certain time this timer job will run, then only you will notice documents are moved to respective libraries as per the rules. We have to wait till the time this job complete:

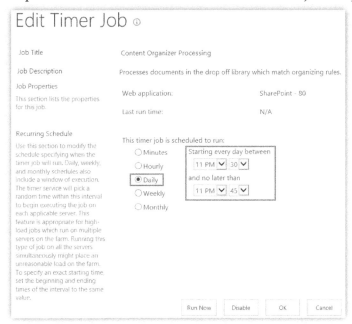

Figure 7.32: *Timer Job Content Organizer Processing*

7. Once timer job **Content Organizer Processing** run, you will see files created using content types are moved to the respective libraries as seen in the following screenshot:

Figure 7.33: *Files moved to Target Location as per Rules*

8. Files with name **Project**, **Tables of Contents**, **Author**, **Project Manager**, **Invoice** that are uploaded, not moved and still in **Drop Off Library** as seen in the following screenshot:

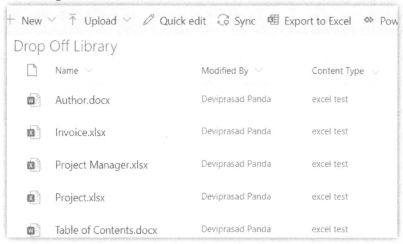

Figure 7.34: *Files Not Moved to Target Location*

9. As per the configuration we did before **Rule Managers** will receive mail for action as seen in the following screenshot:

Figure 7.35: *Rule Managers Mail*

10. Click on any one of the documents link out of 5 links will redirect to view item properties as seen in the following screenshot:

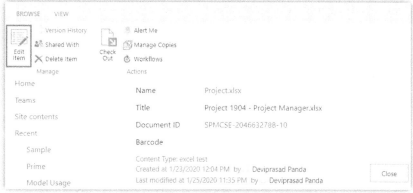

Figure 7.36: Edit Item

11. Click on **Edit Item**. Select the content type as **Project** since its project type. You will notice a message at the top **This document will be automatically moved to the correct library and folder after required properties are filled out**. Click on **Save** or **Submit** as seen in the following screenshot:

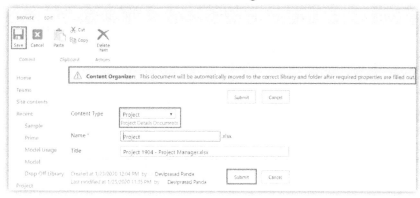

Figure 7.37: Change Content Type Field for Item

12. After that you will see another page with the URL to access the file as seen in the following screenshot. The file is moved to the target location as per the ruleset.

Figure 7.38: Saved to Final Location

13. Similarly, you can edit respective **Content Types** for other items still present in the **Drop Off Library** from **Details Pane** as seen in the following screenshot. All items will be moved to the target location:

Figure 7.39: Edit Item Properties

Conclusion

In this chapter, we had a glance on the content organizer feature all about, what is the purpose of using this. Understood the dependent features for the content organizer. Discussed step by step to activate site features related to the content organizer, to create site content type and adding content type to the library. How to configure content organizer settings, content organizer rules. Also checked how the content organizer rules work. Next in *Chapter 8, Manage Permission* will discuss managing permission in SharePoint.

Points to remember

- SharePoint Server Standard Site Collection features site collection feature activation is must to active **Content Organizer** site feature.

- Adding content type to target library must be done because when we will create **Content Organizer Rules** and will select **Target Location** then we will get an error if the selected content type is not present in the target library.

- Users need to upload documents in **Drop Off Library**.

- Uploaded documents will not move to target locations immediately. Once timer job **Content Organizer Processing** scheduled **Daily** runs documents will be moved.

- In this chapter wherever its mentioned like this format _layouts/15/****. aspx, means this section is added after the site URL http:// <site url> /_layouts/15/****.aspx.

- Regular changes are applied in Office 365 and SharePoint Online by which there may be changes happen in the template or some other features.

CHAPTER 8

Manage Permission

Introduction

In the previous chapter, we discussed all the content organization features. In this chapter, we will discuss SharePoint permission management. We know SharePoint provides a collaborative platform for content management. Users upload documents in the library, access content to work collaboratively. Since all contents present and accessed through the SharePoint site, managing the security of the content is very important so as to make sure that only users authorized to those contents should access. SharePoint Permission management comes into picture which plays the most critical role so as to manage content security. We need to control who can access the content and who should be restricted. We need to control what action users can take based on their roles. So, SharePoint provides options to control permission for the contents stored in sites and manage security.

Structure

In this chapter, we will discuss the following:

- Introduction to permission in SharePoint
- SharePoint groups by default

- Permission levels in SharePoint
- Different settings in permission management
- Permission management modern experience

Objective

During the end of the chapter, you will get a clear understanding of the following:

- Permission overview
- Default groups in SharePoint
- Groups dependent on features
- Different permission levels
- Different settings available for permission management
- Modern experiences in permission management

SharePoint groups by default

Till now we discussed site collection, sites, subsites, list, library, how to upload documents in the library, store information in the list but how can we restrict the access of these contents based on user roles so that only authorized people can access the content in site or library or list, is not discussed yet. In this chapter we are going to discuss how to manage the security of SharePoint content.

Once a site is created, there are some default groups created on the site. Let's perform the following steps to check the default groups in SharePoint:

1. Click on **Settings** (gear icon) ⚙ from site. Click on **Site permissions** from the dropdown as seen in the following screenshot:

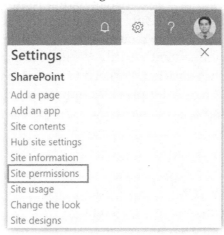

Figure 8.1: Site Permissions

2. You will get another window with information like **Invite people, Site owners, Site members, Site visitors, Change sharing settings, Advanced permissions settings**. Click on **Advanced permissions settings** (`<_layouts/15/user.aspx>`) as seen in the following screenshot:

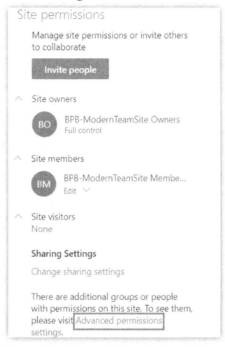

Figure 8.2: Advanced Permissions Settings

3. You will be redirected to the **User** page where you can find three SharePoint groups `BPB-ModernTeamSite Members`, `BPB-ModernTeamSite Owners`, `BPB-ModernTeamSite Visitors` by default as seen in the following screenshot. Group name is in format **<Site Name> Owner, <Site Name> Members, <Site Name> Visitors**:

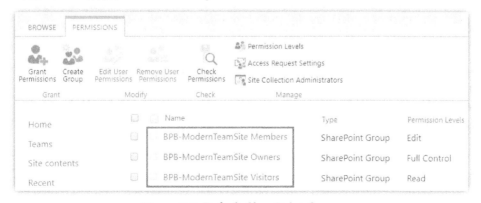

Figure 8.3: Default SharePoint Groups

4. You see each group is assigned to a permission level. The user needs to be added to a particular group to manage the task as per the role. We will discuss this in detail later sections.

5. Activating site collection features will create a few SharePoint groups. Activating **SharePoint Server Publishing Infrastructure** feature will create groups **Translation Managers**, **Restricted Readers**, **Hierarchy Managers**, **Approvers**, **Designers** as seen in the below screenshot.

6. Activating **SharePoint Server Enterprise Site Collection features** will create group **Excel Services Viewers** as seen in the below screenshot.

7. When we will create record center, another group **Records Center Web Service Submitters** will be created as seen in the below screenshot:

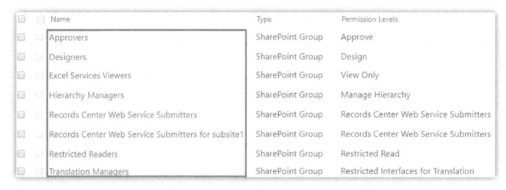

Name	Type	Permission Levels
Approvers	SharePoint Group	Approve
Designers	SharePoint Group	Design
Excel Services Viewers	SharePoint Group	View Only
Hierarchy Managers	SharePoint Group	Manage Hierarchy
Records Center Web Service Submitters	SharePoint Group	Records Center Web Service Submitters
Records Center Web Service Submitters for subsite1	SharePoint Group	Records Center Web Service Submitters
Restricted Readers	SharePoint Group	Restricted Read
Translation Managers	SharePoint Group	Restricted Interfaces for Translation

Figure 8.4: Groups Created After Activating Features

Permission levels

There are specific actions in the site that can be taken by specific group of people assigned with specific permission level. As per the roles and responsibility, users are assigned permission to that group so as to manage specific tasks.

You see every SharePoint group is assigned with a permission level. Different permission level in SharePoint are **View Only**, **Read**, **Edit**, **Full Control**, **Approve**, **Design**, **Manage Hierarchy**, **Restricted Read**, **Records Center Web Service Submitters**, **Restricted Interfaces for Translation**, **Limited Access** as seen in the following screenshot:

Figure 8.5: Permission Levels

Click on **Permission Levels** (https://<site url>/_layouts/15/role.aspx) from ribbon present under **PERMISSIONS** tab as seen in the following screenshot to see all permission levels:

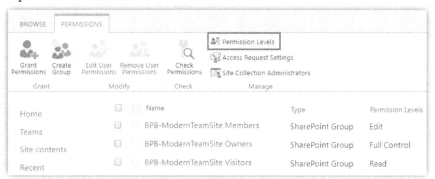

Figure 8.6: Permission Level Settings

Read permission level

Click on any one of the permission levels, let's say **Read** as seen in the following screenshot. You will see the type of actions that users with read permission can take:

Permission Levels ‣ Edit Permission Level

Name and Description

Type a name and description for your permission level. The name is shown on the permissions page. The name and description are shown on the add users page.

Name:

Read

Description:

Can view pages and list items and download documents.

Figure 8.7: Read Permission Level

Users having **Read** permission can open, read list items, documents present in library. They can view application pages and document versions as well as seen in the following screenshot:

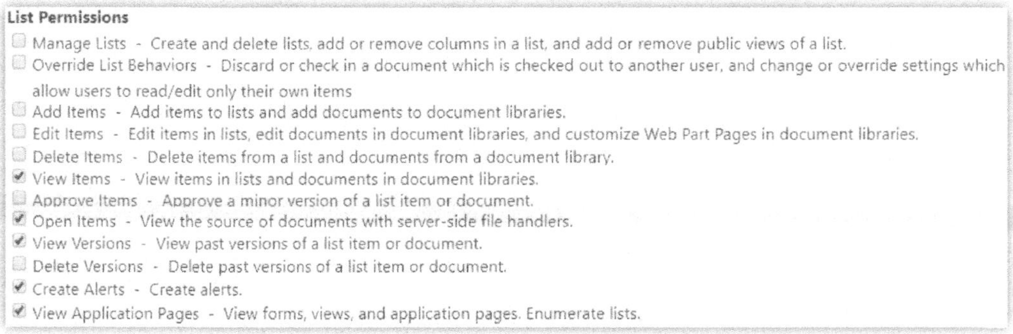

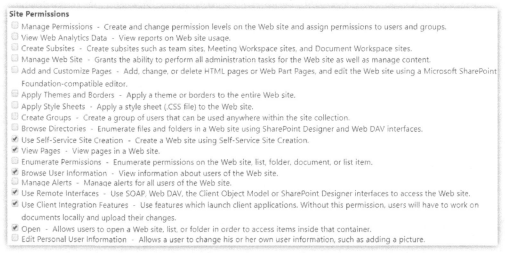

Figure 8.8: List Permissions Read Permission Level

At site level user can open site, access all lists, libraries, folders, pages, and can browse user information as seen in the following screenshot:

Figure 8.9: Site Permissions Read Permission Level

There is no action that can be taken by user at **Personal Permissions** as seen in the following screenshot:

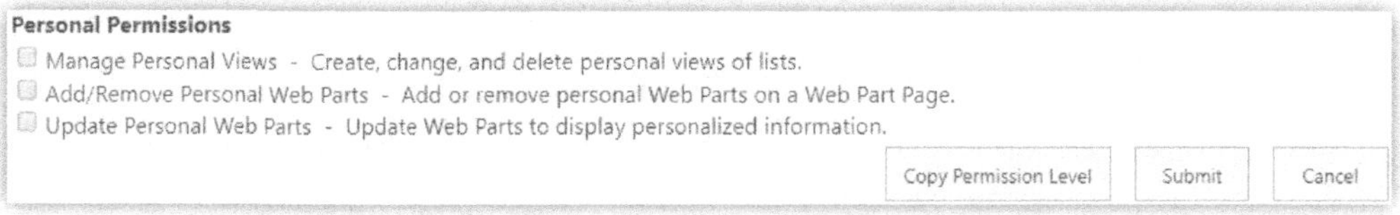

Figure 8.10: Personal Permissions Read Permission Level

View only permission level

Click on the permission level **View Only**, you will see the actions that can be taken by user having view only permission. Users can view site pages and content in site but cannot download the files as seen in the following screenshot:

Figure 8.11: *View Only Permission Level*

User can view items, list item and document versions, application pages. User can create alerts as well as seen in the following screenshot:

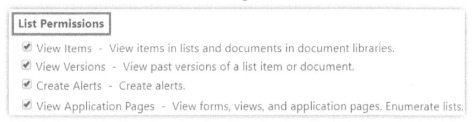

Figure 8.12: *List Permissions View Only Permission Level*

At site level permissions user can view pages, list, libraries, user information as seen in the following screenshot:

Figure 8.13: *Site Permissions View Only Permission Level*

There is no action that can be taken by user at **Personal Permissions**. This permission level is applicable for the group **Excel Services Viewers**. This permission level has lower permission then **Read** permission level.

Edit permission level

Click on the permission level **Edit** as seen in the following screenshot which is superior permission to **Read** permission:

Figure 8.14: Edit Permission Level

User can create list, delete list, add list columns, and views in list. User can view list or document versions and delete versions as well as seen in the following screenshot:

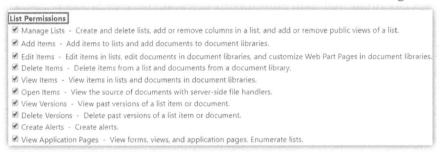

Figure 8.15: List Permissions Edit Permission Level

User can browse directories, files, folders using designer, also can view user information and can edit own information. User can edit the document and can upload in the library as seen in the following screenshot:

Figure 8.16: Site Permissions Edit Permission Level

User can manage their personal view, add or remove webparts, can update to show personalized information as seen in the following screenshot:

Figure 8.17: Personal Permissions Edit Permission Level

Contribute permission level

Click on the permission level **Contribute** as seen in the following screenshot:

Figure 8.18: Contribute Permission Level

If you compare **Contribute** permission with **Edit** permission, then you see contribute has same level of permission except **Manage Lists** permission means user cannot create and delete list, cannot add or remove columns, cannot add or remove views. User can view pages, list or document items, item versions and delete items from list or library as well as seen in the following screenshot:

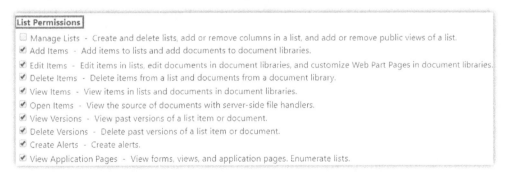

Figure 8.19: List Permissions Contribute Permission Level

User can browse directories, files, folders using designer. User can browse user information and can edit own information. User can edit the document and can upload in the library which is same as of **Edit** permission level as seen in the following screenshot:

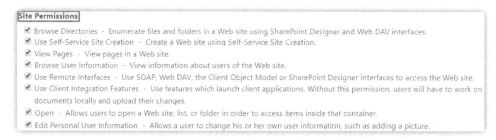

Figure 8.20: Site Permissions Contribute Permission Level

User can manage their personal view, add or remove webparts, can update to show personalized information as seen in the following screenshot:

Figure 8.21: Personal Permissions Contribute Permission Level

Full control permission level

Full control is the highest level permission in site. Users with full control permission level are authorized to do all activities in the site and subsite level. Click on the permission level **Full Control**. You see under category **List Permissions** all options are enabled. User can **Manage Lists, Override List Behaviors, Add Items, Edit Items, Delete Items, View Items, Approve Items, Open Items, View Versions, Delete Versions, Create Alert, View Application Pages** as seen in the following screenshot:

List Permissions

- Manage Lists - Create and delete lists, add or remove columns in a list, and add or remove public views of a list.
- Override List Behaviors - Discard or check in a document which is checked out to another user, and change or override settings which allow users to read/edit only their own items
- Add Items - Add items to lists and add documents to document libraries.
- Edit Items - Edit items in lists, edit documents in document libraries, and customize Web Part Pages in document libraries.
- Delete Items - Delete items from a list and documents from a document library.
- View Items - View items in lists and documents in document libraries.
- Approve Items - Approve a minor version of a list item or document.
- Open Items - View the source of documents with server-side file handlers.
- View Versions - View past versions of a list item or document.
- Delete Versions - Delete past versions of a list item or document.
- Create Alerts - Create alerts.
- View Application Pages - View forms, views, and application pages. Enumerate lists.

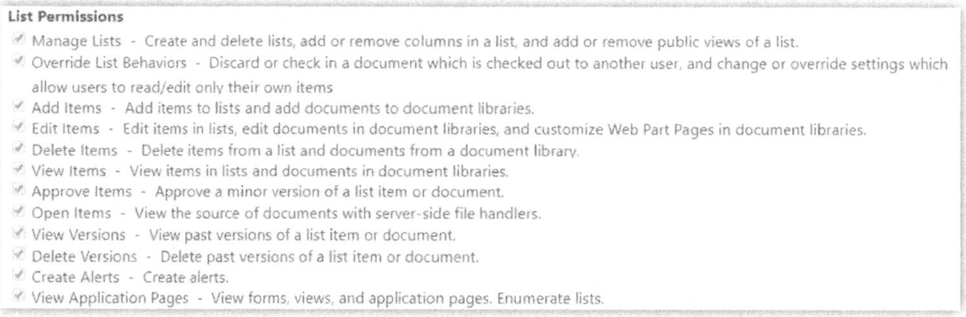

Figure 8.22: List Permissions Full Control Permission Level

At site permission level user can **Manage Permissions, View Web Analytics Data, Create Subsites, Manage Web Site, Add and Customize Pages, Apply Themes and Borders, Apply Style Sheets, Create Groups, Browse Directories, Use Self-Service**

Site Creation, View Pages, Enumerate Permissions, Browse User Information, Manage Alerts, Use Remote Interfaces, Use Client Integration Features, Open, Edit Personal User Information as seen in the following screenshot:

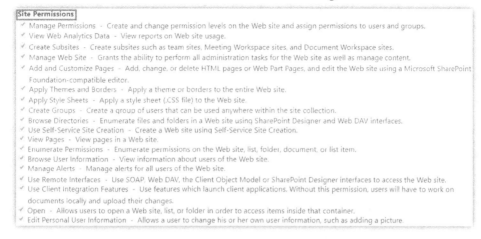

Figure 8.23: Site Permissions Full Control Permission Level

User can manage their personal view, add or remove webparts, can update to show personalized information as seen in the following screenshot:

Figure 8.24: Personal Permissions Full Control Permission Level

Design permission level

User with **Design** permission are mainly responsible to add, delete, customize pages, apply themes and borders, apply style sheets, add and remove webparts as seen in the following screenshot:

Permission Levels › Edit Permission Level

Name and Description

Type a name and description for your permission level. The name is shown on the permissions page. The name and description are shown on the add users page.

Name:

Design

Description:

Can view, add, update, delete, approve, and customize.

Figure 8.25: Design Permission Level

User having **Design** permission, all options are enabled at list permissions level similar to user having **Full Control**. User can **Manage Lists, Override List Behaviors, Add Items, Edit Items, Delete Items, View Items, Approve Items, Open Items, View Versions, Delete Versions, Create Alert, View Application Pages** as seen in the following screenshot:

List Permissions

☑ Manage Lists - Create and delete lists, add or remove columns in a list, and add or remove public views of a list.
☑ Override List Behaviors - Discard or check in a document which is checked out to another user, and change or override settings which allow users to read/edit only their own items
☑ Add Items - Add items to lists and add documents to document libraries.
☑ Edit Items - Edit items in lists, edit documents in document libraries, and customize Web Part Pages in document libraries.
☑ Delete Items - Delete items from a list and documents from a document library.
☑ View Items - View items in lists and documents in document libraries.
☑ Approve Items - Approve a minor version of a list item or document.
☑ Open Items - View the source of documents with server-side file handlers.
☑ View Versions - View past versions of a list item or document.
☑ Delete Versions - Delete past versions of a list item or document.
☑ Create Alerts - Create alerts.
☑ View Application Pages - View forms, views, and application pages. Enumerate lists.

Figure 8.26: List Permissions Design Permission Level

At site permission level user can **Add and Customize Pages, Apply Themes and Borders, Apply Style Sheets, Browse Directories, Use Self-Service Site Creation, View Pages, Browse User Information, Use Remote Interfaces, Use Client Integration Features, Open, Edit Personal User Information** as seen in the following screenshot:

Site Permissions

☑ Add and Customize Pages - Add, change, or delete HTML pages or Web Part Pages, and edit the Web site using a Microsoft SharePoint Foundation-compatible editor.
☑ Apply Themes and Borders - Apply a theme or borders to the entire Web site.
☑ Apply Style Sheets - Apply a style sheet (.CSS file) to the Web site.
☑ Browse Directories - Enumerate files and folders in a Web site using SharePoint Designer and Web DAV interfaces.
☑ Use Self-Service Site Creation - Create a Web site using Self-Service Site Creation.
☑ View Pages - View pages in a Web site.
☑ Browse User Information - View information about users of the Web site.
☑ Use Remote Interfaces - Use SOAP, Web DAV, the Client Object Model or SharePoint Designer interfaces to access the Web site.
☑ Use Client Integration Features - Use features which launch client applications. Without this permission, users will have to work on documents locally and upload their changes.
☑ Open - Allows users to open a Web site, list, or folder in order to access items inside that container.
☑ Edit Personal User Information - Allows a user to change his or her own user information, such as adding a picture.

Figure 8.27: Site Permissions Design Permission Level

User can manage their personal view, add or remove webparts, can update to show personalized information as seen in the following screenshot:

Personal Permissions

☑ Manage Personal Views - Create, change, and delete personal views of lists.
☑ Add/Remove Personal Web Parts - Add or remove personal Web Parts on a Web Part Page.
☑ Update Personal Web Parts - Update Web Parts to display personalized information.

Figure 8.28: Personal Permissions Design Permission Level

Approve permission level

Permission level **Approve** is mainly assigned to users who are primarily responsible for review the contents and can do the needful by approving or rejecting or sending back to owner of the content for review and submit again for approval as seen in the following screenshot. The approval is done by the authorized persons, so a dedicated group creation might be required as per business requirement:

Figure 8.29: Approve Permission Level

User can **Override List Behaviors**, **Add Items**, **Edit Items**, **Delete Items**, **View Items**, **Approve Items**, **Open Items**, **View Versions**, **Delete Versions**, **Create Alert**, **View Application Pages** as seen in the following screenshot:

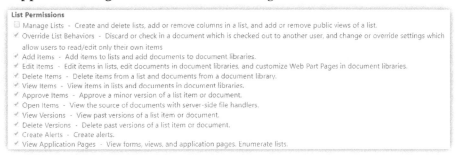

Figure 8.30: List Permissions Approve Permission Level

At site permission level user can **Browse Directories**, **Use Self-Service Site Creation**, **View Pages**, **Browse User Information**, **Use Remote Interfaces**, **Use Client Integration Features**, **Open**, **Edit Personal User Information** as seen in the following screenshot:

Site Permissions
- ☑ Browse Directories - Enumerate files and folders in a Web site using SharePoint Designer and Web DAV interfaces.
- ☑ Use Self-Service Site Creation - Create a Web site using Self-Service Site Creation.
- ☑ View Pages - View pages in a Web site.
- ☑ Browse User Information - View information about users of the Web site.
- ☑ Use Remote Interfaces - Use SOAP, Web DAV, the Client Object Model or SharePoint Designer interfaces to access the Web site.
- ☑ Use Client Integration Features - Use features which launch client applications. Without this permission, users will have to work on documents locally and upload their changes.
- ☑ Open - Allows users to open a Web site, list, or folder in order to access items inside that container.
- ☑ Edit Personal User Information - Allows a user to change his or her own user information, such as adding a picture.

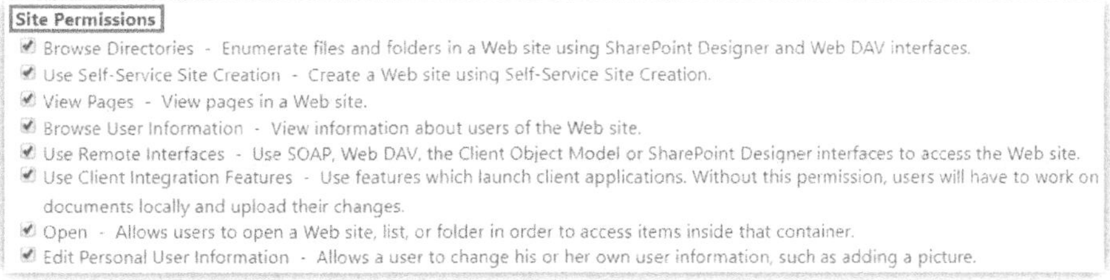

Figure 8.31: Site Permissions Approve Permission Level

User can manage their personal view, add or remove webparts, can update to show personalized information as seen in the following screenshot:

Figure 8.32: Personal Permissions Approve Permission Level

Manage hierarchy permission level

User with **Manage Hierarchy** permission can create sites, edit site pages including items in list and library as seen in the following screenshot:

Figure 8.33: Manage Hierarchy Permission Level

User can **Manage Lists, Override List Behaviors, Add Items, Edit Items, Delete Items, View Items, Open Items, View Versions, Delete Versions, Create Alert, View Application Pages** as seen in the following screenshot:

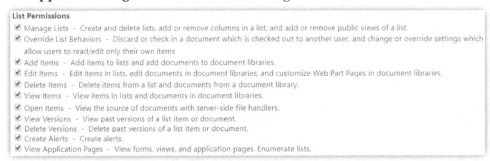

Figure 8.34: List Permissions Manage Hierarchy Permission Level

At site permission level user can **Manage Permissions, View Web Analytics Data, Create Subsites, Manage Web Site, Add and Customize Pages, Browse Directories, Use Self-Service Site Creation, View Pages, Enumerate Permissions, Browse User Information, Manage Alerts, Use Remote Interfaces, Use Client Integration Features, Open, Edit Personal User Information** as seen in the following screenshot:

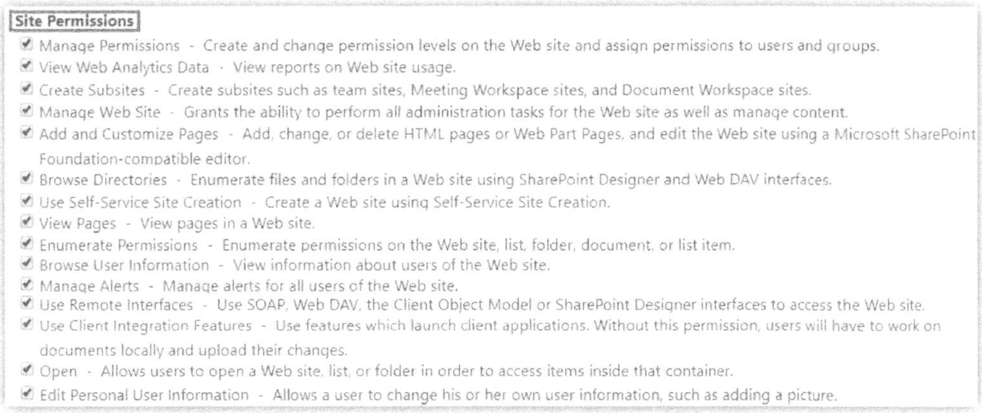

Site Permissions
Manage Permissions - Create and change permission levels on the Web site and assign permissions to users and groups.
View Web Analytics Data - View reports on Web site usage.
Create Subsites - Create subsites such as team sites, Meeting Workspace sites, and Document Workspace sites.
Manage Web Site - Grants the ability to perform all administration tasks for the Web site as well as manage content.
Add and Customize Pages - Add, change, or delete HTML pages or Web Part Pages, and edit the Web site using a Microsoft SharePoint Foundation-compatible editor.
Browse Directories - Enumerate files and folders in a Web site using SharePoint Designer and Web DAV interfaces.
Use Self-Service Site Creation - Create a Web site using Self-Service Site Creation.
View Pages - View pages in a Web site.
Enumerate Permissions - Enumerate permissions on the Web site, list, folder, document, or list item.
Browse User Information - View information about users of the Web site.
Manage Alerts - Manage alerts for all users of the Web site.
Use Remote Interfaces - Use SOAP, Web DAV, the Client Object Model or SharePoint Designer interfaces to access the Web site.
Use Client Integration Features - Use features which launch client applications. Without this permission, users will have to work on documents locally and upload their changes.
Open - Allows users to open a Web site, list, or folder in order to access items inside that container.
Edit Personal User Information - Allows a user to change his or her own user information, such as adding a picture.

Figure 8.35: *Site Permissions Manage Hierarchy Permission Level*

User can manage their personal view, add or remove webparts, can update to show personalized information as seen in the following screenshot:

Personal Permissions
Manage Personal Views - Create, change, and delete personal views of lists.
Add/Remove Personal Web Parts - Add or remove personal Web Parts on a Web Part Page.
Update Personal Web Parts - Update Web Parts to display personalized information.

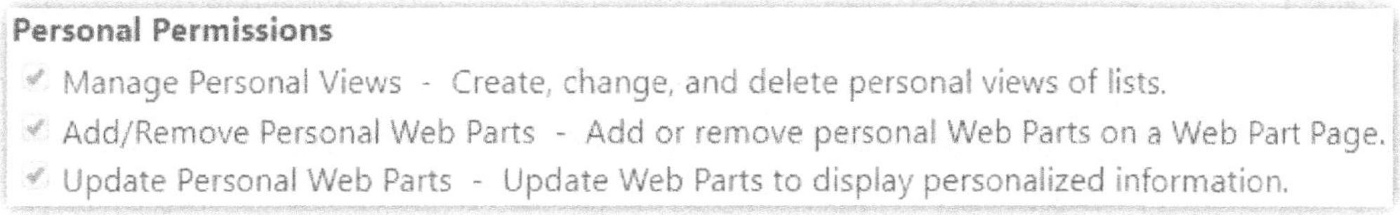

Figure 8.36: *Personal Permissions Manage Hierarchy Permission Level*

Restricted read permission level

User with **Restricted Read** permission is restricted primarily with list item or document versions, user permissions as seen in the following screenshot:

Permission Levels › Edit Permission Level
Name and Description
Type a name and description for your permission level. The name is shown on the permissions page. The name and description are shown on the add users page.
Name:
Restricted Read
Description:
Can view pages and documents, but cannot view historical versions or user permissions.

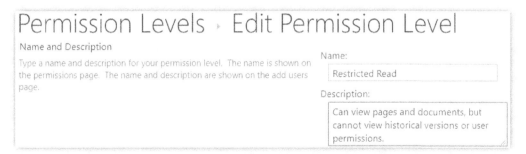

Figure 8.37: *Restricted Read Permission Level*

At list permissions level, user can view list items, documents, open items as well as seen in the following screenshot:

List Permissions

☑ View Items - View items in lists and documents in document libraries.

☑ Open Items - View the source of documents with server-side file handlers.

Figure 8.38: List Permissions Restricted Read Permission Level

At site permissions level user can view pages, open list, library, and folders to view items as seen in the following screenshot:

Site Permissions

☑ View Pages - View pages in a Web site.

☑ Open - Allows users to open a Web site, list, or folder in order to access items inside that container.

Figure 8.39: Site Permissions Restricted Read Permission Level

Restricted interfaces for translation permission level

The permission **Restricted Interfaces for Translation** is mostly applicable for SharePoint developers. Open **Restricted Interfaces for Translation** permission level as seen in the following screenshot:

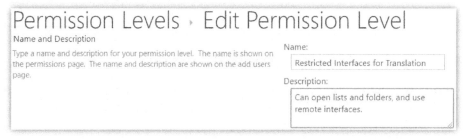

Figure 8.40: Restricted Interfaces for Translation Permission Level

User can **User Remote Interfaces** and **Open** site, list, library, folder. User having **Contribute** permission only in library will not allow to open the item. User must have minimum **Restricted Interfaces for Translation** permission at site level and **Contribute** at library or list level will allow users to open items. This allows to view list or library properties using remote interfaces like REST API, Web Services, Client Object Model, and SharePoint Designer as seen in the following screenshot:

Site Permissions

☑ Use Remote Interfaces - Use SOAP, Web DAV, the Client Object Model or SharePoint Designer interfaces to access the Web site.

☑ Open - Allows users to open a Web site, list, or folder in order to access items inside that container.

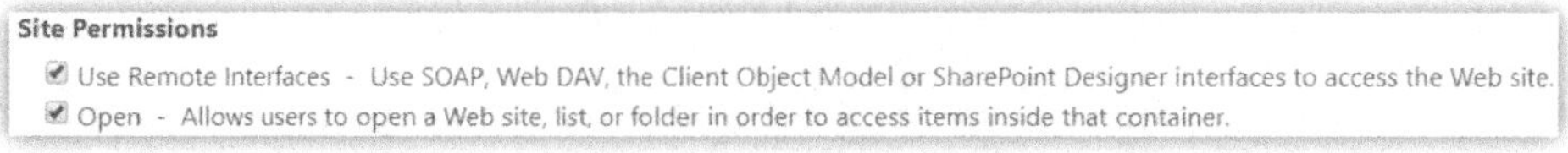

Figure 8.41: Site Permissions Restricted Interfaces for Translation Permission Level

Records center web service submitters permission level

The permission **Records Center Web Service Submitters** allows users to submit content to site using web services as seen in the following screenshot:

Figure 8.42: Records Center Web Service Submitters Permission Level

User can **User Remote Interfaces** and **Open** site, list, library, folder to access items as seen in the following screenshot:

Figure 8.43: Site Permissions Records Center Web Service Submitters

Custom permission level

We discussed about different permission level that are created by default or by activating any feature. We can create a custom permission level as per business requirement by which we can allow or restrict any specific permission to a dedicated group of people.

Let's say I want to create custom permission level (contribute without delete) where users will have contribute permission but want to restrict users from deleting items from list or library. Let's perform the following steps to create custom permission level:

1. Click on **Contribute** (<_layouts/15/editrole.aspx?role=Contribute >) from permission level.

2. Scroll down to bottom of the page and click on **Copy Permission Level** as seen in the following screenshot:

Figure 8.44: Copy Permission

3. You will be redirected to copy role page (<_layouts/15/copyrole. aspx?role=Contribute >) where you need to enter **Name** (Contribute Without Delete) of the permission level that you want to create and **Description** of the page.

4. You will see same permissions **List Permissions, Site Permissions, Personal Permissions** are checked in. Identify **Delete Items** from **List Permissions** and **Uncheck** that option as seen in the following screenshot:

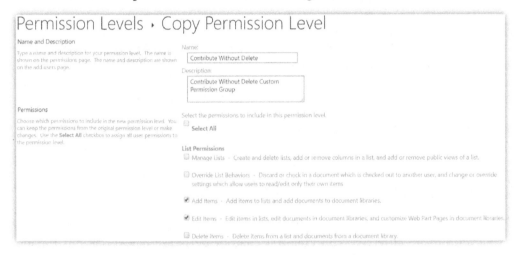

Figure 8.45: Copy Permission Level

5. Click on **Create** button present at the bottom of page.

6. Custom permission level **Contribute Without Delete** created now to apply.

Access request settings

Access Request Settings provides sharing option in site. Let's perform the following steps to see different settings available and will see how it works:

1. Click on **Access Request Settings** from ribbon under user page as seen in the following screenshot:

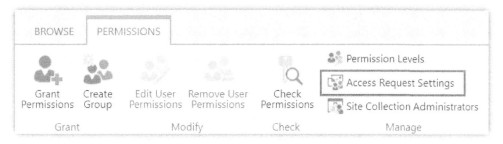

Figure 8.46: Access Request Swttings

2. Another dialog box will open where you will find options **Allow members to share the site and individual files and folders, Allow members to invite others to the site members group, BPB-ModernTeamSite Members. This setting must be enabled to let members share the site** which allows to share site, files, folders are enabled by default as seen in the below screenshot:

3. Next option **Allow access requests** where you can configure **who will receive access requests** for the site. By default, all members of the group **BPB-ModernTeamSite Admins** will receive approval request for access request as seen in the below screenshot.

4. If you need to dedicate one user who is responsible for providing and handling access request for better management and additional security, select next radio button and enter e-mail address of that person as seen in below screenshot:

Figure 8.47: Allow Access Request

5. Navigate to **Settings** (gear icon) from home page of modern site. Click on **Site Permissions** from drop down.

6. Click on **Change sharing settings** then you see the sharing option is same as we discussed with a new look as seen in the following screenshot:

Figure 8.48: Sharing Settings

First option in new sharing option allows **site owner and member** can share files, folder, and site. People with edit permission can share files and folders:

1. Second option allows **site owner and member, people with edit permission** can share files and folders. Site owner only can share site.

2. Third option allows only site owner can share file, folders, site.

Site collection administrators

Next setting under **Permissions** tab is **Site Collection Administrators** who has admin level permission over the site collection to handle all actions in site collection as well as sites present under that site collection. Click on **Site Collection Administrators** from ribbon, you see owner group BPB-ModernTeamSite Owners is added as site collection administrator by default as seen in the following screenshot. You can modify this and can add dedicated users or groups here:

Figure 8.49: *Site Collection Administrator*

Check user permission

When we need to check, which user is having what type of permission in the site then we can click on **Check Permission** from ribbon under permission tab. Enter **Name or Mail Address** in the people picker box and click on **Check Now**. You will see the user permission level and part of the group related to that permission level as seen in the following screenshot. If you will not find anything after search means, user or group has no permission. User or group need to raise request to get access in the site or library or list or item:

Figure 8.50: *Check User Permission*

Remove user permission

If any user or group is no more part of authorized group, then we need to follow this option **Remove User Permissions** present in ribbon under the tab **PERMISSIONS** to remove permission from site. Select the **User or Group** and click on **Remove User Permissions**. You will get one message which you need to confirm by clicking **OK** as seen in the following screenshot. Permission will be removed:

Figure 8.51: *Remove User Permission*

Edit user permissions

If you want to change the permission of an existing user already having permission level assigned and part of one SharePoint group, then we need to follow **Edit User Permissions**. Let's perform the following steps to edit user permission:

1. Select any user or group that you want to edit permission.

2. Click on **Edit User Permissions** from ribbon.

3. Select permission level you want to assign by selecting checkbox and click **OK** as seen in the following screenshot:

Figure 8.52: Edit User Permission

Grant permissions

When users' need access to site or list of libraries, they need to contact the authorized person (site owners having full control or any dedicated user responsible to assign permission) responsible for this and create a request for access with type of permission level. Authorized person responsible for providing access need to follow these below steps to assign permission:

1. Click on **Grant Permissions** from the ribbon.

2. Enter **Name or Mail ID** of the user whom you are going to give permission.

3. Click on **Show Options**.

4. Choose one permission level from the dropdown option **Select a permission level**. Select a group having a permission level which will add the user into that group else you can add the user directly to a permission level with no groups linked (**Read, Contribute, Full Control**, and so on) as seen in the following screenshot. As per the best practice its always recommended to create a group and assign users to that user instead of adding directly to the user:

Figure 8.53: Grant Permission

Create a group

As per the best practice its always recommended to create a group if you want to assign permission to users apart from default permission. As an example, we have created a custom permission level **Contribute Without Delete** by making a small change in the permission level **Contribute** that is restricted the delete permission for items in the library or list. If you want to assign **Contribute Without Delete** permission to any user then better you create a group, assign **Contribute Without Delete** permission level to the group and add users to the custom group. Let's perform the following steps to create a group:

1. Click on **Create Group** from ribbon as seen in the following screenshot:

Figure 8.54: Create Group

2. Enter **Name** (BPB-ModernTeamSite Custom) and **About Me** of the group.

3. There should be an owner of the group. Enter owner **Name or Mail ID** in the box **Group Owner**.

4. From the next option **Group Settings**, select **Who can view the membership of the group** as **Group Members** by which only members of this group can see all members present in this group. There is another option **Who can edit the membership of the group** which you need to select as **Group Owner** as seen in the following screenshot:

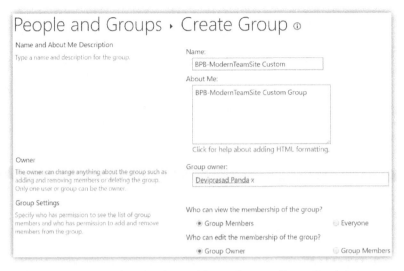

Figure 8.55: Custom Group Name, Owner, Group Settings

5. From next option **Membership Requests**, select **Allow requests to join/leave this group** as **Yes** and in the field **Send membership requests to the following e-mail address,** enter the e-mail address of the person who will receive a mail when any user want to be added into his group. The reason for this setting like adding users into this group needs to be done by a specific user for additional security.

6. Select the type of permission level that needs to be assigned to the group. Select the custom permission level **Contribute Without Delete** that we created before as seen in the following screenshot. From next time onwards whenever any user needs to be assigned to **Contribute Without Delete** permission then add users to this custom group BPB-ModernTeamSite Custom.

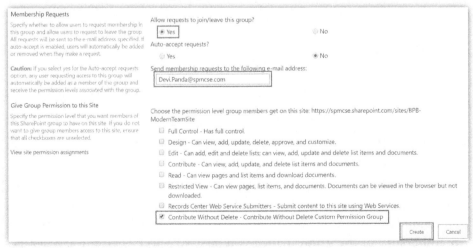

Figure 8.56: Membership Requests and Group Permission Details For Custom Group

7. You see the custom group `BPB-ModernTeamSite Custom` is added as seen in the following screenshot:

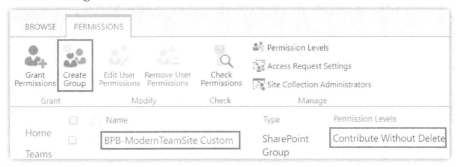

Figure 8.57: Custom Group Created

Permission inheritance

If we see the hierarchy in SharePoint from lower to a higher level it comes like list or library items present in list or library, respectively. Library or list present in a subsite. Subsite is under the next higher-level site or site collection. If we assign permission (**Contribute**) to the user at site collection, by default all subsite present under that site collection inherit the same permission (**Contribute**) as of site collection. All lists, libraries present under that subsite inherit the same permission (**Contribute**) as of subsite. All items present under list or library inherit the same permission (**Contribute**) as of the list or library respectively. So, we can control permission at any level from site collection to list or library item level. Let's perform the following steps to achieve this:

1. If you want to restrict users for access at any level (site, list/library, and item) and assign permission to specific users as per business requirement then we need to break inheritance by selecting **Stop Inheriting Permissions** from the ribbon. We call it as unique permission means subsite has its permission management and not inheriting permission from the higher-level site. Next, you will get a message for confirmation to proceed, click on **OK** as seen in the following screenshot:

Figure 8.58: Stop Inheriting Permission

2. You will be redirected to the permission set up a page where you have options to create new groups for the site you want to set unique permission. You can create a new group by clicking **Create a new group** or can proceed with the same group clicking on **OK** as seen in the following screenshot. Permission inheritance is broken and now you can assign permission to the user for that site manually by following the normal process.

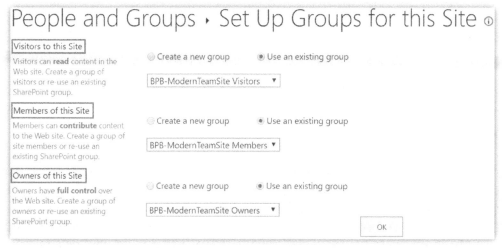

Figure 8.59: Set Up Group

3. This is very critical to **Stop Inheriting Permissions** because all users including owners will also lose permission. So, while creating a site or site owner should plan for this option for permission management, else everything needs to be set up manually which might be very difficult for large sites.

4. Similarly, we can stop permission at the library or list level or item level following the same steps discussed. If you want to inherit the next higher-level site permission again, you need to select the option **Delete Unique Permissions** from the ribbon. You will get a confirmation message of losing permission, once confirmed by clicking **OK** as seen in the following screenshot, inheritance is established again:

Figure 8.60: Delete Unique Permissions

Permission management modern experience

There are new experiences in which permission is introduced that makes sharing, assigning permission simple. Users can be added to certain groups like owners, members by option **Invite People**. Easy to add a user to SharePoint groups by the option by **Share Site Only**. New Experience in sharing introduced. Let's discuss each option in detail.

Invite people

Option **Invite People** to allow to add users in groups like **Owner**, **Member**. Navigate to **Settings** (gear icon) from the home page of the modern site. Click on **Site Permissions** from the dropdown. You will find an option **Invite People** button, just click on **Invite People** button. You will notice two options **Add members to group** and **Share site only** as a dropdown. Let's discuss on **Add members to group** and **Share site only** in details.

Add members to the group

When you will click **Invite People** button, you will get an option **Add members to group**. Let's perform the following steps to see the options available to add members to the group:

1. Click on **Add members to group**.

2. From the next option under **Group Membership** click on **Add members**.

3. Enter **Name or email address** in the box and click on **Save** as seen in the following screenshot:

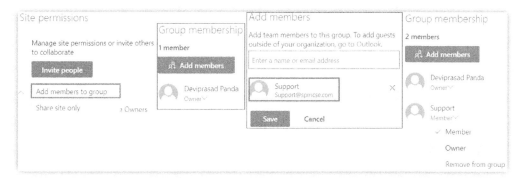

Figure 8.61: Add Members to Group

4. Users will be added as **Member** by default and the number of members is updated.

5. We can further change the permission level. Click on the expand option by clicking **Member** or **Owner** present below the username, select the type of membership. Membership will be updated.

6. If you want to remove from the group, then click on **Remove from group**.

7. By **Add members to group** option we can change the membership between **Owner** and **Member** only not with other permission levels.

8. When any user is added by **Add members to group** option these users are added to the **Office 365 Group/Microsoft Teams (BPB-ModernTeamSite)** as seen in the following screenshot:

Figure 8.62: Office 365 Group Members Added

Share site only

Let's perform the following steps to see how **Share Site Only** works:

1. Click on **Share site only** option from the dropdown under **Invite People**.

2. Enter **Name or email ID** of the user, you see by default user will be showing **Edit** permission.

3. Click on button **Add**, the user will be added to the group **BPB-ModernTeamSite Members**.

4. If you click on the **Edit** permission level, you will see the dropdown option to change to different permission level **Read** or **Full Control**. If you select **Read**, the user will be added to the group **Site Visitors** as seen in the following screenshot:

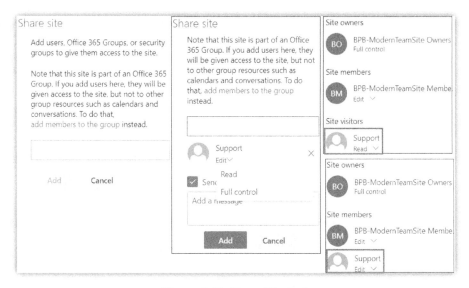

Figure 8.63: Share Site Only

5. When any user is added by **Share site only**, these users are added to the SharePoint groups (**Owners**, **Members**, and **Visitors**) present in the site, not in office 365 group.

Sharing options

Sharing options provides a link to users by which they can access a specific file or folder directly. Let's perform the following steps to check how sharing options work exactly:

1. Click on the file or folder that you want to share.
2. Click on **Share** from the command bar.
3. Another way you can get the **Share** ↗ option side to the file or folder name or by clicking **Show Action** ⋮ button as seen in the following screenshot:

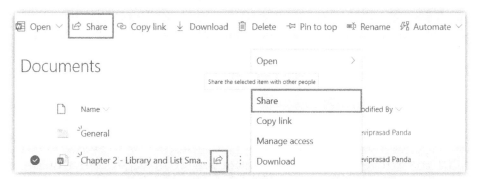

Figure 8.64: Share

4. On clicking **Share**, another dialog box will open where you need to enter the email ID of the user to which file needs to be shared.

5. Click on the option **People in SPmcse with the link can view** the present above user.

6. There will be 4 types of options under link settings as seen in the below screenshot. You need to select any one and click on **Send**.

    *   **Anyone with the link**: Anyone who has the link can access the file. There is no requirement of authentication and access is not audited for this type of link. This is used for sharing external users outside the organization.

    *   **People in the organization with the link**: People in your organization only can access the file if they have the link.

    *   **People with existing access**: People having access already are shared with the link. This has no impact on the type of permission that users already have.

    *   **Specific people**: Specific people are shared with the link. By default, the user will have view permission. We can select the checkbox **Allow Editing** to give edit permission to a specific user as per the mail ID entered.

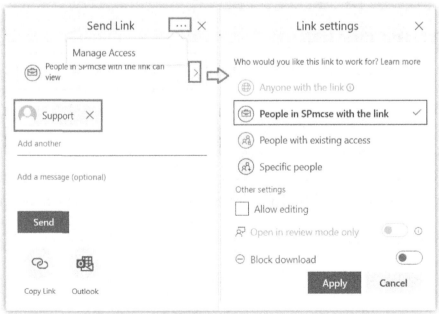

Figure 8.65: Send Link

7. There is an option **Manage Access** in the dialog box **Send Link**. If you click on that you will get another dialog where you see manage access window in for of categories like **Stop Sharing, Links Giving Access, Direct Access**.

8. **Direct Access** category showing users, groups having access to sites. Click on **Plus** sign ➕ will open one dialog box to grant permission. Enter user you want to grant access in people picker field. Below that you will find the option to choose the type of access like **Can Edit** or **Can View**. Select one option and click on grant access to apply changes. Permission will be assigned to the user.

9. If you click on the **Share** 🔗 present side to **Links Giving Access**, you will get the same **Send Link** dialog box to share the link. Select the checkbox **Allow editing** will give edit permission to the user receiving the link. You can enable the option **Block Download** to restrict the user from downloading as seen in the following screenshot:

Figure 8.66: Manage Access

10. Click on **Stop Sharing** to stop inheriting permission and configure unique permission. You will get a message as dialog box, that all user permissions will be removed except **Owner** group, for confirmation, click on **Stop Sharing** will apply changes. If you click on **Advanced** option present at the bottom will redirect you to permission page (`https://<site url>/_layouts/15/user.aspx`) and you will notice the owner group present.

Conclusion

In this chapter we had a glance at permission all about, what is permission management. Understood default groups available in SharePoint, different permission levels. Understood the dependent features on group creation. Discussed how to create group, permission levels. Discussed in detail different settings available for managing permission in SharePoint. Discussed permission inheritance. Also discussed the modern experiences in permission management and sharing. Next in *Chapter 9, Managed Metadata Concept* will discuss all managed metadata.

Points to remember

- Activating **SharePoint Server Publishing Infrastructure**, **SharePoint Server Enterprise Site Collection features** feature and during the creation of record center few dependent groups will be created.

- By **Add members to group** option we can change the membership between **Owner** and **Member** only.

- When any user is added by **Add members to group** option, actually these users are added to the **Office 365 Group/Microsoft Teams**.

- When any user is added by **Share site only**, these users are added to the SharePoint groups (**Owners**, **Members**, and **Visitors**) present in the site not in the office 365 group.

CHAPTER 9

Managed Metadata Concept

In the previous chapter, we discussed all managing permission in SharePoint online. In this chapter, we will discuss managed metadata. Metadata is nothing but information/data about Information/data that plays an important role in quick and most relevant content searching, refining content, and building global navigation that can apply to all sites under one site collection for better user experience. We can create metadata, keywords by tagging, following that ultimately helpful for searching and getting information quickly and most relevantly.

Structure

In this chapter we will discuss the following:

- Introduction to managed metadata
- Term store administration
- Creating a metadata column
- Metadata navigation settings
- Testing metadata navigation settings
- Create metadata navigation

Objective

During the end of the chapter you will get a clear understanding of the following:

- Managed metadata overview
- How to create a new group, term set, term
- Application of reuse terms, copy term set, merge terms, move term set
- Hoe to create metadata column
- Application of metadata in navigation settings and filtering
- Create and apply metadata navigation

Term store administration

Terms can be managed centrally from the **Term store** present under the **SharePoint Admin Center**. Under the **SharePoint Admin Center** you will find option **More features**, click on that. You will see the **Term store**, click on **Open** as seen in the following screenshot. You will be redirected to term store manager page (`https://< SharePoint admin center url>/_layouts/15/TermStoreManager.aspx`) which is the central location for creating, storing, configuring, and managing taxonomy or metadata:

Figure 9.1: Term Store in SharePoint Admin Center

Creating a new group

The group is the top-level folder that is created based on the usability and to keep related terms at one place. Let's perform the following steps to create a group under **New Group** (`Employee`):

1. Right-click on **Managed Metadata Service** (`Taxonomy_SBvqjHawxODOt szfaHuoeQ==`) or click on the right end side where you will find an option to expand.

2. Click on the **New Group** option appeared from the dropdown.

3. Enter **Name** of the group as **Employee** as seen in the following screenshot:

Figure 9.2: Create New Group

4. New group **Employee** will be created and right to that you will find another window with options **Group Name, Description, Group Manager, Contributors, Unique Identifier** as seen in the following screenshot:

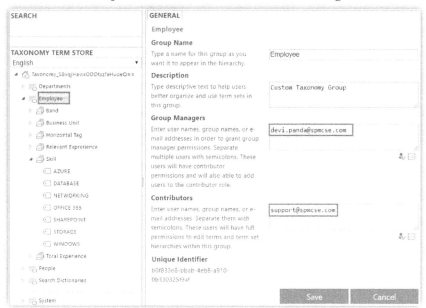

Figure 9.3: New Group General Properties

5. Enter the user name or email ID in the field of **Contributors** who are authorized to **Add or Modify** the term set.

6. Enter the user name or email ID in the field of **Group Managers** who can do all activities that a user with contributor can do apart from that can **Add or Remove** contributors. Click on **Save** finally.

Creating a term set

Under the new group **Employee** we can create a group of **Term Set**. Let's perform the following steps to create a term set under group **Employee**:

1. Right-click or **Expand** the new group created **Employee**.

2. Select the option **New Term Set** from the dropdown.

3. Enter the name of the term set as **Business Unit** as seen in below screenshot:

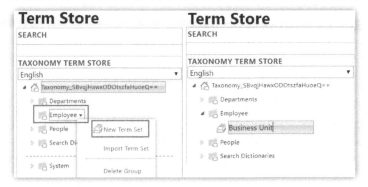

Figure 9.4: New Term Set

4. The new term set **Business Unit** created and right to that you will find another window with options **Term Set Name**, **Description**, **Owner**, **Contact**, **Stakeholder**, **Submission Policy**, **Unique Identifier** under category **GENERAL** as seen in the following screenshot:

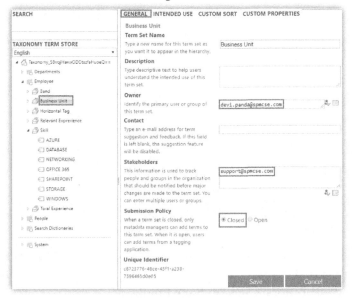

Figure 9.5: Term Store General Properties Tab

5. Enter the name or email of one user or group under the field **Owner** who is/ are going to be the owner of the term set.

6. Enter the name or email of one user or group under the field **Stakeholders** who will receive notification mail if any major changes in term set happen.

7. Next option **Submission Policy** enables who can add terms to the term set. Selecting the option **Closed** will allows only administrators, contributors, metadata managers to add terms. Selecting the option **Open** will allow all users to add terms in the term set.

8. Click on the next tab of category **INTENDED USE** right to the tab **GENERAL**. You will find options **Term set Usage, Available for Tagging, Use This Term Set for Site Navigation, Use This Term Set for Faceted Navigation** as seen in the following screenshot:

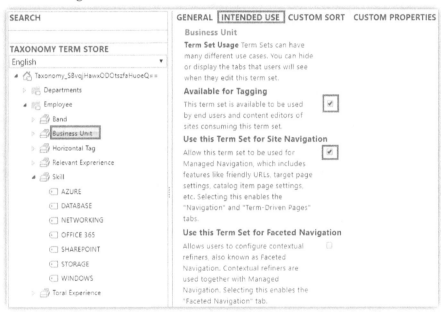

Figure 9.6: *Term Store Intended Use Properties Tab*

9. Select the checkbox **Available for Tagging** that will enable that term set to be available for tagging for end users.

10. Select the checkbox **Use This Term Set for Site Navigation** which will enable the term set to be available for site navigation.

11. Next tab side to **INTENDED USE** is **CUSTOM SORT** that has options **Use default sort order according to current language, Use custom sort order** for sorting the terms.

12. By default, the option **Use default sort order according to current language** is selected, we can choose **Use custom sort order** for changing the order as seen in the following screenshot:

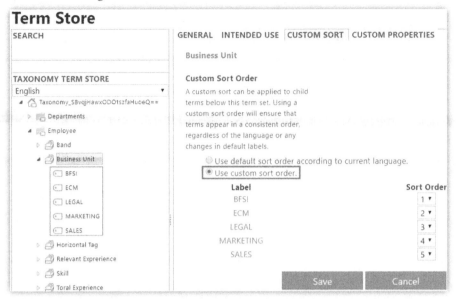

Figure 9.7: Term Store Custom Sort Properties Tab

13. The next tab side to **CUSTOM SORT** is **CUSTOM PROPERTIES**. We can add **CUSTOM PROPERTIES** which are additional information about the term set as seen in the following screenshot:

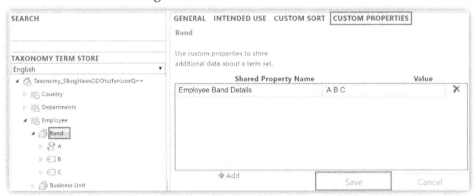

Figure 9.8: Custom Properties

14. Custom properties can be used in webpart **Term Property**. Edit one classic page like **Wiki Page** or **Web Part Page** present in page library and click on **Webpart** under the tab **Insert** from the ribbon. Click on webpart **Term Property** present under the category **Content Rollup** as seen in the following screenshot:

Figure 9.9: *Term Property Webpart*

15. Edit that webpart, you will find one option **Custom Property** where we can use custom properties as seen in the following screenshot:

Figure 9.10: *Custom Property Option in Term Property Webpart*

16. Create a few more term sets named **Band**, **Horizontal Tag**, **Relevant Experience**, **Skill**, **Total Experience**, **Relevant Experience** under group **Employee**.

Creating a term

Under each term set we can create a group of terms. Let's perform the following steps to create the term:

1. Right-click or expand the term set **Business Unit**.

2. Click on **Create Term** from the dropdown option.

3. Enter the name as **BFSI** as seen in the following screenshot:

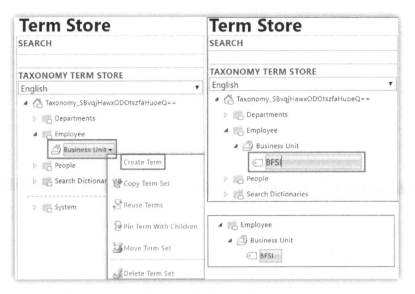

Figure 9.11: Create Term

4. Similarly create few more terms like **ECM, MARKETING, SALES, LEGAL** under term set **Business Unit**.

5. Similarly create terms **MAS, DIGITAL, INSURANCE, FINANCE** under term set **Horizontal Tag**.

6. Similarly create terms **SHAREPOINT, OFFICE 365, WINDOWS, DATABSE, STORAGE, NETWORKING, AZURE** under term set **Skill**.

7. Similarly create terms **0-3, 3-6, 6-9, 9-12**, under term set **Relevant Experience**.

8. Similarly create terms **0-3, 3-6, 6-9, 9-12** under term set **Total Experience**.

9. Similarly create terms **A, B, C, D** under term set **Band**. Under term, **A** creates more terms **A1, A2, A3**. Similarly create terms further under each term **B, C, D** as seen in the following screenshot:

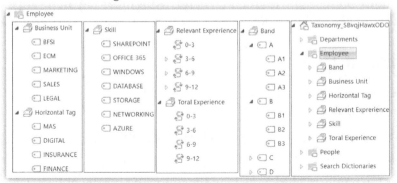

Figure 9.12: All Term Set and Terms Created

10. Click on one term (**Database**) you will find 2 tabs **GENERAL** and **CUSTOM PROPERTIES**. Under the tab, **GENERAL** select the option **Available for Tagging** which will make this term available for tagging.

11. You will find the field **Default Label** as the term name (**DATABASE**). You can give another fort label under the field **Other Labels (DB)** as seen in the below screenshot:

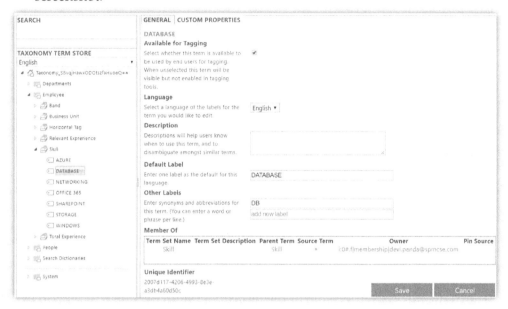

Figure 9.13: *Term Properties General Tab*

Reuse terms

Since we are putting the same terms for both **Relevant Experience** and **Total Experience** we can reuse terms of another term set. If we want to use the terms present under **Relevant Experience** in **Total Experience** then we can follow the steps below:

1. Right-click on the term set **Total Experience**, select term **Reuse Terms**.

2. You will get a dialog window **Term Reuse**, navigate to the term set **Relevant Experience** present under the group **Employee**.

3. Select one term and click **OK**. The term will be added to the term set **Total Experience**. Similarly, we need to select each term one by one and click on **OK** to add multiple terms as per the requirement as seen in the following screenshot:

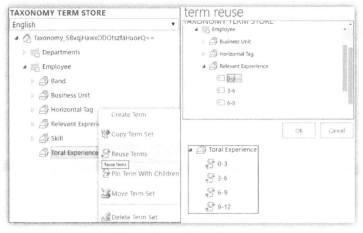

Figure 9.14: Reuse Terms

Copy term set

Another option we can use is the **Copy Term Set** that is used to create another term set. Let's perform the following steps to copy the term set:

1. Right-click on the term set **Band**.

2. Click on **Copy Term Set**.

3. You will get a message **Copying this term set will make a new term set that will include reused version of the terms. The source terms will remain in the original term set. To proceed select OK otherwise select Cancel**. Click on **OK**.

4. New term set **Copy of Band** will be created including terms present in the term set as seen in the following screenshot:

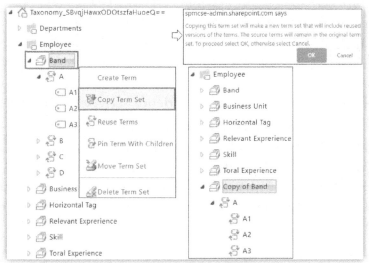

Figure 9.15: Copy Term Set

5. Similarly, if you want to copy the terms, then right-click on one term **A** under term set **Band**.

6. Select the option **Copy Term with Children** will create another term **Copy of A** including all child terms present under term **A** as seen in the following screenshot:

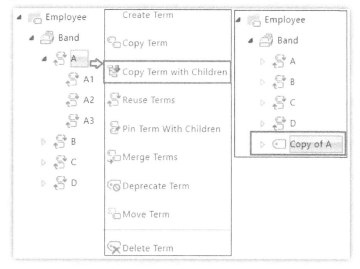

Figure 9.16: *Copy Term Set with Children*

Merge terms

We can merge 2 terms using this option. Let's perform the following steps to merge terms and see how it works:

1. Right-click on term **Copy of A**.
2. Select the option **Merge Terms**.
3. You will get another dialog window **select term to merge into (D)** where you need to select the term to which terms will be merged.
4. After selection of term, you see the terms are merged with **D**. Under the term **D**, you see child terms both **A** and **D** as seen in the following screenshot:

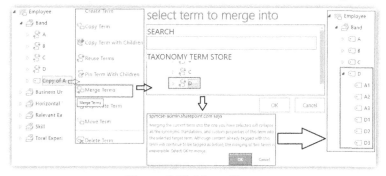

Figure 9.17: *Merge Terms*

Move term set

We can move the term set from one group to another group using this option. Let's perform the following steps to move the term set:

1. Right-click on term set **Copy of Band**.

2. Select **Move Term Set**.

3. You will get another dialog box *term set move*, where you need to select the location to which term set will move.

4. Select a different group **Departments** as the location to move and click on **OK**.

5. You see the term set is moved to the new group **Departments** including all terms present in the term set as seen in the following screenshot:

Figure 9.18: Move Term Set

Creating a metadata column

We created a group, term set, and terms. Now we will see how these are usable on-site. We can use these in the library or list by creating a metadata column. There are two conditions **Submission Policy Closed** and **Submission Policy Open**. Few settings are enabled by making the **Submission Policy Open**. Let's create a metadata column and will see in both cases the difference.

Metadata column with submission policy closed

First, we need to verify the settings selected for the **Submission Policy**. Navigate to **Term Store** and check **Submission Policy** for term set **Business Unit** which is selected **Closed** by default as seen in the following screenshot:

Figure 9.19: Submission Policy Settings

Let's create a metadata column in a list. Let's perform the following steps to create metadata column with submission policy closed:

1. Navigate to **List Settings** of any list.

2. Click on **Create column** (https://<site url>/_layouts/15/fldNew. aspx? List=**) present under the option **Columns** as seen in the following screenshot:

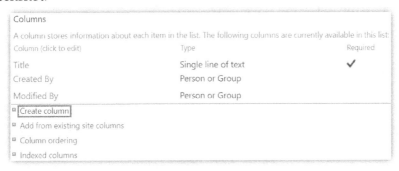

Figure 9.20: Create Metadata Column

3. Enter **Name** of the column as BU India and choose column type as **Managed Metadata** as seen in the following screenshot:

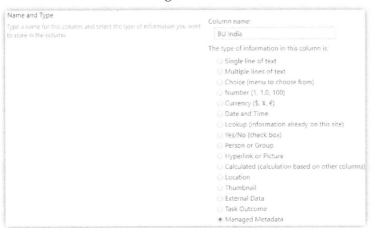

Figure 9.21: Managed Metadata Field Type

4. Keep options under **Additional Column Settings** as default as seen in the following screenshot:

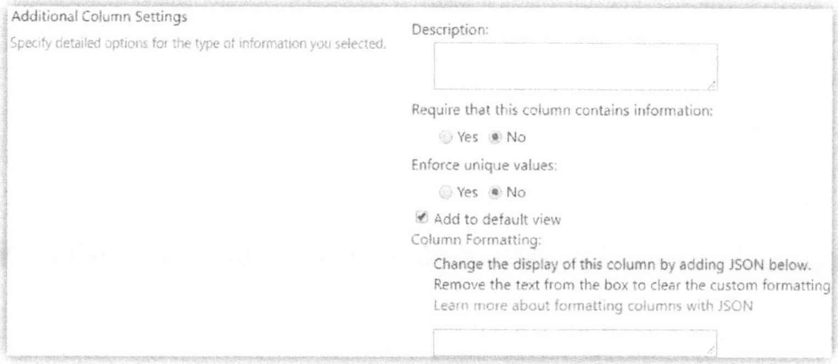

Figure 9.22: Additional Column Settings

5. Keep the options **Multiple Value Field** and **Display Format** selected as default as seen in the following screenshot:

Figure 9.23: Display Format

6. Next, select the option **Use a managed term set** under the option **Term Set Settings**.

7. Expand the group **Employee** and select the term set **Business Unit** as seen in the following screenshot:

Figure 9.24: Term Set Settings

8. Next option **Allow 'Fill-in' choice** is selected **No** as default and notice the option is disabled. Later I will tell you the reason for this. Finally, click on **OK** as seen in the following screenshot:

Figure 9.25: Allow Fill-in Choice

9. A metadata column is created. Now create a list item in which the metadata column is created. Fill the details in the list. Notice the filed **Enterprise Keywords** where you entered a keyword (BU).

10. In the metadata column, if you type the term and present in the global term set will appear as suggestions. Else click on the *icon* tag as seen in the following screenshot:

Figure 9.26: Tag from Auto Display as Drop Down Suggested

11. Another dialog box will open. Select the term **BFSI**, click on **Select** and finally click on **OK** to apply the selection as seen in the following screenshot:

Figure 9.27: Tagging

12. The **Enterprise Keywords**, we entered, is stored under **Keywords** in taxonomy term store as seen in the following screenshot:

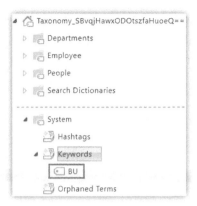

Figure 9.28: Enterprise Keywords

Metadata column with submission policy open

Now let's perform the following steps to create metadata column with submission policy open and will the difference:

1. Navigate to **Term Store** and check the **Submission Policy** for the term set **Business Unit** which is selected **Closed** by default. Change to **Open** and click on **Save** as seen in the following screenshot:

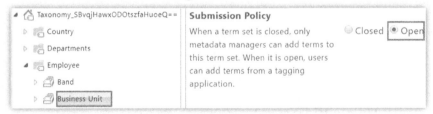

Figure 9.29: Submission Policy Opened

2. If submission policy is open, then during creating metadata column you will find the option **Allow 'Fill-in' choices** as **Yes** as seen in the following screenshot:

Figure 9.30: Allow Fill-in Choice Enabled

3. When you will select the option **Use a managed term set** after following *steps 1* to *step 10* as described in the above section **Metadata Column with Submission Policy Closed**, you will notice an option **Add New Item** enabled. This option **Add New Item** enables to create term from here as seen in the following screenshot:

Select : BU India
New items are added under the currently selected item.
Add New Item
Business Unit
BFSI
ECM
LEGAL
MARKETING
SALES
Select >>
BFSI
OK
Cancel

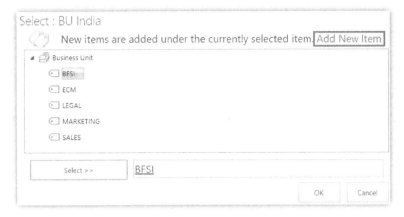

***Figure 9.31:** Add New Item Enabled*

Creating local term set

We can create terms from site collection as well that are usable for all sites present under that site collection for which we are calling it as local term set. Let's perform the following steps to create a local term set:

1. Follow the same *step 1* to *step 5* as described in sections above the *Metadata column with submission policy closed* for metadata column creation.
2. Next step to that, select the option to **Customize your term set** under the option **Term Set Settings**. The moment you select the option **Customize your term set**, a term set with the same name (`BU India`) as of metadata column name will be created.
3. We can create terms from there following the same procedure discussed before as seen in the following screenshot:

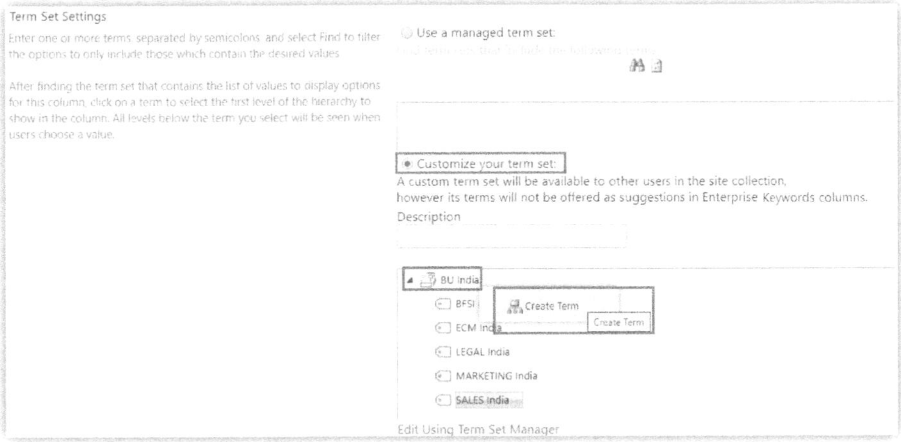

Term Set Settings
Enter one or more terms separated by semicolons and select Find to filter the options to only include those which contain the desired values.
After finding the term set that contains the list of values to display options for this column, click on a term to select the first level of the hierarchy to show in the column. All levels below the term you select will be seen when users choose a value.
Use a managed term set:
Customize your term set:
A custom term set will be available to other users in the site collection, however its terms will not be offered as suggestions in Enterprise Keywords columns.
Description
BU India
BFSI
Create Term
Create Term
ECM India
LEGAL India
MARKETING India
SALES India
Edit Using Term Set Manager

***Figure 9.32:** Create Local Terms*

4. When we are creating terms under this **Customize your term set**, these are called local terms sets because these are created, and its application limited within site collection and below the hierarchy.

5. If you want to see the terms created, then navigate to **Site Settings** (`<_ layouts/15/settings.aspx>`).

6. Click on **Term store management** (`https://<site url>/_layouts/15/ termstoremanager.aspx`) present under **Site Administration** as seen in the following screenshot:

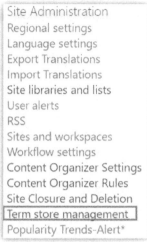

Figure 9.33: Term Store Management

7. You will notice a new group created with site collection name **Site Collection - spmcse.sharepoint.com-sites-BPB-ModernTeamSite** as seen in the below screenshot:

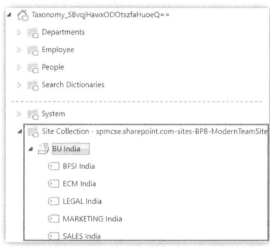

Figure 9.34: Local Term Sets Created Under Site Collection

8. Similarly, if any local term set created under subsite present under site collection then the term set will be available under this site collection group and applicable for the site collection and below the hierarchy, as seen in the following screenshot:

Figure 9.35: Local Term Sets Created Under Subsite

Creating a global term set from the site collection

We created a term set navigating from **SharePoint Admin Center** ❘ **More Features** ❘ **Term Store** (https://<sharepoint admin center url>/_layouts/15/ TermStoreManager.aspx) directly which we call as global term set and created terms during metadata column creation which we call as local term set. Users having permission can create a global term set from site collection as well following the steps below. Let's perform the following steps to create a global term set from site collection:

1. Navigate to **Site Settings** (<_layouts/15/settings.aspx>).

2. Click on **Term store management** (https://<site url>/_layouts/15/term storemanager.aspx) present under **Site Administration** as seen in the following screenshot:

Figure 9.36: Term Store Management

3. User will be redirected to the **Term Store Manager** page to create **Term Set**, **Term** following the same procedure as discussed before as seen in the following screenshot:

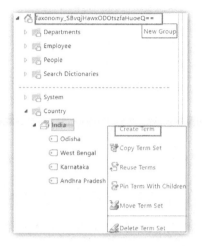

Figure 9.37: Global Terms Created

Metadata navigation settings

We can use the metadata term set, terms for navigation, and filtering. We will see the application of these metadata in navigation. We will activate one feature, create site content type, create site metadata column, and add columns to the content type. We will configure to allow content type in the library, add existing columns to the library, and configure metadata navigation settings from library settings.

Activate feature first

We need to activate one site feature to make available the option **Metadata Navigation Settings** under library settings otherwise you will find this setting missing in library settings. Let's perform the following steps to activate the site feature:

1. Navigate to **Site Settings** (<_layouts/15/settings.aspx>) and click on **Manage site features** (<_layouts/15/ManageFeatures.aspx>) present under **Site Actions**:

Figure 9.38: Manage Site Features

2. Identify the feature **Metadata Navigation and Filtering** and activate the feature:

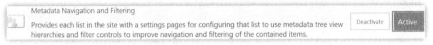

Figure 9.39: Activate Site Feature

Create metadata site columns

We already created a metadata column in the section *Metadata column with the submission policy closed*. Follow *step 3* to *step 8* for metadata column creation once navigated to **Site Settings** (`<_layouts/15/settings.aspx>`) and click on **Site Columns** present under **Web Designer Galleries**.

We are creating site columns and it's the best practice to create site columns to make it reusable. Create metadata column with names **Band**, **Business Unit**, **Horizontal Tag**, **Relevant Experience**, **Skill**, **Total Experience**.

Create a site content type

Since we are planning to categorize and filter based multiple content types, we will create multiple content types. Navigate to **Site Settings** (`<_layouts/15/settings.aspx>`) and click on **Site content types** (`https://<site url>/_layouts/15/mngctype.aspx`) present under **Web Designer Galleries**:

Figure 9.40: Site Content Types

We already discussed how to create content type before, follow the same step. Create site content type with names **Business Unit**, **Horizontal Tag**, **Skill**, **Total Experience**, **Relevant Experience** as seen in the following screenshot:

Figure 9.41: New Content Type

Add columns to content type

Once the content type is created, then we need to add the site column to content type so that when we add that content type in the library those columns will also be added to the library. Let's perform the following steps to add columns to content-type:

1. Open site content type **Business Unit**, click on **Add from existing site columns** present under content type settings as seen in the following screenshot:

Figure 9.42: Add from Existing Site Columns

2. Select the site column **Business Unit, Horizontal Tag, Skill, Total Experience, Relevant Experience, Band** from next window, click on **Add** and click on **OK** finally to apply the changes.

3. Metadata site columns **Business Unit, Horizontal Tag, Skill, Total Experience, Relevant Experience, Band** are added to content type **Business Unit** as seen in the screenshot below:

Figure 9.43: Metadata Columns Added

4. Click on **Manage publishing for this content type,** you see option **Publish** is selected. Click on **OK** to publish the content type as seen in the screenshot below:

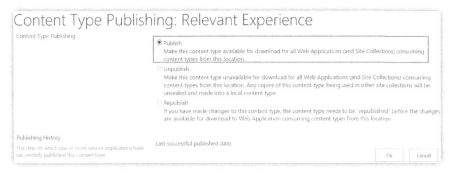

Figure 9.44: Publish Content Type

5. Similarly, add metadata site column **Band** to content type **Band**, add metadata site column **Horizontal Tag** to content type **Horizontal Tag**, add metadata site column **Skill** to content type **Skill**, add metadata site column **Relevant Experience** to content type **Relevant Experience**, add metadata site column **Total Experience** to content type **Total Experience** and publish those content types:

Allow management of content types in the library

First, we need to allow the management of content types in the library. Let's perform the following steps to allow content type in the library:

1. Open one document library **Documents**, navigate to **Library Settings**.
2. Click on **Advanced Settings** present under the **General Settings** category.
3. Select the checkbox **Allow management of content types** as **Yes** and click on **OK**.

Add site content types to the library

The next step is to add content types to the library. Let's perform the following steps to add site content type in the library:

1. Under library settings (`https://<site url>/_layouts/15/listedit.aspx?List=**`) click on the option **Add from existing site content types** (`https://<site url>/_layouts/15/AddContentTypeToList.aspx?List=**`) present under category **Content Types**.
2. Select the site content types **Business Unit**, **Horizontal Tag**, **Relevant Experience**, **Skill**, **Total Experience** that we created from another window, and apply changes by clicking **OK**.

3. All content types will be added and under columns and you will find all metadata columns that are present in the content types are available in library columns.

Configure metadata navigation settings

Next, we need to configure the actual settings present in the library for metadata navigation. Let's perform the following steps to configure metadata navigation settings:

1. Navigate to **Library Settings** (`https://<site url>/_layouts/15/listedit.aspx?List=**`).

2. Click on **Metadata Navigation Settings** (`https://<site url>/_layouts/15/MetaNavSettings.aspx?List={**}`) present under the category **General Settings** as seen in the screenshot below:

Figure 9.45: Metadata Navigation Settings

3. From **Available Hierarchy Fields** select **Content Type, Business Unit, Skill, Band, Horizontal Tag, Relevant Experience, Total Experience** and click on **Add** as seen in the screenshot below:

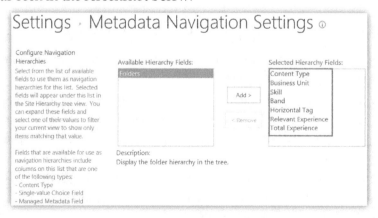

Figure 9.46: Selected Hierarchy Fields

4. From **Available Key Filter Fields** select **Content Type, Business Unit, Skill, Band, Horizontal Tag, Relevant Experience, Total Experience,** and click on **Add**. Finally, click on **OK** to apply changes as seen in the screenshot below:

Figure 9.47: *Selected Key Filter Fields*

Testing metadata navigation settings

We created the metadata navigation and filtering. Let's perform the following steps to see how metadata filtering works:

1. Now upload documents in the library.

2. Select one item and click on **Details Pane**. Click on **Edit All** properties as seen in the screenshot below:

Figure 9.48: *Edit All Propertied From Details Pane*

3. All document properties will open which you need to fill up. You will see all the metadata columns that we created are present and can be selected as seen in the screenshot below. Upload more documents and select terms for all fields present in the library:

Figure 9.49: Metadata Properties of Item

4. Now open the document library and click on **Filter Pane** from the command bar. You will see all metadata properties are available as seen in the screenshot below:

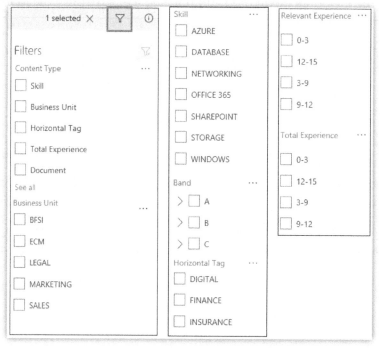

Figure 9.50: Metadata Properties Filtering

5. Click on any of the metadata properties to filter files based on **Content Type, Business Unit, Skill, Band, Horizontal Tag, Relevant Experience, Total Experience** as seen in the screenshot below:

Figure 9.51: Filter Items Based on Content Types

6. We can filter by selecting multiple metadata properties like select content type as well as skill to check the items matching that criteria.

7. If you switch the library to classic mode, you see navigation like this as shown in the screenshot below. You can filter based on any properties by selecting them:

Figure 9.52: Classic Experience Metadata Navigation Filtering

Metadata navigation

We can use the term set as navigation which widely used as global navigation in SharePoint sites. Let's perform the following steps to see how metadata navigation works.

Enable term set for site navigation

First, we need to enable one setting from the term store. Let's perform the below steps to enable:

1. Navigate to the term set **Skill** term store.

2. Click on the tab **INTENDED USE**.

3. Select the checkbox present under the option **Use this Term Set for Site Navigation** and click on **Save** to apply changes as shown in the screenshot below:

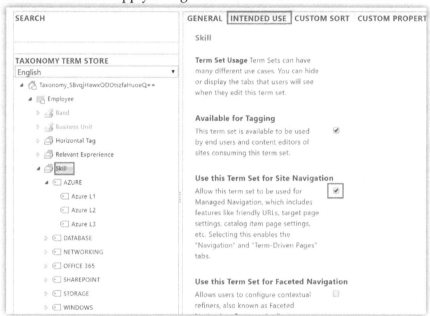

Figure 9.53: Enable Term Set For Site Navigation

Set term driven pages

The next step is to configure **Term Driven** pages. Let's perform below steps to configure term driven pages for all terms and child terms:

1. Once settings **Use this Term Set for Site Navigation** is enabled as discussed above, you will find another tab **TERM DRIVEN PAGE** is enabled for the term set **Skill**.

2. Click on the tab **TERM DRIVEN PAGE** and select the checkbox **Change target page for terms in this term set**.

3. Enter **Site Page URL** (/sites/BPB-ModernTeamSite/Pages/Skill.aspx) created under the library **Pages** and click **Save** as show in screenshot below:

Figure 9.54: Term Driven Pages

4. Click on the term **AZURE** and click on the **NAVIGATION** tab.

5. Select option **Navigation Node Type** as **Term-Driven Page with Friendly URL**.

6. You see the filed **Navigation Node Title** is showing with same name **AZURE** as off term under term set **Skill** as shown in the screenshot below:

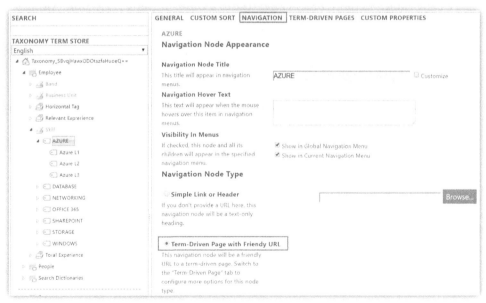

Figure 9.55: Term Driven Pages with Friendly URL

7. Click on the tab **TERM-DRIVEN PAGES**.

8. Click on the checkbox **Change target page for this term**. Enter **Site Page URL** (/sites/BPB-ModernTeamSite/Pages/Azure.aspx) created under the site-library **Pages**.

9. Under option **Configure Friendly URL for this term** you will find the friendly URL /azure and click on **Save** as shown in the screenshot below. When you click on term **AZURE** from navigation you will be redirected to the URL https://spmcse.sharepoint.com/sites/BPB-ModernTeamSite/azure.

Figure 9.56: Target Page Settings

10. Click on the child term **Azure L1** present under the term **Azure**.

11. Click on the checkbox **Change target page for this term**. Enter **Site Page URL** (/sites/BPB-ModernTeamSite/Pages/AzureL1.aspx) created under the site-library **Pages**.

12. Under option **Configure Friendly URL for this term** you will find the friendly URL /azure/azure-l1 as shown in the screenshot below. When you click on term **Axure L1** from navigation you will be redirected to the URL https://spmcse.sharepoint.com/sites/BPB-ModernTeamSite/azure/azure-l1:

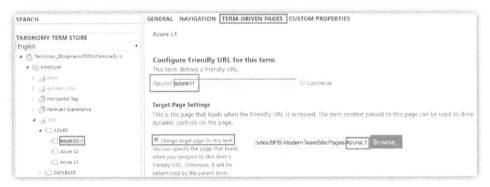

Figure 9.57: Target Driven Page for Terms

13. Similarly configure setting **Change target page for this term** for all other terms and child terms.

Configure site navigation settings

Next will discuss configure navigation settings. Let's perform the following steps to configure site navigation settings:

1. Navigate to **Site Settings** (`<_layouts/15/settings.aspx>`).

2. Click on **Navigation** (`https://<site url>/_layouts/15/ AreaNavigationSettings.aspx`) present under the category **Look and Feel**.

3. From **Global Navigation**, select the option **Managed Navigation: The navigation items will be represented using a Managed Metadata term set** as shown in the screenshot below:

Figure 9.58: Global Navigation

4. Keep the option **Current Navigation** as default for the moment as shown in the screenshot below:

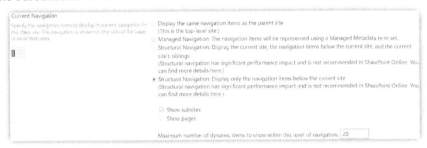

Figure 9.59: Current Navigation

5. From the option **Managed Navigation: Term Set**, select one term set **Skill** and click **OK** to apply changes as shown in the screenshot below:

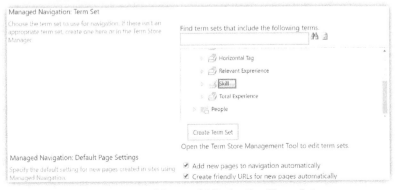

Figure 9.60: Managed Navigation Term Set

6. Open site home page, you see metadata navigation is created based on the terms as shown in the screenshot below. Click on any term will redirect to respective configured term driven page:

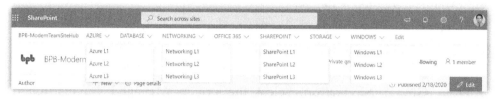

Figure 9.61: Metadata Navigation

7. Now change the option for **Current Navigation** from default to **Managed Navigation: The navigation items will be represented using a Managed Metadata term set** and click **OK** as shown in the screenshot below:

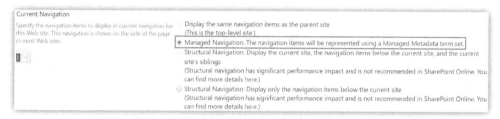

Figure 9.62: Current Navigation with Metadata Option Selected

8. Now you will notice under left navigation metadata navigation is created as shown in the screenshot below:

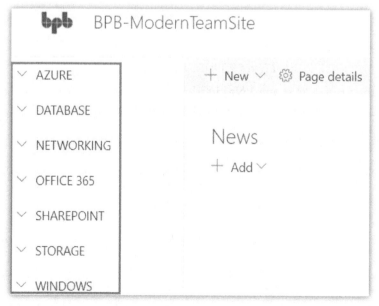

Figure 9.63: Left Navigation Using Metadata

Conclusion

In this chapter we discussed metadata all about, term store. How to create groups, term sets, terms from **Term Store** present at SharePoint admin center as well as from site collection. Understood global term sets and local term sets. Created metadata column and understood and how it's reusable and applicable in metadata navigation filtering. Created metadata navigation and discussed its application. Next in *Chapter 10: SharePoint Server Publishing Infrastructure Feature* will discuss all publishing features in SharePoint.

Points to remember

- Site collection feature *SharePoint Server Publishing Infracture* and site feature *SharePoint Server Publishing* are enabled in site collection which we will discuss in detail in the next chapter.

- Administrators, contributors, metadata managers can add term set, terms.

- Site feature *Metadata Navigation and Filtering* needs to be activated to use navigations based on terms and term set. This feature will make available the option **Metadata Navigation Settings** under the document library.

- Best practice to create site columns of type metadata and site content types to be added to these site columns.

- New feature *Tree view* related to modern managed metadata experience is rolling out, between May to June, for a list or library that will give a tree view experience for metadata during metadata tagging and filtering.

- In this chapter wherever its mentioned like this format `_layouts/15/****.aspx`, means this section is added after the site URL `http:// <site url> /_layouts/15/****.aspx`.

- Regular changes are applied in Office 365 and SharePoint Online by which there may be changes happening in a template or some other features.

CHAPTER 10
SharePoint Server Publishing Infrastructure Feature

In the previous chapter, we discussed all the managed metadata in SharePoint Online. In this chapter, we will discuss the publishing feature. The publishing feature is a unique feature that will make a lot of changes in the site. Mostly we create team sites, communication sites. The type of contents available by default, settings available for managing site will change a lot, which will provide additional options to apply custom branding, themes, metadata navigations on your site, at the same time will make it difficult to manage by an administrator that needs complete understanding. In this chapter, we will discuss the changes happening on the site due to the activation of the publishing feature.

Structure

In this chapter, we will discuss the following topics:

- Activating Features
- Changes in Site Contents
- Changes in Content Type
- Changes in Site Column
- Changes in Look and Feel
- Changes in Page Layouts

- Change in permission levels
- Changes in Webparts

Objective

During the end of the chapter, you will get a clear understanding of the following topics:

- How to activate the features
- What are the changes happening in the site after activating the feature

Activate Feature First

There is a feature **SharePoint Server Publishing Infrastructure**, which needs to be activated first in the site if we want to get the benefits of publishing features on the team site. Let's perform the following steps to activate the feature.

1. Navigate to **Site Settings** (<_layouts/15/settings.aspx>) page from site (**Modern Team Site**).

2. Click on **Site collection features** (<_layouts/15/ManageFeatures. aspx?Scope =Site>) present under **Site Collection Administration**, as seen in the following screenshot:

Figure 10.1: Click on Site collection features

3. If you scroll down, identify the feature **SharePoint Server Publishing Infrastructure**. You will find a button **Activate** at the right, as seen in the following screenshot. Click on that button. It will take a few minutes to activate:

Figure 10.2: Activate SharePoint Server Publishing Infrastructure site collection feature

4. Similarly, click on **Manage site features** (<_layouts/15/ManageFeatures. aspx>) present under **Site Actions** as seen in the following screenshot:

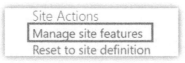

Figure 10.3: Manage site features

5. Identify the feature **SharePoint Server Publishing** and click on **Active**, as seen in the following screenshot. The feature will be activated:

SharePoint Server Publishing
Create a Web page library as well as supporting libraries to create and publish pages based on page layouts.   Deactivate Active

Figure 10.4: Activate SharePoint Server Publishing site feature

Changes in Site Contents

After features activated, you will notice a few changes in Site Contents. Let's discuss the changes below:

1. Before features activated, contents available under **Site Contents** are **Documents**, **Form Templates**, **Site Assets**, **Style Library**, **Site Pages**.

2. After site collection publishing feature (**SharePoint Server Publishing Infrastructure**) activated, additional contents like **Reusable Content** list, **Site Collection Documents** library, **Site Collection Images** library, **Workflow Tasks** added under **Site Contents**.

3. After activating publishing feature under site feature (**SharePoint Server Publishing**) additional contents like **Pages** library, **Images** library added under **Site Contents** as seen in the following screenshot:

Figure 10.5: Added contents after publishing feature activated

Changes in Content Type

There will be changes in **Content Types**. Let's discuss the changes below:

1. Navigate to **Site Contents**, identify the library **Pages**, and click on it.

2. Open **Library Settings** for **Page** library.

3. You will see under **Content Types,** four pages like **Page, Article Page, Welcome Page, Error Page** added, as seen in the following screenshot:

Figure 10.6: Changes in Content Types

4. Navigate to **Site Settings** (`<_layouts/15/settings.aspx>`).

5. Click on **Site content types** (`https://<site url>/_layouts/15/mngctype.aspx`) present under **Web Designer Galleries** as seen in the following screenshot:

Figure 10.7: Site content types under Web Designer Galleries

6. If you scroll down, you will notice additional content types **Article Page, Catalog-Item Reuse, Enterprise Wiki Page, Error Page, Project Page, Redirect Page, Welcome Page** under **Page Layout Content Types**.

7. **ASP NET Master Page, Html Master Page, Html Page Layout, Page, Page Layout** under **Publishing Content Types** as seen in the following screenshot:

Page Layout Content Types		
Article Page	Page	BPB-ModernTeamSite
Catalog-Item Reuse	Page	BPB-ModernTeamSite
Enterprise Wiki Page	Page	BPB-ModernTeamSite
Error Page	Page	BPB-ModernTeamSite
Project Page	Enterprise Wiki Page	BPB-ModernTeamSite
Redirect Page	Page	BPB-ModernTeamSite
Welcome Page	Page	BPB-ModernTeamSite
Publishing Content Types		
ASP NET Master Page	System Master Page	BPB-ModernTeamSite
Html Master Page	ASP NET Master Page	BPB-ModernTeamSite
Html Page Layout	Page Layout	BPB-ModernTeamSite
Page	System Page	BPB-ModernTeamSite
Page Layout	System Page Layout	BPB-ModernTeamSite

Figure 10.8: Additional content types

Changes in Site Column

There will be changes in **Columns**. Let's discuss about the changes below:

1. Navigate to **Site Contents** (`https://<site url>/_layouts/15/viewlsts.aspx`), identify the library **Pages** (`https://<site  url>/Pages/Forms/AllItems. aspx`) and click on it.

2. Open **Library Settings** for **Page** library.

3. You will see under **Columns** like **Article Date**, **Byline**, **Comments**, **Contact**, **Contact E-Mail Address**, **Contact Name**, **Contact Picture**, **Created**, **Hide physical URLs from search**, **Image Caption**, **Number of Ratings**, **Page Content**, **Page Image**, **Rating (0-5)**, **Rollup Image**, **Summary Links**, **Summary Links 2**, **Target Audiences**, **Title**, **Wiki Categories** added as seen in the following screenshot:

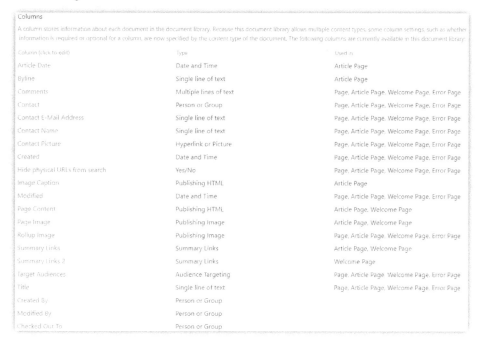

Columns

A column stores information about each document in the document library. Because this document library allows multiple content types, some column settings, such as whether information is required or optional for a column, are now specified by the content type of the document. The following columns are currently available in this document library:

Column (click to edit)	Type	Used in
Article Date	Date and Time	Article Page
Byline	Single line of text	Article Page
Comments	Multiple lines of text	Page, Article Page, Welcome Page, Error Page
Contact	Person or Group	Page, Article Page, Welcome Page, Error Page
Contact E-Mail Address	Single line of text	Page, Article Page, Welcome Page, Error Page
Contact Name	Single line of text	Page, Article Page, Welcome Page, Error Page
Contact Picture	Hyperlink or Picture	Page, Article Page, Welcome Page, Error Page
Created	Date and Time	Page, Article Page, Welcome Page, Error Page
Hide physical URLs from search	Yes/No	Page, Article Page, Welcome Page, Error Page
Image Caption	Publishing HTML	Article Page
Modified	Date and Time	Page, Article Page, Welcome Page, Error Page
Page Content	Publishing HTML	Article Page, Welcome Page
Page Image	Publishing Image	Article Page, Welcome Page
Rollup Image	Publishing Image	Page, Article Page, Welcome Page, Error Page
Summary Links	Summary Links	Article Page, Welcome Page
Summary Links 2	Summary Links	Welcome Page
Target Audiences	Audience Targeting	Page, Article Page, Welcome Page, Error Page
Title	Single line of text	Page, Article Page, Welcome Page, Error Page
Created By	Person or Group	
Modified By	Person or Group	
Checked Out To	Person or Group	

Figure 10.9: Changes in Columns

Changes in Look and Feel

You will notice additional options under site settings **Look and Feel**, after feature activation, like **Design Manager** (`https://<site  url>/_layouts  /15/Design WelcomePage.aspx`), **Master page** (`<_layouts/15/ChangeSiteMasterPage. aspx>`), **Page layouts and site templates** (`<_layouts/15/AreaTemplateSettings.`

aspx>), **Navigation** (<_layouts/15/AreaNavigationSettings.aspx>), **Import Design Package** (<_layouts/15/DesignPackageInstall.aspx>), **Welcome Page** (<_layouts/15/AreaWelcomePage.aspx>), **Device Channels** (https://<site url >/DeviceChannels/AllItems.aspx), **Image Renditions** (<_layouts/15/Image RenditionSettings.aspx>) as seen in the following screenshot that reflects change in settings with no publishing feature activated, publishing feature under site collection feature activated and publishing feature under site feature activated respectively:

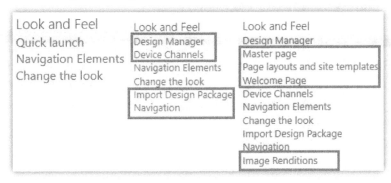

Figure 10.10: Changes in Look and Feel

Click on **Master page** (<_layouts/15/ChangeSiteMasterPage.aspx>) from **Look and Feel**. You will be redirected to the **Site Master Page Settings** page and will see an option **Inherit the theme from the parent of this site** under category **Theme**, which got enabled due to the publishing feature. Select the checkbox to enable the inheriting theme of the site from a higher-level site that we call as parent site as seen in the following screenshot:

Figure 10.11: Changes in Master Page under option Theme

Changes in Page Layouts

After publishing feature activated, there are few page layouts created to make the intranet site proper branding and structured. Let's see the step by step process to create a site page using layout created after the publishing feature activated:

1. Navigate to **Site Contents** (`<_layouts/15/viewlsts.aspx>`), identify the library **Pages** (`<Forms/AllItems.aspx>`) and click on it.

2. Click on **New** from command bar; you will content types like **Page**, **Article Page**, **Welcome Page**, **Error Page** will be available.

3. Click on the page **Article Page** as seen in the following screenshot:

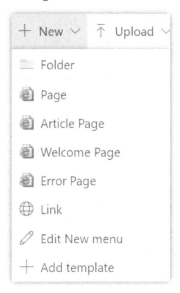

Figure 10.12: *New Content Types Added*

4. We will get the option to create a page. Enter the name of the page in the field **Title** (`ImageOnleftpage`) and description under field **Description**.

5. Under option **Page Layout** you will multiple layouts like **(Article Page) Body only, (Article Page) Image on left, (Article Page) Image on right, (Article Page) Summary links, (Catalog-Item Reuse) Blank Catalog Item, (Catalog-Item Reuse) Catalog Item Image in Left, (Enterprise Wiki Page) Basic Page, (Error Page) Error, (Project Page) Basic Project Page, (Redirect Page) Redirect, (Welcome Page) Blank Web Part Page, (Welcome Page) Splash, (Welcome Page) Summary links**.

6. Select the layout **(Article Page) Image on left** and click on **Create** as seen in the following screenshot:

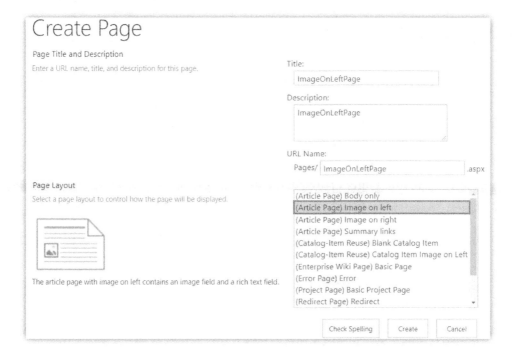

Figure 10.13: Create Page

7. You will get redirected to page layout option where you can find zones to enter contact details like **Title**, **Page Image**, **Article Date**, **Byline**, **Image Caption**, **Page Content**. You will see the message at the top of this page is **Checked out to you. Only you can see the recent changes** as seen in the following screenshot:

Figure 10.14: Insert Picture in Page

8. Click on the option. **Click here to insert a picture from SharePoint** to insert page image. You will get a dialog box to choose properties related to the image.

9. Click on **Browse** option present side to **Selected Image** as seen in the following screenshot:

Figure 10.15: Insert image dialog box

10. Click on library **Images** from left navigation, select one image, and click on **Insert** as seen in the following screenshot:

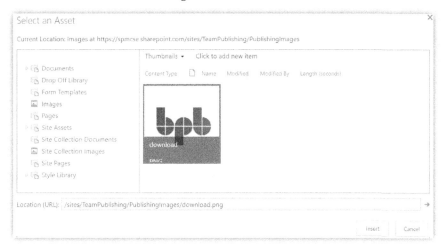

Figure 10.16: Select image from Images library

11. Click on **Browse** present side to **Hyperlink**, as shown in *Figure 10.15*.

12. Click on **Pages** from left navigation, select one page (**AboutUs**) and click on **Insert** as seen in the following screenshot:

Figure 10.17: Insert link

13. We can adjust the **Layout** and **Size** as shown in *Figure 10.15* and finally click on **OK**.

14. Enter other properties as well, like **Article Date**, **Byline**, **Image Caption**, **Page Content**.

15. Click on **Save** present in the ribbon. Still, we will see the message at the top of this page is **Checked out to you. Only you can see the recent changes** as seen in the following screenshot:

Figure 10.18: Add Page Content, Caption, Article Date, Byline

16. Click on the tab **Publish**, click on **Publish** from the drop-down as seen in the following screenshot:

Figure 10.19: Publish page

17. You will get a dialog box to enter a comment. Enter your comment and click on **Continue** option as seen in the following screenshot:

Figure 10.20: Enter comments

18. The page will be published, and changes will be available for all users as seen in the following screenshot:

Figure 10.21: Published page

Change in permission levels

There will be few changes in the SharePoint permission level once the publishing feature is activated. Navigate to **Settings** ⚙ present at the top right corner of the site. From next option click on **Advanced permission settings**, you will see new groups like **Approvers**, **Designers**, **Hierarchy Managers**, **Restricted Readers** as seen in the following screenshot:

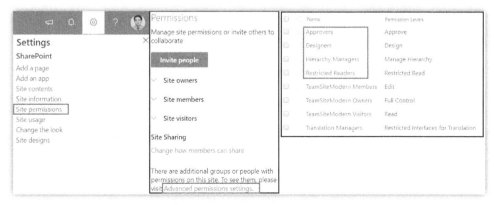

Figure 10.22: Changes in permission level

Changes in Webparts

There will be a few webparts added. Webparts like **Content Query** Web Part, **Summary Links** Web Part, **Table of Contents** Web Part are the mostly used webparts created under category **Content Rollup**.

If you add webpart **Table Of Contents**; you will see the same links present under left navigational elements as seen in the following screenshot:

Figure 10.23: Table Of Contents Web part

If you add webpart **Summary Links** and enter images, links, descriptions will look like as shown in the figure below. Left side image, description at the right side of that image with the link at the top of the description as seen in the following screenshot:

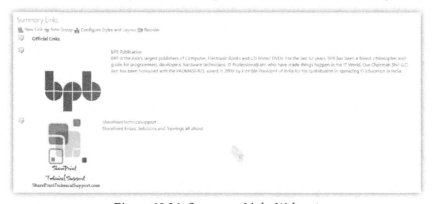

Figure 10.24: Summary Links Webpart

Change in Site Settings options

If you notice site settings (<_layouts/15/settings.aspx >) and compare the options, you see there will be a change in options available under site settings with no publishing feature activated, publishing feature under site collection feature activated and publishing feature under site feature activated respectively as described below steps:

1. Under site settings option **Web Designer Galleries**, you will notice an additional option **Master pages and page layouts** (https://<site url>/_catalogs/masterpage/Forms/AllItems.aspx):

Web Designer Galleries | Web Designer Galleries | Web Designer Galleries
Site columns | Site columns | Site columns
Site content types | Site content types | Site content types
| | Master pages and page layouts

Figure 10.25: Change in Web Designer Galleries options

2. Under site settings option **Site Actions**, you will notice the option **Enable search configuration export** is not available:

Site Actions | Site Actions | Site Actions
Manage site features | Manage site features | Manage site features
Enable search configuration export | Enable search configuration export | Reset to site definition
Reset to site definition | Reset to site definition |

Figure 10.26: Change in Site Actions options

3. Under site settings option **Site Administration**; you will notice few options more available like **Translation Status** (https://<site url>/Translation%20Status/All%20Users.aspx), **Site output cache** (<_layouts/15/areacachesettings.aspx>), **Manage catalog connections** (<_layouts/15/ManageCatalogSources.aspx>), **Site variation settings** (<_layouts/15/VariationsSiteSettings.aspx?Source=**>):

Figure 10.27: Change in Site Administration options

4. Under site settings option **Site Collection Administration**; you will see few more options available like **Site collection navigation** (<_layouts/15/ SiteNavigationSettings.aspx>), **Content Type Policy Templates** (<_ layouts/15/Policylist.aspx>), **Variations Settings** (<_layouts/15/ VariationSettings.aspx>), **Variation labels** (<_layouts/15/ vsubwebs.aspx>), **Translatable Columns**, **Variation logs** (<_layouts/15/ VariationLogs.aspx>), **Suggested Content Browser Locations** (https://<site url>/PublishedLinks/AllItems.aspx), **Site collection output cache** (<_layouts/15/sitecachesettings.aspx>):

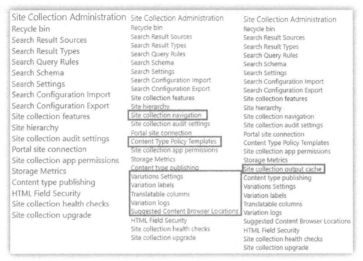

Figure 10.28: Change in Site Collection Administration

Conclusion

In this chapter, we discussed activating features related to publishing. Discussed the changes happening in site contents, content type, site column, changes in look and feel, page layouts, permission levels, webparts. Next, in *Chapter 11, Application of Business Connectivity Services* will discuss the external content type.

Points to remember

- Only focused on changes happening due to activating the publishing feature.
- In this chapter, wherever its mentioned like this format _layouts/15/****. aspx, means this section is added after the site URL http:// <site url> /_layouts/15/****.aspx.
- Regular changes are applied in Office 365 and SharePoint Online by which there may be changes happening in the template or some other features.

CHAPTER 11
Application of Business Connectivity Services

In the previous chapter, we discussed all publishing features in SharePoint Online. In this chapter, we will discuss business connectivity services. Business Connectivity Service allows users to connect to external data using web services. We can integrate external content databases (Azure SQL DB, On-premises SQL DB). We can use a SharePoint designer to create an external content database and use it in the SharePoint list. Let's discuss the business connectivity services configuration step by step.

Structure

In this chapter, we will discuss:

- Create an external content type
- Integrate external content type with SharePoint list

Objective

During the end of the chapter, you will get a clear understanding of:

- How to create an external content type
- How to integrate external content type with SharePoint

Create an external content type

We need to create an external content type using SharePoint Designer. Let's follow the step by step process to create an external content type.

1. Open SharePoint Designer. Click on **Open Site**.

2. Enter the site URL "`https://spmcse.sharepoint.com/sites/bpb-modern teamsite` where you want to create the external content-type:

Figure 11.1: Open SharePoint Site in Designer

3. The site will open and click on **External Content Type** from navigation or ribbon:

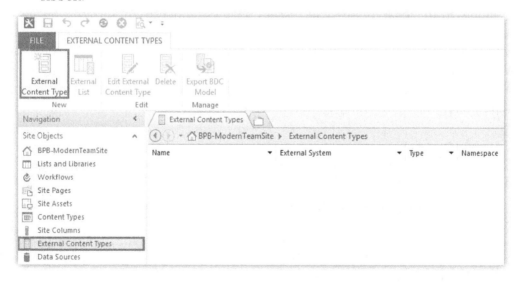

Figure 11.2: Click on External Content Type

4. Enter external content type **Name** (`EmployeeExternalContentType`) and click on **Click here to discover external sources and define operations**:

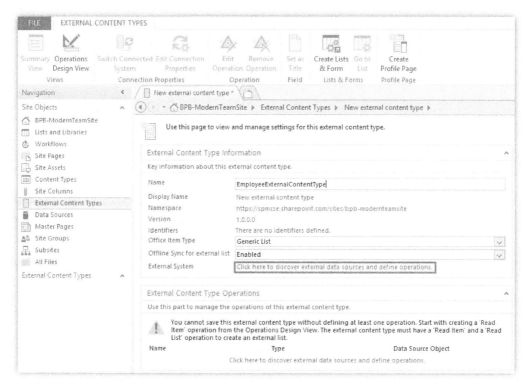

Figure 11.3: Enter Name of External Content Type

5. Click on **Add Connection**. One pop up will open to select **Data Source Type** from **External Data Source Type Selection**. Select the **SQL Server** as **Data Source Type**:

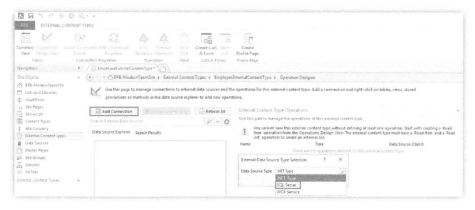

Figure 11.4: Add Connection to SQL Server

6. We need to enter the **SQL Server Connection** details. Enter the **Database Server** name as **Azure SQL Server Name** and **Database Name** created under the Azure SQL database (**EmployeeDB**).

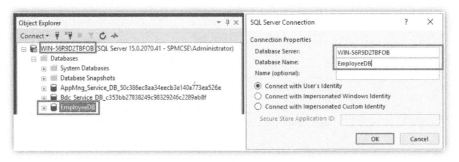

Figure 11.5: Enter Connection Properties Details

7. The connection will be established to the content database **EmployeeDB**. Expand the content database and select the table **Employee**. Right-click on the table **Employee** and click on the option **Create All Options**:

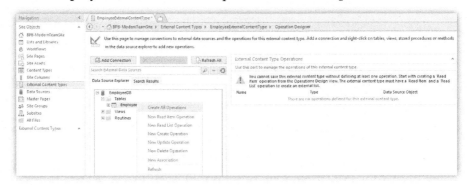

Figure 11.6: Create All Operations

8. Option **Operation Properties** will appear. Click on **Next**:

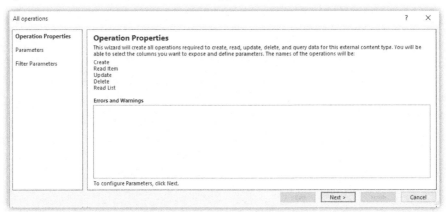

Figure 11.7: Operation Properties

9. The Parameters Configuration option will appear. You will see table columns **EmployeeId, FirstName, LastName, Address, PhoneNumber, DepartmentId** under **Data Source Elements**.

10. Select the checkbox **Map to Identifier** and choose **Identifier** as one field **EmployeeId** from **Properties**. Click **Next**:

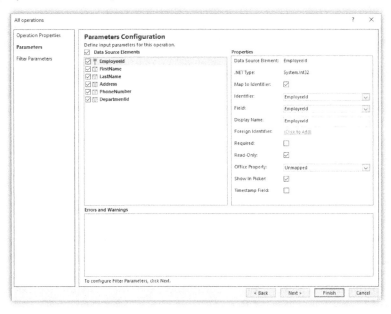

Figure 11.8: Parameters Configurations

11. Click on **Finish** from **Filter Parameters Configuration**:

Figure 11.9: Filter Parameters Configurations

12. Click on **Save** 🖫 present at the top left corner. Content-type is created now and ready to be applied in the external list:

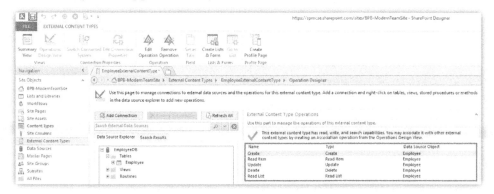

Figure 11.10: Connection established

Application of external content type

We need to apply the created external content type in an external list. Let's follow the step by step to create an external list:

1. Navigate to site URL `https://spmcse.sharepoint.com/sites/bpb-modernteamsite` under which we created an external content type.

2. Click on **New** from the ribbon, select **App**.

3. Click on **External List** one dialog box related to **Adding External List** will open.

4. Enter the **Name** of the external list. Select the option **Select External Content Type**.

5. Option **External Content Type Picker** will open where you can find existing external content types. Select the content type and click on **OK**:

Figure 11.11: Create External List

6. External list **Employee External CT** will be created with added external content type:

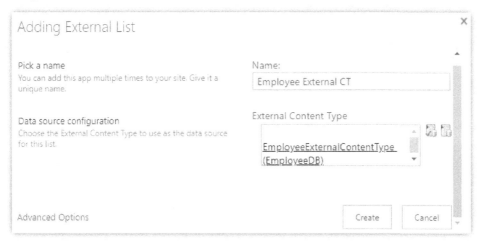

Figure 11.12: Select External Content Type

7. Now you can open the external list created from site contents:

Figure 11.13: External List Created

Conclusion

In this chapter, we discussed the use of business connectivity services. Discussed step by step procedure to create an external content type. Understood how to integrate external content type with the SharePoint external list. Next, in *Chapter 13, Site Designing and Enhancement* will discuss all editing, modifying, designing the SharePoint site.

Points to remember

- We can add Azure DB or on-premises SQL DB as an external data source following the same process of adding a server name and database name; there should not be any problem in that.

- In this chapter wherever its mentioned like this format `_layouts/15/****.aspx`, means this section is added after the site URL `http://` `<site url>/_layouts/15/****.aspx`.
- Regular changes are applied in Office 365 and SharePoint Online by which there may be changes happening in the template or some other features.

CHAPTER 12

Site Designing and Enhancement

In the previous chapter, we discussed business connectivity services in SharePoint online. In this chapter, we will discuss the designing site and steps to modify the site. Each site is having pages in it that are stored in a specific library. Each site has specific default contents available based on the type of template we choose. Those contents are applied in the pages as a webpart under a specific zone. We can edit that page to add or remove or modify contents on the page as per our requirement. Let's discuss how to design or modify any site pages.

Structure

In this chapter we will discuss the following:

- Site pages
- Section layouts
- Modern site webparts
- Structural navigation caching
- Hub site

Objective

During the end of the chapter, you will get a clear understanding of the following:
- How to create and edit site pages
- Section layouts and terminologies
- New modern webparts in details
- How to structural navigation cache works
- How to register hub site, associate other sites with a hub site, application of webparts in hub site,

Site page

Once you access a site in SharePoint, the landing page you access is called the home page. So, in SharePoint every site is having one home page. Users can create a new site page and can set any one of the pages as the home page. You can customize the site by editing the site page and applying different webparts in it. Let's perform the following steps to create a site page:

1. Access the modern site collection URL (`https://spmcse.sharepoint.com/sites/BPB-ModernTeamSite`) that we created previously.

2. Click on **Site Contents** from left navigation. Alternatively, you can open site content by adding `<_layouts/15/viewlsts.aspx>` after the site URL (`http://<site url>/_layouts/15/viewlsts.aspx`). Here will be the link for site contents `https://spmcse.sharepoint.com/sites/BPB-ModernTeamSite/_layouts/15/viewlsts.aspx`. You will notice default contents (**Documents, Form Templates, Site Assets, Style Library, Site Pages**) of type list or library available.

3. Click on the library **Site Pages**.

4. You will see the home page `Home.aspx` for this site as seen in the following screenshot:

Figure 12.1: Site Pages Library

5. Click on **New** from the command bar. You will see 3 templates **Wiki Page**, **Web Part Page**, **Site Page**.

6. Select a page template **Wiki Page** from the dropdown as seen in the following screenshot:

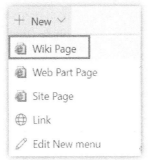

Figure 12.2: Select Page Template

7. You will be redirected to create web page where you need to enter the name of the site page and click on **Create** as seen in the following screenshot:

Figure 12.3: Page Name

8. You will be redirected to traditional SharePoint edit option to customize page further like adding webparts, contents, etc. as seen in the following screenshot:

Figure 12.4: SharePoint Ribbon

9. After adding webparts and all click on **Publish** following the tab publish from ribbon as seen in the following screenshot:

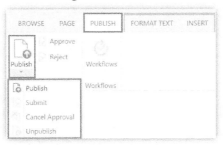

Figure 12.5: Publish Page

10. Next select a page template **Web Part Page** from the dropdown. You will be redirected next to traditional way of entering details like page **Name, Layout, Save Location** as seen in the following screenshot:

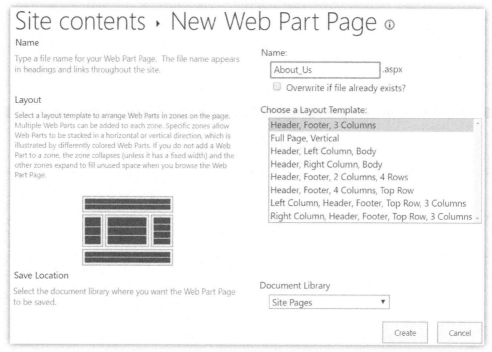

Figure 12.6: Layout Templates

11. You need to select the type of layout template. Layout provides webpart zones where you can add webparts in the page. The number of webpart you need to add and type of UI you need, you can select one of these predefined layouts as seen in the following screenshot:

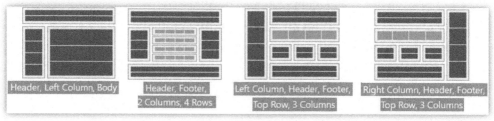

Figure 12.7: Different Layouts

12. Select the library **Site Pages** to store this page under the option **Save Location** and click on **Create**. Next you will get option to add webpart and customize your site as seen in the following screenshot:

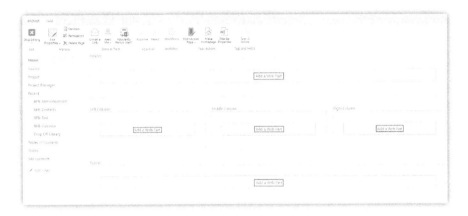

Figure 12.8: Webpart Zone

13. Click on **Add a Web Part**, you will notice additional options under traditional ribbon to select webpart and click on **Add** as seen in the following screenshot:

Figure 12.9: Classic Site Webparts

14. All webparts are placed under specific categories like **Apps**, **Blog**, **Business Data**, **Community**, **Content Rollup**, **Document Sets**, **Data Enterprise**, **Filters**, **Forms**, **Media and Content**, **Search**, **Search-Driven Content**, **Social Collaboration**.

15. Under each category you will find number of webparts which you need to select and click on **Add** to insert into page.

16. I will not discuss any of these webparts present here because we are moving to the new webparts which are going to be adopted for future uses and gradually more webparts will be released.

17. Next select a page template **Site Page** from drop down under **New**.

18. New page is added with new way of edit your page. Click on **Edit** from left, you will see more options will be available to fill details like **Layout**, **Alignment**, **Text above title**, **Show text block above title**, **Show published date**, **Alternate text**.

19. Enter name of the page directly at title field as `BPB Publication`.

20. Select one **Layout** option to display. Each layout option will show beautiful header in page which you can select as per choice.

21. Select the option **Alignment** to align **Left**, **Center**.

22. Enter details in **Text above title** as `Asia's largest publishers of Books`.

23. Enable the option **Text above title** and **Show text block above title**.

24. Click on **Edit Image** option from left to add header image as seen in the following screenshot:

Figure 12.10: Edit Page

25. Click on **Page details** from command bar will show the page properties.

26. Change thumbnail fill other page properties like **Description**, **Owner**, **Location**.

27. **Audience** is now available for page property which we can fill by entering any user or group ID. We can select **Managed Column** details also in page property as seen in the following screenshot:

Figure 12.11: Page Properties

28. Finally click on **Publish** from command bar. After that you will get option like **Save as page template, Email, Add page to navigation, Post as News on this site** as seen in the following screenshot:

Figure 12.12: After Publish Options

29. Click on the option **Save as page template**, enter template name as **About Us** and click on **Save page template** from command bar as seen in the following screenshot:

Figure 12.13: Save as Template

30. Click on **Template details** will show **Template Properties** which we can fill and save as seen in the following screenshot:

Figure 12.14: Template Properties

31. Click on **Email** will share link to users or group as seen in the following screenshot:

Figure 12.15: Email to user

32. If you click on the option **Add page to navigation** then this page will be added to left navigation of the site.

33. You can add site page by navigating to **New** from home page command bar or from site settings as well. You will find 2 more templates for different user experience as seen in the following screenshot:

Figure 12.16: Site Page Modern Template

Section layout

We discussed how to create site page. In this section we will discuss how to add webpart in site page. Webpart holds content in site page. So as to add webpart or do any modification in page, we need to edit the page first. Click on **Edit** option from command bar to put page in edit mode as seen in the following screenshot. You will find different sections to customize the site:

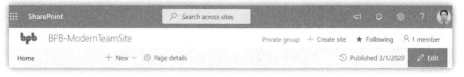

Figure 12.17: Edit Modern Site Page

Once the site page in edit mode you will find sign like **+** in page. Click on the sign **+** present at the left will show option like **One Column, Two Column, Three Column, One-third left column, One-third right column, Vertical section** as section layout. Section layout provides zones to add webpart in page. Select one section layout first as seen in the following screenshot:

Figure 12.18: Selection Layout

Add a new section

Once section layout (**Two columns**) is selected you will see two column section is added into the site page.

You will find few more options like **Add a new section** , **Edit section** , **Move section** , **Duplicate section** , **Delete section** , **Add a new webpart in column one** , **Add a new webpart in column two** as sign, available in that section. Hover over those signs will show actions related to those signs as seen in the following screenshot:

Figure 12.19: Add New Section

Click on the option **Add a new section** will show same option to choose one section layout.

Edit section

SharePoint provides an option to edit each section at any moment of time. Let us perform the following steps to edit the section:

1. Click on the option **Edit** section 📖.

2. You will find option to choose **Layout** options with current option selected. If you want to change the layout, you need to select another layout.

3. Now you can select background color for each section from the option **Section background**. Select any one of the backgrounds and publish the page as seen in the following screenshot:

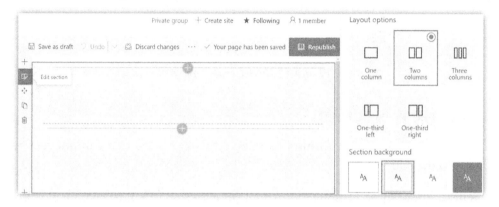

Figure 12.20: Edit Section

Move section

You can move the webparts present under once column under one section to other column present under another section by following the option **Move** section ✥.

If you want to move the section, click on the section will show similar **Move** section ✥ and same step is applicable.

Click on the section/webpart that you want to move, select the option **Move** section ✥, drag and drop to the column present under any other section in that page.

Duplicate section

If you want to create similar section including webparts then you can follow the option **Duplicate** section 🗐. There will be a duplicate section created including all webparts in it. Means all webparts in source section will also be present in the duplicated section which can further be modified as per your requirement.

Delete section

You can delete section or webpart from page following the option **Delete** section 🗑.

Add a new webpart in column

Under each section and under each column you will find an option **Add a new webpart in column two** ⊕ which is used to add webparts in columns under that section in site page. Remember this option which we will click to add webparts in every column that we will discuss next.

Modern site webparts

Now come to most important part that is webpart which is the actual building block of site page. Modern site provides modern webparts with new beautiful UI, new features, easy to configure considering the best use of it. Classic old webparts are getting replaced with this modern webparts gradually. Let's follow the steps below to check list of modern webparts available in sharepoint online:

1. Click on the option **Add a new webpart in column two** ⊕ in any column under the section will open one dialog with list of different webparts.

2. You can search the webpart from list by typing name of webpart in search box instead of scrolling down. Also, there is an option **Expand** ↗ to expand dialog box to see more webparts. Click on that sign **Expand** ↗ as seen in the following screenshot:

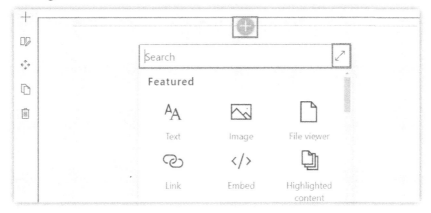

Figure 12.21: Click to add Webpart

3. Once you expand you can see all webparts are present categorically. Click on the dropdown **All by Category** will all categories like **Featured, Text, Media and Content** as seen in the following screenshot:

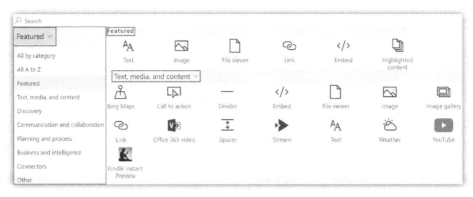

Figure 12.22: Featured Webpart, Text, Media and Content Webpart

4. Categories like **Communication and Collaboration, Planning and Process, Business and Intelligence** as seen in the following screenshot:

Figure 12.23: Communication and Collaboration, Planning and Process, Business and Intelligence Webpart

5. Categories like **Connectors, Discovery** as seen in the following screenshot:

Figure 12.24: Connectors Webpart and Discovery Webpart

6. Finally, few webparts under category **Other** as seen in the following screenshot:

Figure 12.25: Other Webparts

Let's discuss about each webparts one by one to understand better.

Featured webparts

Category **Featured** webparts includes webparts like **Text**, **Image**, **File Viewer**, **Link**, **Embed**, **Highlighted Content**. Let's discuss about each featured webparts in details one-by-one.

Text

Text webpart is the modern webpart used for adding text content, other content like link, table. It will be replacement for classic content editor webpart. Let's perform the following steps to edit webpart **Text**:

1. Click on the option **Add a new webpart in column two** ⊕ in any column under the section will open one dialog box.

2. You can search webpart **Text** in search box. Else click on that sign **Expand** ↗.

3. Click on the drop down **All by Category**, select the webpart **Text** under category **Featured** will add that webpart in column with settings visible.

4. Enter text in the webpart directly as per requirement. Formatting the text available directly from the options appearing in webpart like **Bold** B, **Italic** I, **Underline** U, **Align** ≡▾, **Bulleted list** ≡▾, **Hyperlink** 🔗 as seen in the following screenshot:

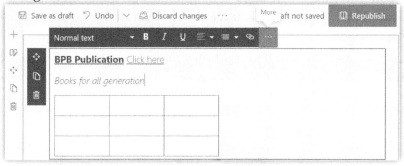

Figure 12.26: Text Webpart

5. There is another option **More** ••• available, click on that will show additional option under **Text and table formatting**.

6. Click on the dropdown **Font Style** to change the text to heading or pull quote or monospaced. Options available to change the **Font size"**, **Font color** and can **Highlight color, Strikethrough, Superscript, Subscript, Clear all formatting** as well.

7. Click on **Hyperlink** to enter links and option **Insert Table** will enter table in the webpart as seen in the following screenshot:

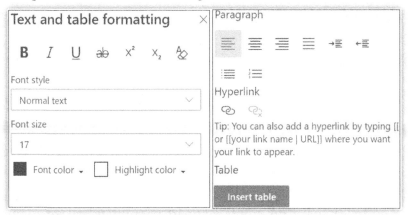

Figure 12.27: Text Webpart Format Options

Image

Image webpart used to include image and multiple actions can be taken on image in the site page. Let's perform the following steps to see detail action on webpart **Image**:

1. Add one image webpart in the column.

2. Click on **Add image** will show you option to add image from **OneDrive**, **Site**, **Upload**, **From a link**, **Stock Images**. Click on upload and select any image from computer.

3. Once uploaded you will find multiple options to edit the photo like **Resize** 🖼 , **Crop** 🔲, **Aspect Ratio** 🔲, **Alignment** 🗄, **Reset** ✕, **Save** 💾 as seen in the following screenshot:

Figure 12.28: Image Webpart

4. Click on **Edit**  will show additional options to enter **Link** (http://sharepointtechnicalsupport.com), so that clicking to the image will open that link.

5. Enable **Add text over image** and enter text (Deviprasad Panda) over image.

6. **Alternative text** ⓘ is suggested over photo. Click on *keep* will add suggested text in the field **Alternative text**.

7. Option to **Add a caption** below image available which can be filled as per requirement.

File viewer

File viewer webpart is used to show files of different formats like word, excel, power point, pdf etc., more than 270 file types, in the site page. This is the modern webpart compared to old classic webpart **Page Viewer** which is going to the replacement webpart. Let's perform the following steps to see detail action on webpart **File Viewer**.

1. Add one **File viewer** webpart in the column.

2. After that will show you option to add files from **OneDrive**, **Site**, **Upload**, **From a link**. Click on upload and select any word file from computer.

3. Below the file you will find **Menu** option to **Download a Copy**, **Print to PDF**, **Accessibility Mode**, **Terms to Use**, **Privacy and Cookies** as seen in the below screenshot.

4. Side to menu option will find an option **Full Screen**. Click on that will open the file in a new tab.

5. **Add a description** (Table of Content) below the file.

6. Under the option **Start Page** select the **Page Number** (1) which will be the start page. You can change the file by following option **Change file**. Click on **Apply** finally:

Figure 12.29: Word File in File Viewer Webpart

7. Similarly add one excel file in file viewer webpart.

8. Click on **Edit** ✏️ will show few options to choose whether you want to show the **Entire workbook, Chart, Table, Range**. Also, you can choose to show file in **Show grid lines, Show row and column headers, Allow sorting and filtering columns** as seen in the following screenshot:

Figure 12.30: Excel File in File Viewer Webpart

9. Below the excel file will show you options like **Download** 📥, **Refresh all data connection** 🔄, **Information about this workbook** 📋, **View full-size workbook** 🔲.

10. Click on the option **Information about this workbook** 📋 will show **URL** and **Embed Code**, as seen in the following screenshot, which cab used in other webparts:

Figure 12.31: Information about this workbook

Link

Link webpart can hold site page link, video link, image link and document link. Insert one webpart **Link**. Enter any link, alternative text and publish as seen in the following screenshot:

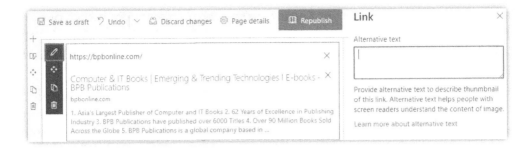

Figure 12.32: Link Webpart

Embed

Webpart **Embed** holds embed code or video URL of other sites like you tube. This is the modern webpart compared to the classic old webpart **Page viewer** also will replace the old classic webpart. When you click on share button of any YouTube video there is an option **Embed**. Click on that will show the code which you can copy and pasted in webpart **Embed** as seen in the following screenshot. Video will be available in the webpart and cab be played:

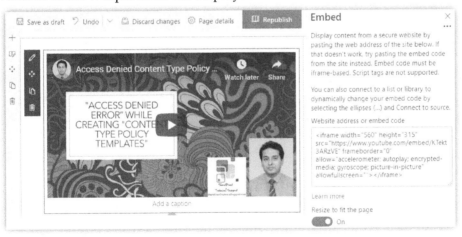

Figure 12.33: Embed Webpart

Highlighted content

Highlighted content webpart automatically shows recent contents in the webpart. At max 200 items will return to be displayed here. It provides options to choose the source from where content needs to be displayed. This is the modern webpart compared to the old classic webparts like **Content query** and **Content search**. We can filter and sort the content. Audience targeting available that can be enabled or disabled to show or hide specific contents to specific group of people or group. We can display the content in different layout like **Grid, List, Carousel, Filmstrip**, also can choose the number of items want to show in the webpart. Let's perform the following steps to see detail action on webpart **Highlighted Content**:

1. We can apply **Filter** or **KQL Code** (Keyword Query Language `https:// docs.microsoft.com/en-us/sharepoint/dev/general-development/ keyword-query-language-kql-syntax-reference`) to query search result.

2. Click on **Edit** ✏️" from webpart. You will see different options to choose either **Filter** or **Custom query**. Click on the option **Filter**.

3. Enable the option **Enable audience targeting** to show content to particular users.

4. Select one of the layouts to display content in different forms.

5. Select how many items you want to display in webpart by entering value in field **Show this many items at a time** as seen in the following screenshot:

Figure 12.34: Highlighted Content Webpart

6. Under the category **Content** you will find options like **Source, Type, Document Type**. Click on the dropdown **Source** and select any one source (`This site`) like **This site, A document library on this site, This site collection, The page library on this site, All site in the hub, Select sites, All sites**.

7. Click on the dropdown **Type**, select any content of type (`Documents`) from **Documents, Pages, News, Videos, Images, Events, Issues, Tasks, Links, Contacts, All**. We can add multiple content types by clicking the option **Add content type**.

8. Click on the dropdown **Document type**. Select one **Document type (Any)** from **Word, Excel, PowerPoint, OneNote, Visio, PDF, Any** as seen in the following screenshot. Multiple **Document type** can be applied:

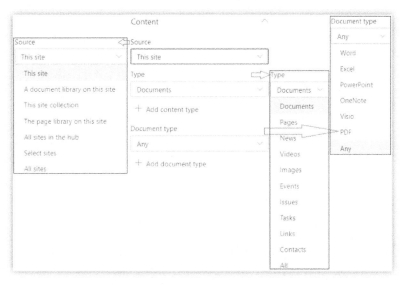

Figure 12.35: Category Content in Highlighted Content

9. Next category is **Filter and sort**. Under the category **Filter** you will find options like **Filter, Since, Sort by**. Click on the dropdown **Filter**, select any one (Recently added) from **Title includes the words, Content includes the words, Recently added, Recently changed, Created by, Modified by, Managed property**.

10. Click on dropdown **Since**, select any one from the options like **Today, Yesterday, Earlier this week, Earlier this month, Last month, Earlier this year, Last year**.

11. Multiple **Filter** can be applied by following the option **Add Filter**.

12. Click on dropdown **Sort by** for sorting results. Select any one from **Sort by** like **Most recent, Most viewed, Trending, Managed property ascending, Managed property descending** as seen in the following screenshot:

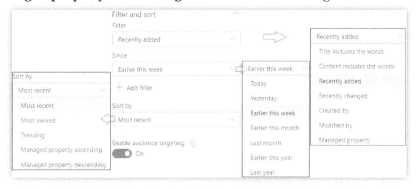

Figure 12.36: Category Filter and Sort in Highlighted Content

13. Select anyone option from **Layout** to display or present the content in form of **Grid, List, Carousel** or **Filmstrip** as seen in the following screenshot:

Figure 12.37: Different Layout In Highlighted Content

14. We can apply **KQL code** or **CAML query** by selecting the option **Custom Query** instead of instead of **Filter**.
15. This webpart is used to create modern blog posts and classic blog site is going to be out of support. We can use this to create modern blog posts.

Text, media, and content webparts

Category **Text, Media, and Content Webparts** webparts includes webparts like **Bing Maps, Call to Action, Divider, Image Gallery, Office 365 Video, Spacer, Stream, Weather, You Tube, Kindle Instant Preview**. Let's discuss about each webparts in details one-by-one.

Bing Maps

Webpart **Bing Maps** is used to add map in site page as per user requirement. Once you add **Bing Maps** webpart, you need enter **Title** of the map under the field **Add a title**. Search anything (BPB Publication) in the search space. Keep the option **Show pin label on map** enabled. You will see **Pin Label** and **Address to display** will show the search location name and address. Now publish to apply in site page as seen in the following screenshot:

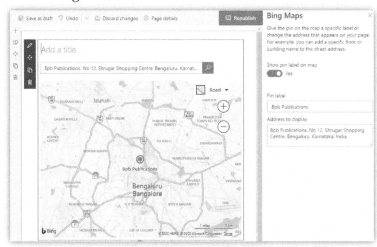

Figure 12.38: Bing Maps Webpart

Call to Action

Webpart **Call to Action** used to create button. Let's perform the following steps to see detail action on webpart **Call to Action**.

1. Add **Call to Action** webpart.

2. Right side you will find option **Change**. Click on that to add or change **Background** image. We can adjust the background image by **Zoon in** 🔍, **Zoom out** 🔍. We can move image to adjust in between that column by follow the option **Set focal point** 🔍.

3. Add button name (BPB Publication) by entering details under the field **Button** label.

4. Add a link to button by entering the URL (https://bpbonline.com) in field button link. Clicking the button will open page (https://bpbonline.com) or any other content (image, document, video, etc.) related to that link in new browser tab.

5. We can add action related to that button (**Click on the button to order online**) under the field **Add your call to action text here**.

6. Select **Alignment** option to align the button and action text **Left**, **Right**, or **Center** as seen in the following screenshot:

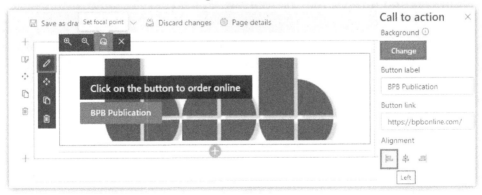

Figure 12.39: Call to Action Webpart

Divider

Webpart **Divider** create a line in between webparts to separate webparts. We can adjust length and width of the line to make the size of the line as per requirement as seen in the following screenshot:

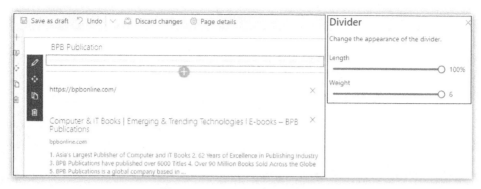

Figure 12.40: Divider Webpart

Image Gallery

Webpart **Image Gallery** used to display number of images at a place with better organized to look better as per user ease. Let's perform the following steps to see detail action on webpart **Image Gallery**:

1. Add the webpart **Image Gallery**.

2. You will find **Image Options** at the right side. By default, **Select Images** option is selected.

3. Enter title of the image gallery in the field **Add a title**.

4. Click on **Add Images** from the webpart. Upload or select any existing image to add in webpart.

5. From **Layout** select the type, either **Brick** or **Grid** or **Carousel**, you want to display the images as seen in the following screenshot:

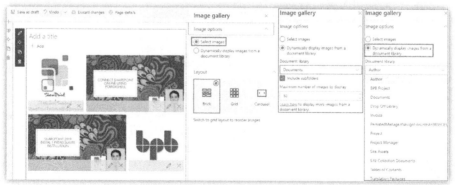

Figure 12.41: Image Gallery Webpart

6. Another option **Dynamically display images from a document library** is available which will show images dynamically from any library present in that site. Means any change in the library images will be reflected immediately in webpart for which we call it as dynamically display.

7. Select any one of the document library from the dropdown.

8. Enable the option **Include subfolders** to display any images present in folder under that selected library.

9. Select number of images that you want to display in the webpart by entering one value in the option **Maximum number of images to display** and publish.

10. Under each image you will find an option **Edit** details ✎. Click on that will show options to edit image properties like **Title**, **Caption**, **Alternative Text**.

Office 365 Video

If you click **All apps** once log in to office365 portal, you will find an app **Video**. If you click on that, will be redirected to a link `https://spmcse.sharepoint.com/portals/hub/_layouts/15/PointPublishing.aspx?app=video&p=h` like this where you will find videos. You can copy link of the video and can use here in webpart **Office 365 Video** as seen in the following screenshot:

Figure 12.42: Office 365 Video webpart

Spacer

Webpart **Spacer** used to adjust the vertical spacing between webparts by dragging the bar up or down as seen in the following screenshot:

Figure 12.43: Spacer Webpart

Stream

Webpart **Stream** is used to add channel or video from **Microsoft Stream**. Let's perform the following steps to see detail action on webpart **Stream**:

1. Add the webpart **Stream**.

2. You will find options available at the right side like **Source, Sort by, Filter search term**.

3. You can select the **Source** like **All of stream** or **Single video** or **Channel**. Select the source **All of stream**.

4. You can select **Sort by** like **Trending, Published date, Views, Likes**. Select **Sort by** as **Trending**.

5. Enter one related term under the option **Filter search term** to get the video quickly while searching as seen in the following screenshot:

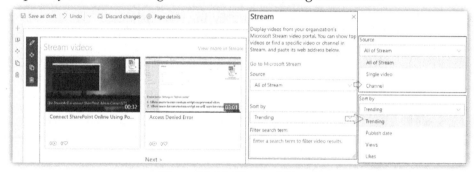

Figure 12.44: Stream Webpart

6. If you are choosing **Source** as **Single video** or **Channel** then you need to enter the **URL** of the single video or channel as seen in the following screenshot:

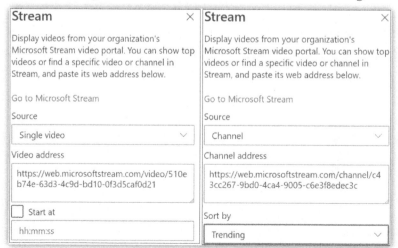

Figure 12.45: Stream Webpart Source

Weather

We can add webpart **Weather** to see weather information for different locations. After adding this webpart, add a location, change the unit as per requirement as seen in the following screenshot:

Figure 12.46: Weather Webpart

YouTube

You can add YouTube videos in the page using this webpart **YouTube**. You can add the video URL or embed code in the webpart to include video in webpart as seen in the following screenshot:

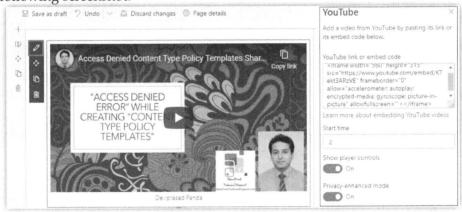

Figure 12.47: YouTube Webpart

Kindle Instant Preview

We can add preview of the kindle book using the webpart **Kindle Instant Preview**. Below the kindle book, under share option, you will see an option **Embed**. Click on that will open another dialog box.

Copy code under **Embed on your site (HTML)**

```
<iframe type="text/html" width="336" height="550" frameborder="0"
allowfullscreen style="max-width:100%" src="https://read.amazon.in/kp/
card?asin=******&preview=inline&linkCode=kpe&ref_=**_**_*_**_**_***"
></iframe>
```
and paste in webpart to include preview in page as seen in the following screenshot:

Figure 12.48: Kindle Instant Preview Webpart

Discovery

Category **Discovery** includes webparts like **Document Library**, **Hero**, **List**, **Highlighted content**, **List Properties**, **Page Properties**, **Quick Links**, **Recent Documents**, **Sites**. Let's discuss about each webparts in details one-by-one.

Document Library

We can include **Document Library** as webpart in the site page. Add this webpart. From the library options select the document library you want to display, select the view for showing documents, select the size **Small**, **Medium**, **Large**, **Authorize** to display documents in library. Option **Show command bar** will enable or disable command bar as per requirement as seen in the following screenshot:

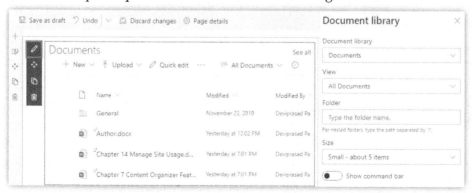

Figure 12.49: Document Library Webpart

Hero

Hero webpart is used to showcase contents like text, image, links in the form of **Tiles** or **Layers**. Let's perform the following steps to see detail action on webpart **Hero**.

1. Add the webpart **Hero** to the page.

2. After adding webpart you will find options **Layout** options on right side.

3. Click on **Tiles** under **Layout** options will get options like **One tile, Two tiles, Three tiles, Four tiles, Five tiles**. Choose one option **Three tiles** as seen in the following screenshot:

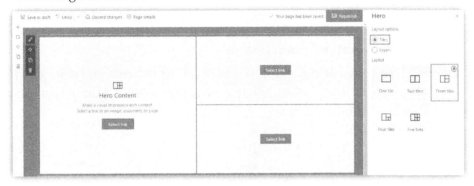

Figure 12.50: Hero Webpart Layout Options

4. Click on the option **Select link** under one tile and add one site page AboutUs as seen in the following screenshot:

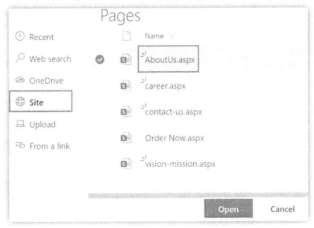

Figure 12.51: Select Link Hero Webpart

5. After page selection you will find an option **Edit details**. Click on that will show additional options in category like **Link, Image, Options**.

6. Under the category you will find link is already updated under the option **Select a link to a document or page**. You can still change the link clicking the option **Change** present below the URL. Clicking anywhere in tile will open that link in browser.

7. Enter **Title** (About Us) for the link that will be displayed in tile. Option **Show title in layout** will allow to show or hide the title in tile.

8. Under next category **Image** you will find option **Auto-selected image** that allow to select image of tile automatically, **Custom image** that allows to upload image, **Color block** will show color in the tile with no image. Enter **Alternative text** for image.

9. Under next category **Options** you will find options to enable or disable call to action like **Show call to action link**.

10. Enter **Call to action text** (Learn more) and **Call to action link** as seen in the following screenshot. Clicking the text **Learn more** will open the link entered in **Call to action link**:

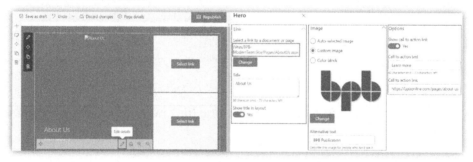

Figure 12.52: Link, Image, Call to Action Options in Hero Webpart

11. Similarly, you can add other tiles as well which will show a view as seen in the following screenshot:

Figure 12.53: Hero Webpart When Layout Option is Tiles

12. If you select **Layers** under **Layout** options you will see additional option **Description**. Text entered under field **Description** will be displayed under title.

13. Option **Show topic heading** to show or hide topic heading available as additional as seen in the following screenshot:

Figure 12.54: Additional Option Description in Hero Webpart When Layout Option is Layers

14. If you add details in all fields under **Layout** options like **Layers**, site page will be displayed as shown in the screenshot below:

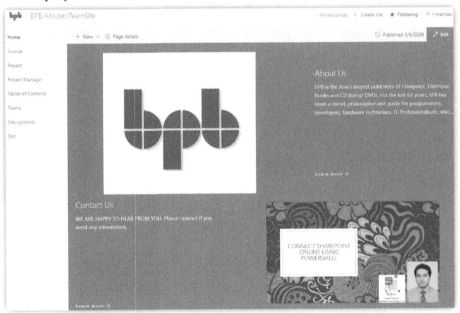

Figure 12.55: Hero Webpart When Layout Option is Layers

List

Similar to document library, we can add **List** as webpart. Add the webpart **List**, select the list that you want to display in webpart, choose the type of view, select size of the items to show, enable or disable command bar from the option as **Show command bar/Hide command bar** per requirement as seen in the following screenshot:

Figure 12.56: List Webpart

List Properties

Webpart **List Properties** displays list properties above the list. Let's perform the following steps to see detail action on webpart **List Properties**.

1. After adding webpart **List** in the page, after that add webpart **List Properties** in same site page.

2. Click on **Connect** from webpart. You will find option at right side, click on **Connect to source** ••• as seen in the following screenshot:

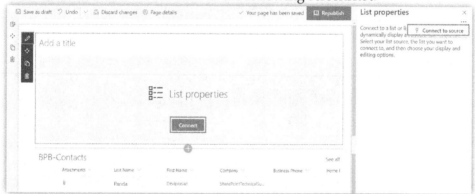

Figure 12.57: Connect Source in List Properties Webpart

3. You will see drop down options **Connect to source** where you need to choose the **List** that exists in the same page.

4. Option **Display** is selected as **Selected item**.

5. You can select the **Size** (Autosize, Small, Medium, Large) of the selected properties.

6. You can enable or disable editing list items from option **Allow users to edit list items**.

7. All columns present in the list will be available for selection. Select the fields or properties to display as seen in the following screenshot:

Figure 12.58: Select List Properties to Display

8. After fields or properties selected click on **Publish**. You will find those properties will be displayed above the list as seen in the following screenshot:

Figure 12.59: List Properties Displayed in Site Page

Page Properties

Similar to **List Properties** we can display page properties in the site using the webpart **Page Properties**. Navigate to **Site Pages** library present under **Site Contents**. The columns present in that library are the page properties as seen in the following screenshot:

Figure 12.60: Page Properties in Site Pages Library

Add the webpart **Page Properties** in the page, click on **Add Properties** present in webpart will open options to **Add** property at the right side. Click on **Add**. Select one property from drop down to add. If you to add more properties, you need to click on **Add** multiple times. Finally click on **Publish** to apply changes as seen in the following screenshot:

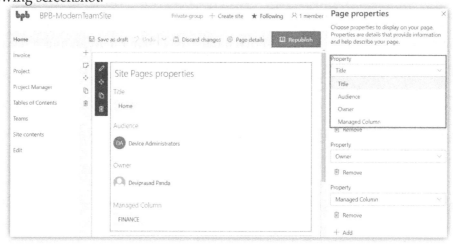

Figure 12.61: Add Page Properties

Quick Links

Webpart **Quick Links** provides option to pin items in the page for quick access or mostly frequently accessing items or links in a simplified way. Let's perform the following steps to see detail action on webpart **Quick Links**.

1. Add webpart **Quick Links** in the page. You will find option to enter name of the quick links. Enter a name `Books Online`.

2. Click on **Edit** ✏ from webpart. You will get options to choose **Layout** options like **Compact**, **Filmstrip**, **Grid**, **Button**, **List**, **Tiles** to represent the pin items in different way. Select the option `Compact`.

3. You will find option **Add links** and **Add a link**. Click anyone as seen in the following screenshot:

Figure 12.62: Quick Links Webpart Layout

4. You will be redirected to choose item that you want pin from **OneDrive**, **Site**, **Upload** or **From a link**. Enter one link `https://bpbonline.com` selecting **From a link** as seen in the following screenshot:

Figure 12.63: Add Link to Quick Webpart

5. After that you will find **Edit** link option at right. If you want to change the link, click on **Change**.

6. Select **Thumbnail**" choosing **Custom image** option.

7. Enter **Alternate text field for thumbnail image** details.

8. Similarly add few more items like document or site page, image, video, external or internal link. You will find the view will be as per screenshot below:

Figure 12.64: Quick Links in Compact Layout

9. If you change **Layout** options as **Filmstrip**, view of the items in page will be as per screenshot below:

Figure 12.65: Quick Links in Filmstrip Layout

10. If you change **Layout** options as **Grid**, view of the items in page will be as per screenshot below:

Figure 12.66: Quick Links in Grid Layout

11. If you change **Layout** options as **Button**, view of the items in page will be as per screenshot below:

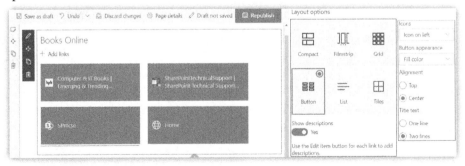

Figure 12.67: Quick Links in Button Layout

12. If you change **Layout** options as **List**, view of the items in page will be as per screenshot below:

Figure 12.68: Quick Links in List Layout

13. If you change **Layout** options as **Tiles**, view of the items in page will be as per screenshot below:

Figure 12.69: Quick Links in Tiles Layout

Recent Documents

Webpart **Recent Documents** displays recently added or modified content. Add the webpart and choose number of files that you want to show in webpart as seen in the following screenshot:

Figure 12.70: Recent Documents Webpart

Sites

Webpart **Sites** used to display sites with recent action happened in that site. This is the modern webpart compared to the classic old webpart **Site aggregator** also will replace the old classic webpart. Let's perform the following steps to see detail action on webpart **Sites**:

1. Once you add webpart **Sites** you can choose option **All sites in the hub** to show all sites in a hub in the webpart.

2. Select one **Layout** to display sites.

3. Limit number of sites to display in webpart from option **Show this many items at a time**.

4. If there is no item to show, you can hide the webpart, enabling the option **Hide this webpart if there is nothing to show**.

5. If you are selecting option **Frequent sites for current user**, you will see frequently visited sites in the webpart.

6. Next option **Select sites** allow user to select sites that to be displayed in webpart as seen in the following screenshot:

Figure 12.71: Sites Webpart

Communication and collaboration

Category **Communication and collaboration** includes webparts like **Conversions, Events, Group Calendar, Highlights, Microsoft Forms, News, People, Twitter**. Let's discuss about each webpart in details one by one.

Conversations

Webpart **Conversations** used to display yammer posts in site page. Let's perform the following steps to see detail action on webpart **Conversations**:

1. Add webpart **Conversations** in page.

2. You will find options **Select conversation source**, **Search for a source** at the right side. You can click on **Get started** to get this options as well as seen in the following screenshot:

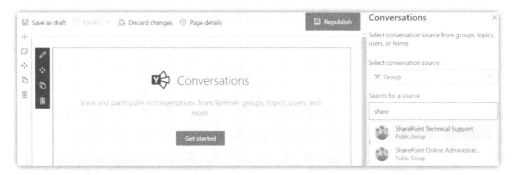

Figure 12.72: *Conversations Webpart*

3. Under **Select conversation source** you will find categories like **Group**, **User**, **Topic**, **Home**. Select the option Group.

4. From next field **Search for a source** search one Yammer group (SharePoint Technical Support) present in Yammer.

5. Select number of conversation, from **Small – 4 conversations**, **Medium – 8 conversations**, **Large – 12 conversations**, that you want to show in the webpart as seen in the following screenshot:

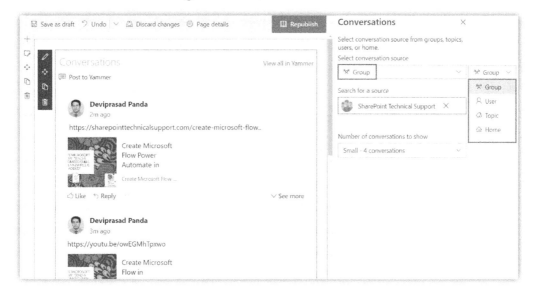

Figure 12.73: *Conversation Source*

6. If we select **Topic** under **Select conversation source** we need to enter the Tag word (#Powerautomate) so that posts linked it that keyword will be displayed in webpart as seen in the following screenshot:

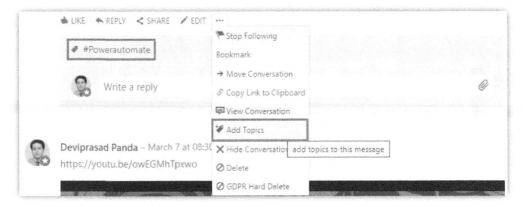

Figure 12.74: Add Topics Conversations Webpart

7. If we select **User** under **Select conversation source** we need to enter the user ID so that post linked with that user will be displayed in webpart as seen in the following screenshot:

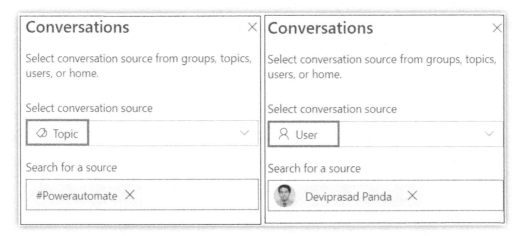

Figure 12.75: Select Different Conversation Source

8. We can add post from webpart directly by clicking the option **Post to Yammer**.

9. Options **Copy Link, Unfollow, View in Yammer** allows to do other action on post as seen in the following screenshot.

10. Expand **See more** to see comments posted or post comment:

Figure 12.76: Post to Yammer

Events

Webpart **Events** used to display events in the page. Let's perform the following steps to see detail action on webpart **Events**:

1. Add webpart **Events** in page.

2. Click on **Edit** 🖉 from webpart. You will get options like **Source**, **Category**, **Date range**, **Layout**, **Show this many items at a time** to choose.

3. Select one option from **Layout** either **Filmstrip** or **Compact** as seen in the following screenshot.

4. Enter number of events (**14**) that you want to display in webpart in the filed **Show this many items at a time**:

Figure 12.77: Add Events Webpart

5. You can select any one source from drop down available as **Events list on this site**, **This site**, **This site collection**, **All sites in the hub**, **All sites**, **Select sites**.

6. Select one category of event that you created from drop down available as **Meeting, Work hours, Business, Holiday, Get-together, Gifts, Birthday, Anniversary**.

7. Select the date range from the dropdown available as **All upcoming events, This week, Next two weeks, This month, This quarter, Select date range** as seen in the following screenshot:

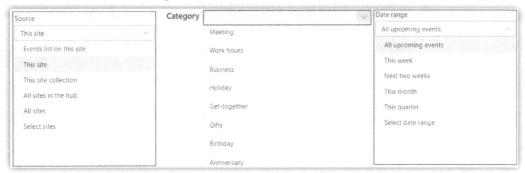

Figure 12.78: Source, Category, Date Range in Events Webpart

8. Click on the option **Add event** from webpart to add event.

9. Enter **Name** of event.

10. Select event start date with time and event end date with time from option **When**. You can choose option **All day** event if it will continue for whole day.

11. Enter meeting joining link under **Address** and display name for that link under **Display** name.

12. Select one event category from the dropdown options available like **Meeting, Work hours, Business, Holiday, Get-together, Gifts, Birthday, Anniversary**.

13. Enter agenda of the option under the field **About this event**.

14. Invite **Users or Groups** to the event entering name or email address in the field as seen in the following screenshot:

Figure 12.79: *Create Events*

Group Calendar

We can add office 365 group calendar in site page using the webpart **Group Calendar**. Click on **Edit** ✏️ will show option to choose office 365 group. Choose one office 365 group (**SharePoint Technical Support**) and select number of events per page to show in group calendar as seen in the following screenshot:

Figure 12.80: *Add Group Calendar*

When there is any event scheduled in the group calendar **SharePoint Technical Support** that event will be shown in webpart **Group Calendar** as seen in the following screenshot:

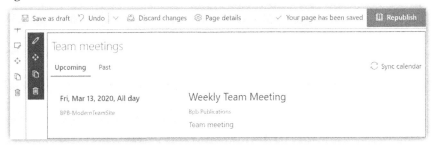

Figure 12.81: *Events in Group Calendar*

Highlights

We can add **Yammer Highlights** in page using webpart **Highlight**. Let's perform the following steps to see detail action on webpart **Highlights**:

1. After adding webpart **Highlights**, click on **Edit** 🖊 will show the option to choose one group.

2. After that choose an option under **Show** to display conversations. You need to choose either **Top Conversations: most popular conversations from the group** or **Latest Conversations: the group's new or more recent conversations** or **Only conversations you choose** as seen in the following screenshot.

3. If you choose **Only conversations you choose**, then you need to pass **Yammer conversation URL**:

Figure 12.82: Highlights Webpart

Microsoft Forms

We can use Microsoft forms and display them in webpart using **Microsoft Forms**. Enter Microsoft form URL in webpart. You can create Microsoft form **Team Event** and passing that URL in webpart to **Collect responses** or **Show form results** as seen in the following screenshot. We can use this webpart to create polls, surveys, quizzes:

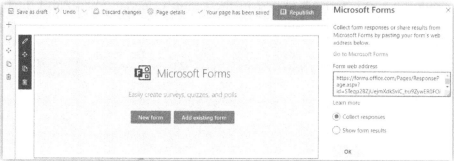

Figure 12.83: Microsoft Forms Webpart

News

The announcement, regular updates on company achievements, policy updates, HR information are shared in the form of news using the webpart **News**. This is the modern webpart compared to the classic old webpart **Announcements** also will replace the old classic webpart. Let's perform the following steps to see detail action on webpart **News**:

1. Add webpart **News** and click on **Edit** 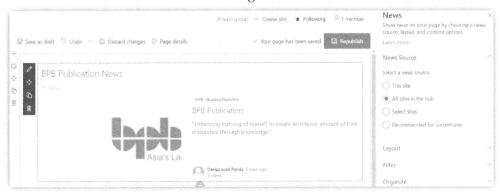.

2. You will find edit options under four categories like **News Source**, **Layout**, **Filter**, **Organize**.

3. Expand category **News Source**. Under option **Select a news source** selects anyone from **This site**, **All sites in the hub**, **Select sites**, **Recommended for current user** as seen in the following screenshot:

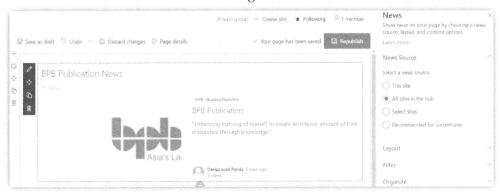

Figure 12.84: News Webpart

4. Expand category **Layout**, select one layout option from **Top story**, **List**, **Side-by-side**, **Hub News**, **Carousel**, **Tiles**.

5. You can enable or disable fields like title and command from option **Show title and commands**.

6. You will find a difference in options in different layouts. In general, you will find options like **Show compact view in narrow widths**, **Show number of views**, **Show author**, **Show first published date**, **Number of news posts to show**, **Show compact view**, **Seconds between each change of news posts**, **Automatically cycle each change of news posts**, **Hide this webpart of there is nothing to show** as seen in the following screenshot. You can choose each layout any see the difference in representation:

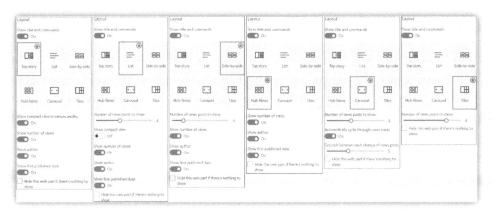

Figure 12.85: New Webpart Layouts

7. Expand category **Filter**, select filtering option from the first dropdown, anyone (`Recently added`) like **Recently added, Title included the words, Recently added, Recently changed, Created by, Modified by, Managed property**.

8. From the second dropdown, select any one related property like **Today, Yesterday, Earlier this week, Earlier this month, Last month, Earlier this year, Last Year** as seen in the following screenshot:

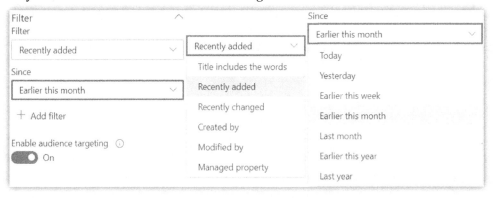

Figure 12.86: Filter Option in News Webpart

9. If we are selecting **Created by** or **Modified by** we need to choose the user name from second the dropdown.

10. We can filter based on the managed property as well. Multiple filtering options are available to refine the search result as per requirement.

11. You can enable or disable audience targeting from the option **Enable audience targeting** to show results to targeted users.

12. The final category is **Organize** to display news in order. Expand the category, click on the option **Select news to organize**.

13. A new dialog box will open with recent news from the selected source. Drag the news and drop to the order that you want to put in as seen in the following screenshot:

Figure 12.87: Ordering in News Webpart

People

Webpart **People** used to show user details on the site page. This is the modern webpart compared to the old classic webpart **Contact details webpart** which is the replacement webpart. Let's perform the following steps to see detailed action on webpart **People**.

1. Add the webpart on the site page.

2. Enter the **Title** of the webpart.

3. Enter the name or email address of the user that wants to display in webpart.

4. The user will be added. Click on the link **Add a profile link** present below the user name.

5. Enter **Link** and **Text to display** in the dialog box opened and save to apply changes.

6. Below the profile link you will find the option to enter a description about the user. You can fill the description.

7. Click on **Edit** 🖉 will show **Layout** options like **Compact** and **Descriptive** on the right side. Select one option from layout as seen in the following screenshot:

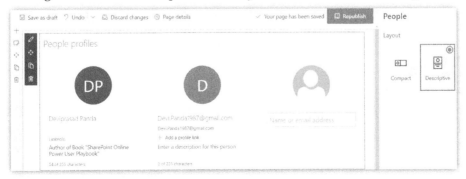

Figure 12.88: People Webpart

8. Click on the user `Deviprasad Panda` will open a dialog box with all details like **Overview, Contact, Organization, Files, LinkedIn** of the user.

9. Click on **Overview** will show details like **Contact, Organization, Files, LinkedIn** one below the other. Scroll down to see each detail.

10. If you click on **Contact** will show details like **Email, Chat, Work phone, Business address, Birthday, About me**.

11. Click on **Organization** will show organization details as seen in the following screenshot:

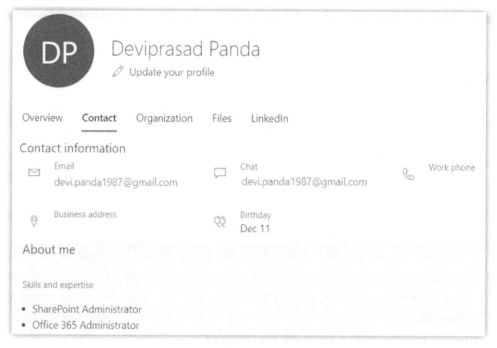

Figure 12.89: People Details

12. Click on **Files** will show files accessed by the users. We can filter the files from the files accessed from the filter option available.

13. Click on the option of **LinkedIn** to access the LinkedIn profile.

Twitter

We can connect to twitter and display tweets on the site page. Once you add twitter, enter twitter id on the right side. Tweets will be added to the webpart. You can select additional settings like **Show Twitter header, Display dividers, Theme color**. As per requirement. Enter number of tweets that you want to display in site page from the option **Maximum number of tweets to show** as seen in the following screenshot:

Figure 12.90: Twitter Webpart

Planning and process

Category **Planning and Process** includes webpart like **Planner**. Let's discuss the webpart in detail.

Planner

We can add a planner on the site page to set a plan, assign tasks, and check status or process on the task assigned for better management. This is the modern webpart compared to the classic old webpart **Tasklist** also will replace the old classic webpart. Let's perform the following steps to see detail action on webpart **Planner**:

1. Add webpart **Planner** on the page.

2. You will get options like **Select an existing plan** and **Display**. Default option under the option **Selects an existing plan** is **Daily Update**.

3. From option **Display** select one the option from **Board, Charts (all), Status chart, Member chart, Bucket chart** to display plan details in webpart.

4. Click on **To do** from webpart.

5. Enter **Task Name, Set due date** of task from the calendar option available below.

6. Assign this task to the user by clicking option **Assign** present below the due date.

7. Once task complete click on the options present at the top right corner to mark it complete as seen in the following screenshot:

Figure 12.91: Add Task to Panner

8. Click on the created task will open more details from where you can change **Bucket (To do, Done)**, **Progress (Not started, In progress, Completed)**, **Due date**, and add **Attachments** as well as seen in the following screenshot. Make changes as per requirement:

Figure 12.92: Task Status in Planner

Business and Intelligence

Category **Business and Intelligence** includes webparts like **Site Activity**, **Quick Chart**, **Power BI**. Let's discuss each webparts in details one-by-one.

Site Activity

We can audit the activity of site contents by adding one webpart on the site. Modern SharePoint provides a webpart called **Site activity**, as seen in the following screenshot below that captures all activities on-site content like contents uploaded, modified, viewed, creation of libraries or lists, etc.

We can see recent activities like files edited, viewed, site pages viewed in the below images. So, this webpart pulls all activities automatically and displays them here to end-users.

Quick Chart

We can represent data in the form of a **Column chart** and **Pie chart** in the site using webpart **Quick Chart**. Let's perform the following steps to see detail action on webpart **Quick Chart**:

1. Add webpart **Quick Chart** on the site page.

2. Select one list **BPB-Task** from where data will be displayed.

3. Click on the dropdown **Column that has the data to display** and select the option **% Complete**.

4. Option **Column with labels for each data point** is selected as **Task Name**.

5. Select the **Sort order** to display the chart.

6. Under category **Layout**, enter the name for **Horizontal axis** (Tasks), **Vertical axis** (Completion Status) as seen in the following screenshot:

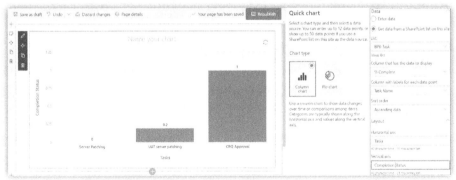

Figure 12.93: Quick Chart Webpart

Power BI

We can display Power BI reports on the site page using this webpart. From the Power BI portal, click on the report name. Then click on **File** and then select **Embed in SharePoint Online**. Copy the link present under **Embed link for SharePoint** and paste in **Power BI** webpart. Enter the **Page name** and select the display ratio. Enable both options **Show Navigation Pane** and **Show Filter Pane**. Finally, click on **Publish** to apply report in webpart as seen in the following screenshot:

Figure 12.94: Power BI Webpart

Connectors

Category **Connectors** include webparts like **Asana, Bitbucket, Bitbucket Server, GitHub, GitHub Enterprise, Google Analytics, Incoming Webhook, JIRA, Microsoft PowerApps, Office 365 Connectors, RSS, Salesforce, Stack Overflow, Trello, UserVoice, Wunderlist**. Let's discuss the **Google Analytics** webpart in detail. Similarly, we need to sign in to other connectors to make it useful.

Google Analytics

We can implement SharePoint sites in Google analytics. Let's perform the following steps to see detail action on webpart **Google Analytics**:

1. Add webpart **Google Analytics** on the site page.

2. You will get the option to log in to **Google Analytics**. Enter user ID and password to log in as seen in the following screenshot:

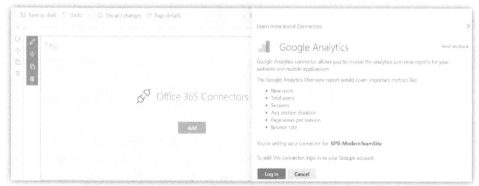

Figure 12.95: Add Google Analytics

3. After sign in you need to enter site URL to use in analytics. Select the frequency to collect information as **Daily**. Finally, click on **Save** as seen in the following screenshot:

Figure 12.96: Enter Site URL in Google Analytics

4. Click on **Edit** ✏, you will get the option to enter details like **Show this many items at a time**. Enter the number of items as 4 and click on **Publish** as seen in the following screenshot:

Figure 12.97: Enter Number of Items to Display

5. Refresh the page, you will see analytics details in webpart as seen in the following screenshot:

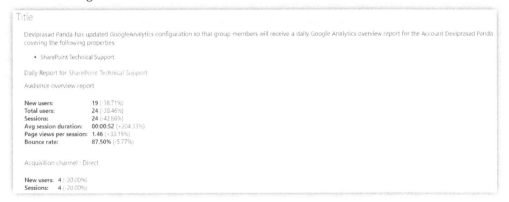

Figure 12.98: Google Analytics Reports Sync to Webpart

Others

Category **Others** include webparts like **Button, Code Snippet, Countdown Timer, Markdown, World Clock**. Let's discuss each webparts in details one-by-one.

Button

You can create a button using the webpart. Add webpart **Button**. Enter button name under the field **Label** and URL related to that button under the filed **Link**. Choose the alignment of the button (**Left**, **Right**, **Center**) choosing the options **Button Alignment** as seen in the following screenshot:

Figure 12.99: Button Webpart

Code Snippet

You can display codes on the site page using webpart **Code Snippet**. After adding webpart, select one language from the dropdown. Enter codes in the code space to display as text format in site page as seen in the following screenshot:

Figure 12.100: Code Snippet Webpart

Countdown Timer

We can display count down of any event on site page using the webpart **Countdown Timer**. Let's perform the following steps to see detail action on webpart **Countdown Timer**:

1. Add the webpart **Countdown Timer**.

2. Enter **Add a title** for the countdown timer.

3. Click on **Edit**, you will get additional options to choose.

4. Enter **Date and time**, Choose one option from **Days** or **Day, hours, minutes** or **Day, hours, minutes, seconds** from the dropdown option **Display timer as**.

5. Enable the option **Call to action** will show 2 more fields **Call to action text** and **Call to action link**.

6. Enter **Call to action text** (Contact Us) and **Call to action link** (https://bpbonline.com/pages/contact-us).

7. Click on **Add** to add a background image. Select one option under **Overlay color** and choose **Overlay opacity** as seen in the following screenshot.

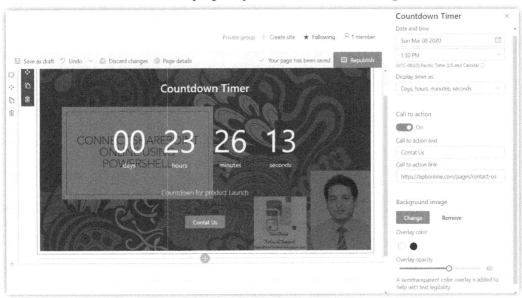

Figure 12.101: Countdown Timer

Markdown

We can add text and format the text using markdown language. Add webpart on the page. You will get a black screen in webpart. Enter text with markup language to format text. If you want to make the text as header add # before the text to make it header 1. Similarly, for Header 2 add ## before the text. Similarly, you can format text using a markup language. Side to the black screen you can see the output in proper format as seen in the following screenshot:

Figure 12.102: Markdown

World Clock

We can add a world clock using the webpart **World Clock**. Once you added the webpart, choose the date and time format. Enable **Show day of the week**. Under the option **Add a location**, enter location name anywhere in the world which will be displayed here in the page as seen in the following screenshot:

Figure 12.103: World Clock

Saved For Later

The new webpart **Saved for later** is under development status. It will hold contents marked as saved for later. This will be rolled out from mid-May to July-end.

Structural navigation caching

Structural navigation caching is a new feature going to be rolled out by the end of May. There will be an introduction of two settings like **Enable structural navigation caching** and **Structural Navigation: Refresh Cache** under **Navigation**. These options will be visible to the SharePoint administrator only. Let's follow the steps below to understand its application:

1. We already discussed in *Chapter 10, SharePoint Server Publishing Infrastructure* feature that enabling publishing feature adds setting **Navigation** (`https://<site url>/_layouts/15/AreaNavigationSettings.aspx`) under **Look and Feel** present in site settings. Click on **Navigation**.

2. Click on the checkbox **Enable Caching** from **Enable structural navigation caching**. This will make the navigation refresh automatically scheduled daily. Any change to navigation will be refreshed daily and cache stored to improve performance.

3. Second option **Structural Navigation: Refresh Cache** will allow us to refresh the navigation manually by clicking option **Refresh**.

Hub site

We already discussed the introduction to the hub site in *Chapter 1: Introduction and Site Information*. In this section we will discuss, how to register the site as a hub site, associate other sites with a hub site, and few settings related to this.

Register as a hub site

Site collection needs to be registered as a hub site first. SharePoint administrators can do this. Let's follow the steps below to understand better:

1. Select one site collection from the SharePoint admin center and click on **Hub** from the command bar.

2. From the dropdown option, select the option **Register as hub site** as seen in the following screenshot:

Figure 12.104: Register as Hub SIte

3. Another window will open where you need to enter people's details who can associate the site with the hub site. In the future, when site owners for other sites want to associate their sites with the hub sites, they can only if added here in this window. Enter people details and click on **Save** to apply changes as seen in the following screenshot:

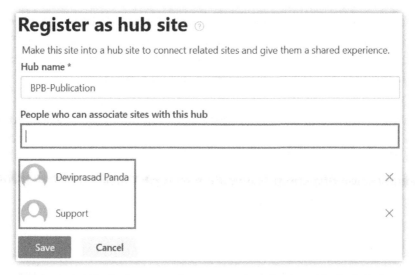

Figure 12.105: Assign user who can associate the site with the hub site

4. Once the site is registered as a hub site, you will find the column **Hub** related to that site will be marked as hub site as seen in the following screenshot:

Figure 12.106: Hub site created

5. Open hub site, you will find a top link navigation bar is added. The hub site will be added as the first link in hub site navigation bar with additional option **Add link** as seen in the following screenshot:

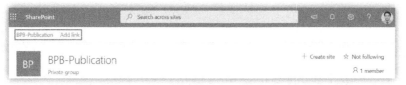

Figure 12.107: Top hub site navigation updated

Hub site association

We can associate other sites with hub sites to make it part of the hub site association. Let's follow the steps below to associate the site with the hub site:

1. Open any other team site (HR) that you want to associate with the hub site (BPB-Publication).

2. Click on **Settings** ⚙ from the top right corner and select **Site Information** from the dropdown option as seen in the following screenshot.

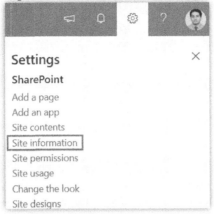

Figure 12.108: Site Information

3. Another dialog box with site information will open. Identify the option **Hub site association**, click on that, and select the hub site `BPB-Publication` as seen in the following screenshot:

Figure 12.109: Hub site association

4. Now open site HR, you will notice the top link hub site navigation bar is added in the site with link **Hub Site** (BPB-Publication) as seen in the following screenshot. HR site is part of hub site association now:

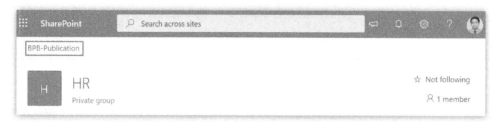

Figure 12.110: Site is associated with the hub site

5. Similarly, you can associate other team sites like **Author**, **Books**, **Career**, **Marketing**, **News**, **Social** with hub site BPB-Publication. In every site, you will find the top hub site navigation bar is added with hub site link BPB-Publication as seen in the following screenshot. Means, if you are accessing any one of the sites part of hub site association, you can navigate to hub site at any time following hub site navigation bar:

Figure 12.111: All associated site with the hub site

6. Now open the hub site BPB-Publication, click on **Add link** from the hub site navigation.

7. Enter any site URL under the field **Address** (https://spmcse.sharepoint. com/sites/HR) and **Display Name** (HR). HR site will be added to the hub site navigation bar as seen in the following screenshot:

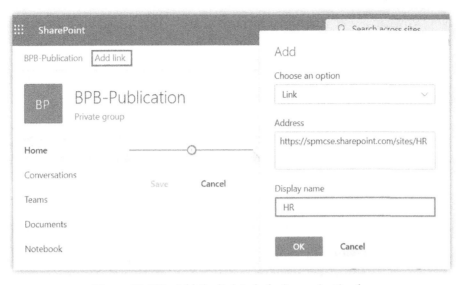

Figure 12.112: Add the link to hub site navigation bar

8. Click on **Edit** from hub site navigation bar then click on **Plus** sign ⊕ multiple times to enter **Address** and **Display Name** details for rest of the sites **Author**, **Books**, **Career**, **Marketing**, **News**, **Social** which is part of hub site association as seen in the following screenshot:

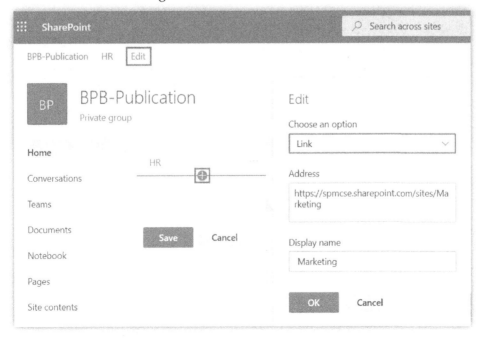

Figure 12.113: Associate multiple sites to hub site navigation bar

9. Now you can see all hub sites are present in the hub site navigation bar as seen in the following screenshot. We added links at hub site only:

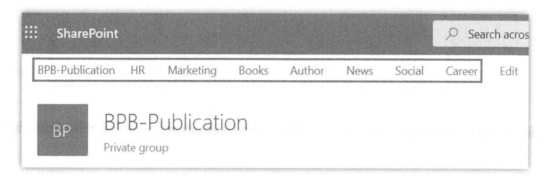

Figure 12.114: All sites associated with the hub site

10. If you open any other site (HR, Author, etc.) associated with the hub site, you will find this hub site navigation which is inheriting from hub site (`BPB-Publication`) as seen in the following screenshot. The benefit of this is like you can easily navigate to any associated site from hub site and vice versa:

Figure 12.115: Shared hub site navigation bar

Hub site settings

Once the site is registered as hub site you will find an additional setting **Hub site settings** under settings. Let's follow the steps below to see different actions that can be taken from hub site settings:

1. Click on **Settings** ⚙ from top right corner and select **Hub site settings** from the dropdown option as seen in the following screenshot:

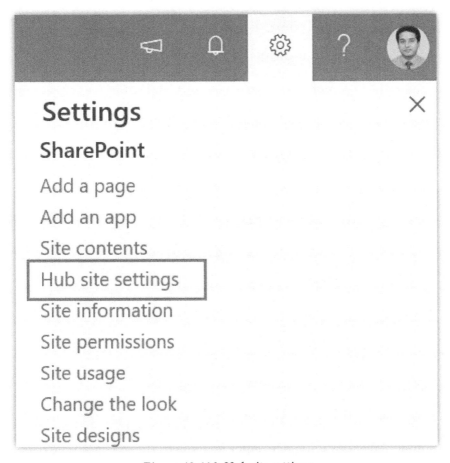

Figure 12.116: Hub site settings

2. Another dialog box will open where you will find options like hub site navigation logo, **Hub name**, **Shown in navigation**, **Require approval for associated sites to join**, **Create flow to require approval**.

3. You will get an option **Upload** under the hub site navigation logo first. Click on that to update the logo. Then you will get option **Change** to update the logo latter.

4. You can rename the hub name from the field **Hub name**.

5. You will get the option to enable to disable **Shown in navigation** which will display or hide the hub site link (BPB-Publication) respectively from the hub site navigation bar.

6. You can enable **Require approval for associated sites to join** by which when users want to associate any site to hub site, it will go for approval. Once this setting is enabled, then you will get an option **Create flow to require approval** is enabled. Click on **Create** as seen in the following screenshot:

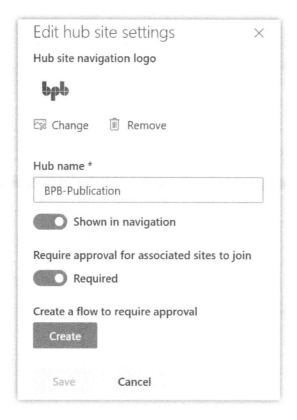

Figure 12.117: *Configure Hub site settings*

7. Another dialog box will open, enter `Approver ID`, and click on **Create** as seen in the following screenshot:

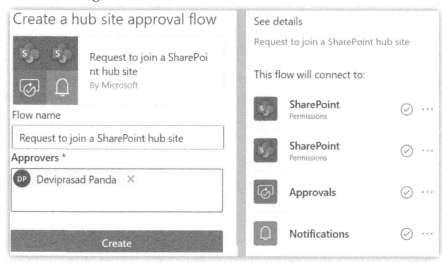

Figure 12.118: *Create Flow*

8. The flow will be created and click on **Save** finally as seen in the following screenshot:

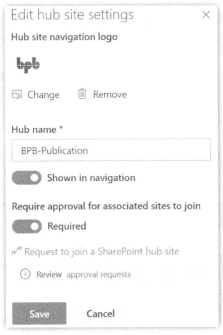

Figure 12.119: Flow created

9. Now onwards when you will try to associate any team site with a hub site, the user will get a dialog box to request for approval. Click on **Continue** form the dialog box appeared as seen in the following screenshot:

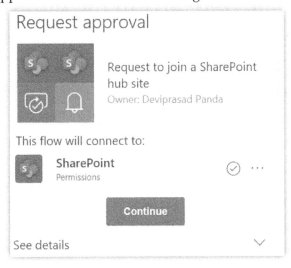

Figure 12.120: Flow initiated when try to associate with the hub site

10. Enter the message for this request and click on **Submit** as seen in the following screenshot. Approver will receive mail to approve. Once approver approved the request then the only site will be associated with hub site:

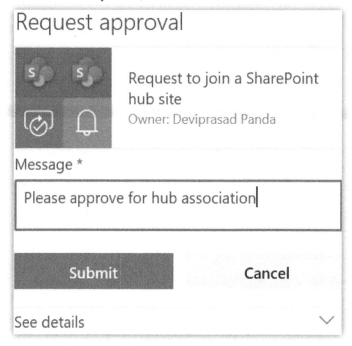

Figure 12.121: Submit requests for approval to associate a site with the hub site

Application of WebParts in the hub site

Hub site connects different sites, with commonly shared navigation, unique branding. It captures information across all associated sites and displays at one place for better collaboration and gets informed about critical tasks, updates, conversations, events, etc. Let's follow the steps below to under better in detail:

1. Edit one site page in the hub site (`BPB-Publication`).
2. Add a webpart **News**. Under news webpart settings you will find an option **All sites in the hub** under **News Source**.
3. Add a webpart **Highlighted Content**. Edit the webpart and select the content source as **All sites in the hub**.
4. Add a webpart **Events** and configure source as **All sites in the hub**.
5. Add a webpart **Sites** and configure the selection option as **All sites in the hub** as seen in the following screenshot:

Figure 12.122: Webparts associated with the hub site

6. Create news posts in all sites like (**HR**, **Books**, **Marketing**, **Author**, etc.), you see those news posts are available in hub site (BPB-Publication) webpart **News**.

9. Similarly, events present in all associates sites will be displayed under webpart **Events** in hub site:

Figure 12.123: News and event webparts hub site

10. Similarly, you add webpart **Sites** to check activities in all sites associated with hub site as seen in the following screenshot:

Figure 12.124: Site webpart associated with the hub site

11. Similarly, you can add webpart highlighted content to display highlighted content of all sites in hub site at one place as seen in the following screenshot:

Figure 12.125: Highlighted webpart associated with the hub site

12. Add webpart **Recent documents** to display recent documents of all sites in hub site:

Figure 12.126: Recent documents webpart associated with the hub site

Search in the hub site

When we will search anything in the hub site it displays results from all sites associated with the hub site. So, the search is limited within the hub site and associated sites. Users having permission on items can see the results. Search something like the *author*. You see results of all type displayed as seen in the following screenshot:

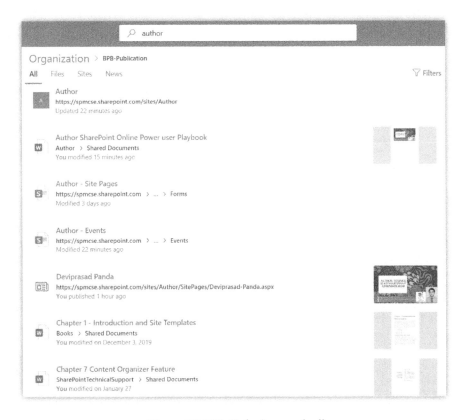

Figure 12.127: *Hub site search all*

Click on category **Files** will show you related documents across hub site and associated sites like **Author**, **Books**:

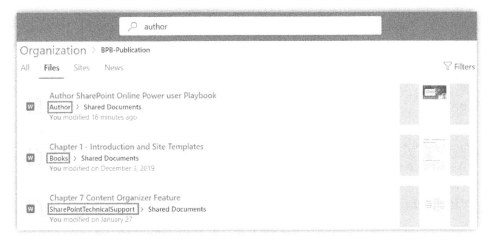

Figure 12.128: *Hub site search files*

Click on category **Sites** will show you related site across hub site and associated sites:

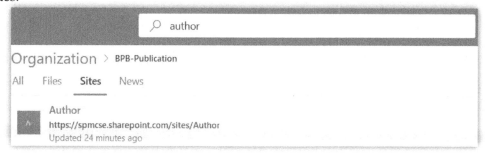

Figure 12.129: Hub site search sites

Click on category **News** will display related news across hub site and associated sites:

Figure 12.130: Hub site search News

Targeting news, files, and navigation

There is a new feature going to be rolled out by which we can target news, files, and navigation to a specific group of peoples. Site owners need to enable the audience targeting to create targeted content. Let's see where this change will be reflected:

1. Targeted contents can be applied in highlighted content webpart and **News** webpart. You will get a field **Audience** in webpart to enter the targeted user or group.

2. Navigate to **Audience targeting settings** present in library settings for the library **Site Pages** and enable audience targeting. There will be a column **Audience** that will be added to the library. You can select any page (**News Page**), click on **Details Pane**, you can find the column **Audience** where you can enter the user or group id to apply targeted changes.

3. Site navigation can also be targeted. You will notice an option **Site navigation audience targeting** at the bottom of left navigation which allows you to enable or disable targeting navigation. You need to enable this option first. Then click

on **Edit** present at the bottom of the left navigation. When you try to edit any existing link item or add a new item, you will find field **Audience targeting** for entering audience details and apply changes. This applies to the site, footer, and hub navigation.

New Footer Navigation

New feature footer navigation is rolling out gradually for communication. Let's see where this change will be reflected:

1. Click on **Change the look** from settings.

2. You will notice additional option **Footer** in the dialog box opened next. Click on **Footer**.

3. Dialog box footer will open. You will find option **Enable** at the first, click on that to enable footer.

4. Choose one **Layout** for footer out of **Simple** or **Extended**.

5. Change the footer logo by selecting **Change** under the option **Logo**.

6. Enter **Display name** of the footer.

7. Select one **Background** theme and click on **Save**, as seen in the following screenshot:

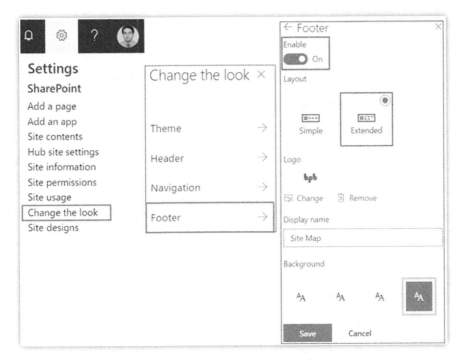

Figure 12.131: Footer Navigation

8. Open communication site, you will find the footer at the bottom with footer logo and display name. You will find an option **Edit** at the right side, click on that.

9. You will find Edit footer dialog box with a **plus** sign ⊕ to add links in footer and option **Enable site navigation audience targeting** to enable audience targeting. Enabling audience targeting will make the navigation visible to only specific group of users only.

10. **Enable site navigation audience targeting** and click on **plus** sign ⊕ to add links to footer.

11. Select option **Link** or **Label** to add link or label respectively in footer.

12. Enter URL if you are choosing **Link**, selecting **Label** do not need any address. Enter **Display name** of link or label.

13. Enter group details in the field **Audience targeting** for targeting footer to specific group of people. You can target up to 10 groups.

14. Click on **OK** to apply changes. Then you will see the footer is updated with Label and links, as seen in the following screenshot:

Figure 12.132: Footer Navigation add Links and Labels

Conclusion

In this chapter we discussed site pages. How to create a site page, design, or modify site pages. We discussed all the new modern webpart introduced. Understood how to add modern webparts, how to configure each webpart in site pages, and get benefits out of that. Then we discussed new feature structural navigation caching. Also discussed all hub site, how to register a hub site, associate site to hub site, application of webparts in the hub site. Next in *Chapter 13: Manage Site Usage* will discuss all site usage analytics.

Points to remember

- Regular updates in webpart are pushed by Microsoft. There might be some additional options in existing webpart appear or new webparts might be added.

- *Image webpart, Image gallery webpart, Hero webpart, File viewer* are the modern webparts compared to the corresponding classic old webparts like *Image webpart, Content editor webpart, Picture library* which are used related to add images.

- *File Viewer, Embed, Stream, Office 365 Video* are the modern webparts compared to the corresponding old classic webparts *Media webpart* used to display videos on the page also will replace classic webpart.

- *Group calendar, Events* are the modern webparts compared to the corresponding old classic webparts *Calendar* used to display date and time, meetings, events on site page also will replace classic webpart.

- *Quick links, Link, Text webpart*, are the modern webparts compared to the corresponding old classic webparts *Promoted links, Links, Content editor webpart, Announcements, Summary Link* used to display other content links in site page also will replace classic webpart.

- Yammer webparts are the modern webpart compared to the classic old webpart *Site feed* also will replace the old classic webpart.

- PowerApps is the modern webpart compared to the classic old webpart *InfoPath Forms* also will replace the old classic webpart.

- In this chapter wherever its mentioned like this format `_layouts/15/****.aspx`, means this section is added after the site URL `http://` `<site url>` `/_layouts/15/****.aspx`.

CHAPTER 13

Manage Site Usage

In the previous chapter, we discussed all site designing and enhancements in SharePoint Online. In this chapter, we will discuss SharePoint site usage and analytics. All activities happening in sites are recorded by SharePoint, which we can analyze to manage the site better with improved performance. Activities like several users visiting the site, several times site are visited, traffic of site at a specified period, popular platforms in site traffic, users accessing content, most viewed content, contents shared with external users, modification of content, deletion of content, and so on, are stores which we can analyze and can act on it for better management and improved performance.

Structure

In this chapter, we will discuss the following topics:

- Site Usage
- File Activity Report
- Site Usage Report
- Site Activity Webpart
- Traditional Audit log report
- Storage Metrics

Objective

During the end of the chapter, you will get a clear understanding of the following:

- How to monitor activities under site usage
- Analyze file activity report
- Analyze site usage report
- Analyze using site activity webpart
- Understand traditional audit log report
- Analyze storage metrics

Site Usage

We can check the usage of the site, which contains information related to unique viewers, site visits, site traffic, popular platforms, most unique viewers, most viewed, shared with external users. Let's perform the following steps to check site usage:

1. Navigate to **Site Contents** (`<_layouts/15/viewlsts.aspx>`) present on site.

2. You will find an option **Site usage** under command bar or from **Site Settings** drop-down. Click on **Site usage** (`https://<site url>/_layouts/15/ siteanalytics.aspx`) as seen in the following screenshot:

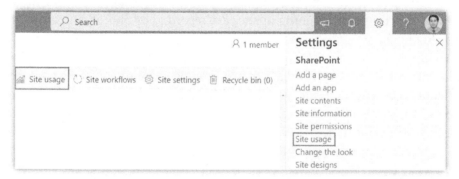

Figure 13.1: Site usage setting

3. You will be redirected to the **siteanalytics** page. The first option under this you will find is **Unique viewers** that logs information regarding the total number of users visited the site to date.

4. Information is displayed in graphical format. If we hover the mouse over any graph will show the number of users visited for that particular date.

5. We can filter the information log in three categories like **Last 7 days**, last **30 days**, last **90 days** that holds information about numbers of users visited in last 7 days, 30 days or last 90 days respectively as seen in the following screenshot:

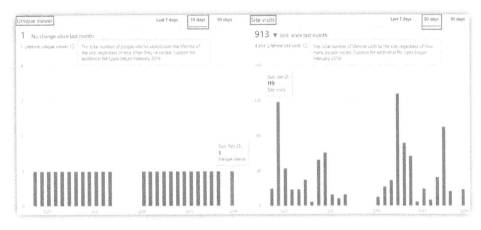

Figure 13.2: Unique viewer and Site visits

6. The next option you will find is **Site visits** that logs information regarding the total number of time sites is visited for a particular date and display in graphical format, as seen in the above screenshot.

7. Hover the mouse over any particular date will show several times the site visited for that particular date.

8. We can filter this information log into three categories like the **Last 7 days**, last **30 days**, last **90 days** similar to option **Unique viewers**.

9. The next option is **Site traffic** that holds information about the number of users visiting the site at a particular time that helps to analyze the load on-site at every moment so that can manage the performance of the site as seen in the following screenshot.

10. This information can be filtered into three categories like **Last 7 days**, **30 days**, **90 days**:

Figure 13.3: Site traffic

11. The next option is **Popular platforms** that hold information regarding the devices used for accessing the site from which we can analyze traffic is from which type of platform, whether desktop, mobile web, mobile app, tablet, or

any other device. This information can be filtered in three categories like **Last 7 days, 30 days, 90 days** as seen in the following screenshot:

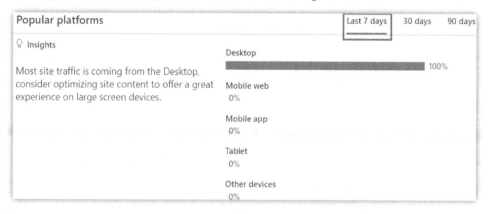

Figure 13.4: Popular platforms

12. Next option **Most unique viewers** that hold information like which content is accessed by how many numbers of viewers for the past 7 days.

13. Option **Most viewed** contains information like which content got how many views and displays most viewed content for past 7 days as seen in the following screenshot:

Most unique viewers	Last 7 days		Most viewed	Last 7 days
Name	Viewers		Name	Views
SPmcse.aspx	1		Project 1904 - Appendix.docx	13
Project 1904 - Appendix.docx	1		Project 1906 - About Author.docx	13
Project 1906 - About Author.docx	1		Project 1906 - About Reviewer.docx	13
Project 1906 - About Reviewer.docx	1		Project 1906 - Appendix.docx	13
Project 1906 - Appendix.docx	1		Project 1906 - Guidelines.docx	13
Project 1906 - Guidelines.docx	1		Project.xlsx	2
Project.xlsx	1		SPmcse.aspx	1

Figure 13.5: Unique viewers and Most viewed

14. Another option you will find is **Shared with external users** that contains information regarding the contents shared with external users.

15. We can generate a report by clicking the option **Run report**, select one library as a storage location for the report, then click in **Run report** as seen in the following screenshot:

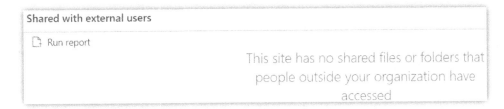

Figure 13.6: Shared with external users

16. There is no item I have shared outside of the organization, so there is no item in the screenshot above. But you can share with the external user and generate it. When you generate a report, it contains information like **Resource Path, Item Type, Permission, User Name, User E-mail, User or Group Type, Link ID, Link Type, AccessViaLinkID**.

File Activity Report

On the **SharePoint admin center** home page, we can now see the reports related to activity on file (**File Activity Report**) and site (**Site Usage Report**). The first report we will see in graphical format is the file activity report. You will find an option **Details** at the top right to that graph. Click on **Details,** as seen in the following screenshot. Let's perform the following steps to check the SharePoint file activity report:

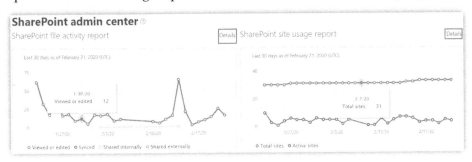

Figure 13.7: Activity report and usage report

1. You will be redirected to the activity page. You will notice the activity reports in the graph can be filtered based on **Files, Pages, Users**.

2. Category **Files** is chosen first. The graph shows the number of files viewed or edited, the number of files shared internally or externally. Click on the option **Export** present at the right sight of the graph; you will find a report containing details like **Report refresh date, Viewed or edited, Synced, Shared internally, Shared externally, Report date, Report period**.

3. Below the graph, you will find a **Details** table. There is an option **Export** at the right sight of that table, clicking on that will generate a report containing

details like **Report refresh date, User principal name, Is deleted, Deleted date, Last activity date, Viewed or edited file count, Synced file count, Shared internally file count, Shared externally file count, Visited page count, Assigned products, Report period**:

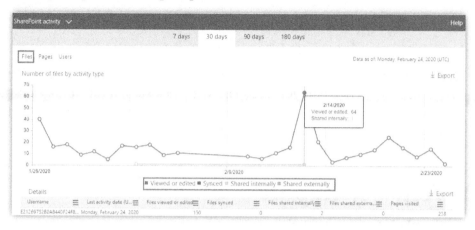

Figure 13.8: Site Activity Report

4. The next category type under site activity is **Pages**. The graph shows the number of pages visited for a particular date.

5. If you export the report from **Details** table you will find the columns in the report as **Report refresh date, Visited page count, Report date, Report period**:

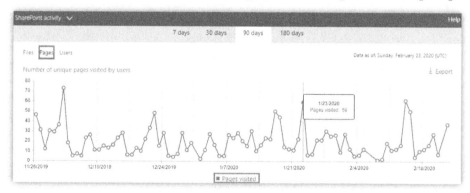

Figure 13.9: Site Activity Report Category Pages

6. The next category type under site activity is **Users**. If you export the report from **Details** table you will find the columns in the report as **Report refresh date, Visited a page, Viewed or edited, Synced, Shared internally, Shared externally, Report date, Report period**:

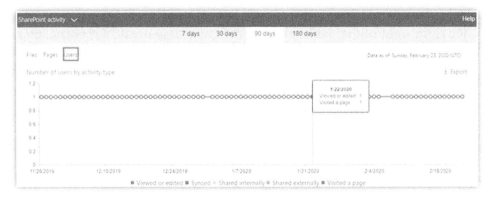

Figure 13.10: Site Activity Reports Category Users

7. Click any one of the fields as shown in the image below, you will find options like **Sort ascending**, **Sort descending**, **Columns**, **Filter**. If you click on the **Columns**, you see all columns. Which of the columns selected those field details will be displayed in the table:

Figure 13.11: Filtering and Displaying Columns

Site Usage Report

The second report we will see in graphical format, on the **SharePoint admin center** home page, is file activity report, which contains activity details for **Sites**, **Files**, **Storage**, **Pages**. Let's perform the following steps to check the **Site Usage report**:

1. You will find an option **Details** at the top right to that graph. Click on **Details**.

2. You will be redirected to the **SharePoint site usage** page. You will notice site usage reports in a graph can be filtered based on **Sites**, **Files**, **Storage**, **Pages**.

3. Category **Sites** is chosen first. The graph shows total sites and active sites trend, as shown in the below screenshot *Figure 13.12*.

4. Click on the option **Export** present at the right sight of the graph; you will find a report containing details like **Report refresh date**, **Site type**, **Total sites**, **Active sites**, **Report date**, **Report period**.

5. Below the graph, you will find a **Details** table. There is an option **Export** at the right sight of that table, clicking on that will generate a report containing details like **Report refresh date, Site Id, Site URL, Owner display name, Is deleted, Last activity date, File count, Active file count, Page view count, Visited page count, Storage used (Byte), Storage allocated (Byte), Root web template, Site owner principal Name, Report period**:

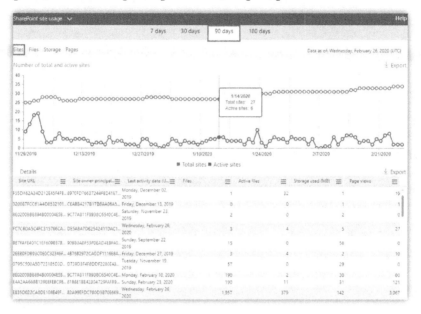

Figure 13.12: Site usage category Sites

6. The next category type under site usage is **Files**. The graph shows total files and active files trend for a particular date, as seen in the following screenshot.

7. If you export the report from **Details** table, you will find the columns in the report as **Report refresh date, Site type, Total, Active, Report date, Report period**:

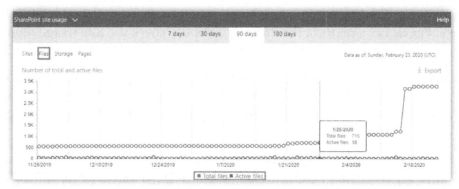

Figure 13.13: Site usage report category Files

8. The next category type under site usage is **Storage**. The graph shows the total storage occupied trend for a particular date, as seen in the following screenshot.

9. If you export the report from **Details** table you will find the columns in the report as **Report Refresh Date, Site Type, Storage Used (Byte), Report Date, Report Period**:

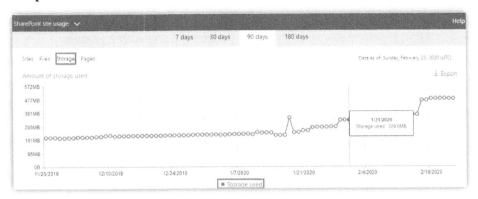

Figure 13.14: Site usage report category Storage

10. The next category type under site usage is **Pages**. The graph shows total page views trend per particular date, as seen in the following screenshot.

11. If you export the report from **Details** table you will find the columns in the report as **Report refresh date, Site type, Page view count, Report date, Report period**:

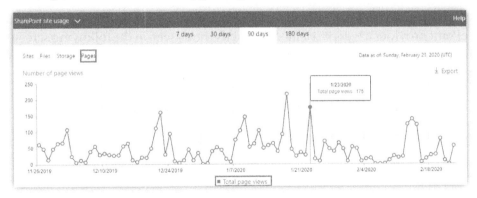

Figure 13.15: Site usage report category Pages

12. Click any one of the fields as shown in the image below, you will find options like **Sort ascending, Sort descending, Columns, Filter**. If you click on the **Columns**, you see all columns. Which of the columns selected those field details will be displayed in the table.

13. Click on the option **Filter** will show different conditions of filtering which we can apply to show data in the **Details** tab as seen in the following screenshot:

Figure 13.16: Filtering and Columns

14. Click on all columns will show all details related to site usage, as seen in the following screenshot, which can be analyzed to manage your site better with improved performance:

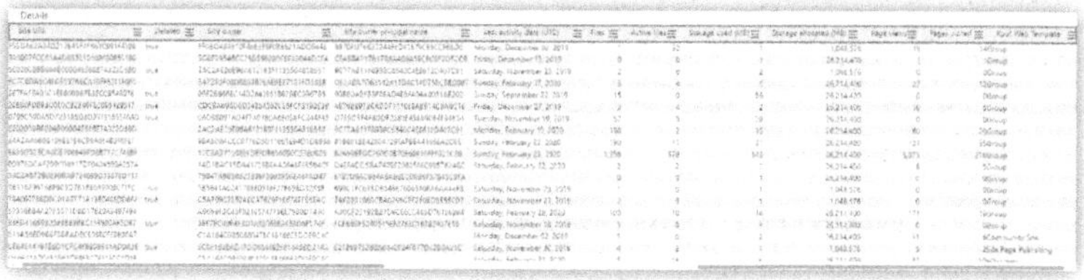

Figure 13.17: Details table

Site Activity Webpart

We can audit the activity of site contents by adding one webpart on the site. Modern SharePoint provides a webpart called **Site activity**, as seen in the following screenshot below, that captures all activities on-site content like contents uploaded, modified, viewed, creation of libraries or lists, and so on:

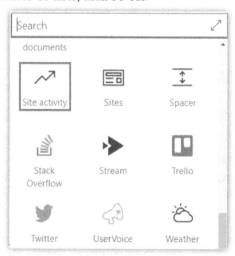

Figure 13.18: Site activity webpart

We can see recent activities like files edited, viewed, site pages viewed in the below images. So, this webpart pulls all activities automatically and display here to end-users as seen in the following screenshot:

Figure 13.19: Activity details

Traditional Audit log reports

In the old way of checking logs from each site, settings are gradually going to be out of use. The new way of checking audit details is becoming so friendly and popular. Let's perform the following steps to check traditional Audit log report:

1. Navigate to **Site Settings** (`<_layouts/15/settings.aspx>`).

2. Click on **Site collection audit settings** (`https://<site url>/_layouts/15/ AuditSettings.aspx`) present under **Site Collection Administration** as seen in the following screenshot:

Figure 13.20: Audit log reports

3. We used to see the settings to enable events like **Editing items, Checking out or checking in items, Moving or copying items to another location in**

the site, Deleting or restoring items related to documents and items and **Editing content types and columns, Searching site content, Editing users and permissions** related to **Lists, Libraries, and Sites** as seen in the following screenshot:

Figure 13.21: Traditional Audit Log Settings

4. SharePoint Online, you will see these settings are going to be out of support and no such setting available to enable as seen in the following screenshot:

Figure 13.22: Audit Log Trimming

5. Next, if you click on **Audit Log Reports** (`https://<site url>/_layouts/15/ Reporting.aspx?Category=Auditing`) present under **Site Collection Administration**, you will see reports **Content viewing, Content modifications, Deletion, Content type and list modifications** under the category **Content Activity Reports**. Reports like **Policy modifications, Expiration and Disposition** under category **Information Management Policy Reports**. Reports **Auditing settings, Security settings** under category **Security And Site Settings Reports**. Reports **Run a custom report** under category **Custom Reports** to audit as seen in the following screenshot:

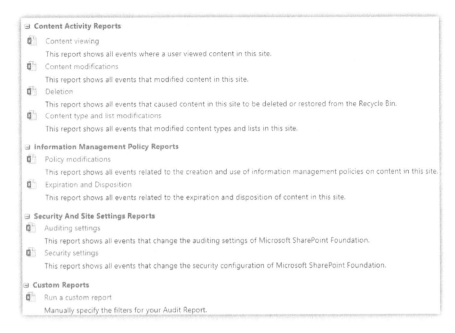

Figure 13.23: Audit Log Report

6. Click any one of the reports will ask a location to save the report. Select one document library to store reports and run to generate the report for audit.

Storage Metrics

Storage Metrics option captures the site collection storage details like what is the current storage occupied, which site, subsite, list, libraries, and other folders occupying how much storage so that we can plan for storage management for better site performance. Let's perform the following steps to check storage metrics:

1. Navigate to **Site Settings** (`<_layouts/15/settings.aspx>`).

2. Click on **Storage Metrics** (`https://<site url>/_layouts/15/storman.aspx`) present under **Site Collection Administration**, as seen in the following screenshot:

Figure 13.24: Storage Metrics Option Under Site Settings

3. You will see the space occupied by the current site; subsites present under that site as seen in the following screenshot:

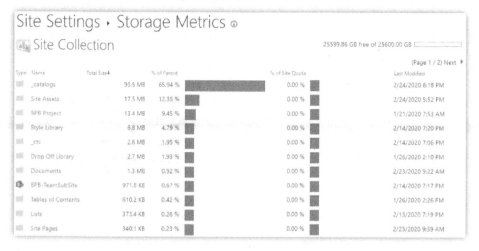

Figure 13.25: Storage Metrics in details

4. If you click any subsite, then it will show a chart of storage occupied by all content types and subsites present under that subsite. So, clicking any of the items will show the storage occupied under those particular items.

Conclusion

In this chapter, we discussed how to check site usages. How to check and analyze different reports like File Activity Report, Site Usage Report. Discussed the use of webpart **Site Activity Webpart** to capture logs. Discussed traditional Audit Log Report also understood how to check storage metrics for site.

Points to remember

- Traditional Audit log report is going to be out of support, and we need to accept the new and modern way of different auditing activities in SharePoint Online.

- In this chapter, wherever its mentioned like this format `_layouts/15/****.aspx`, means this section is added after the site URL `http://` `<site url>` `/_layouts/15/****.aspx`.

- Regular changes are applied in Office 365 and SharePoint Online by which there may be changes happening in the template or some other features.

Made in the USA
Columbia, SC
02 November 2020